Destination Branding

Destination Branding

Creating the unique destination proposition

Edited by

Nigel Morgan, Annette Pritchard and Roger Pride

OXFORD AMSTERDAM BOSTON LONDON NEW YORK PARIS
SAN DIEGO SAN FRANCISCO SINGAPORE SYDNEY TOKYO

Butterworth-Heinemann
An imprint of Elsevier Science
Linacre House, Jordan Hill, Oxford OX2 8DP
200 Wheeler Road, Burlington, MA 01803

First published 2002
Reprinted 2003

British Library Cataloguing in Publication Data
A catalogue record for this book is available from the British Library

Library of Congress Cataloguing in Publication Data
A catalogue record for this book is available from the Library of Congress

ISBN 0 7506 4994 1

For information on all Butterworth-Heinemann publications
visit our website at www.bh.com

Typeset by Genesis Typesetting, Rochester, Kent
Printed and bound in Great Britain by MPG Books Ltd, Bodmin, Cornwall

Contents

Contributors

Simon Anholt is a founder and Planning Director of Cave Anholt Jonason, a London-based international advertising agency. He has been described as 'one of the world's leading consultants for companies wishing to market their brands abroad' and is the best-selling author *of Another One Bites the Grass: Making Sense of International Advertising,* published in 2000 in the AdWeek Books series by Wiley, New York.

Graham Brown is Associate Professor in the School of Tourism and Hospitality Management at Southern Cross University in New South Wales, Australia. Dr Brown has published widely on tourism planning and marketing and has served on a number of editorial boards and acted as the regional editor, Asia/Pacific for the *International Journal of Contemporary Hospitality Management.* He is particularly interested in events and tourism marketing, and worked closely with industry groups in the lead-up to the Sydney 2000 Olympic Games. He was a member of the Tourism Olympic Forum Mission to Atlanta in 1997 and worked on a major research project in collaboration with the Australian Tourist Commission and the International Olympic Committee (IOC) to examine the market characteristics of sponsor guests attending the Sydney Games.

Laurence Chalip is Associate Professor in the School of Marketing and Management at Griffith University, Australia, where he convenes the sport management major and serves as Coordinator of Postgraduate Studies. He currently co-ordinates the Olympic research projects for Australia's Cooperative Research Centre for Sustainable Tourism, and was a Principal Investigator with the research team evaluating the volunteer programme at the Sydney Olympics. He has published over fifty scholarly articles and book chapters, as well as two books. He is editor of the *Sport Management Review* and associate editor of the *Journal of Sport Management.* In 2000, he was awarded the International Chair of Olympism by the Centre d'Etudis Olímpics i de l'Esport at the Universitat Autónoma de Barcelona in co-operation with the IOC.

Shane R. Crockett is the former Chief Executive Officer of the Western Australian Tourism Commission where he was responsible for the formation and implementation of the comprehensive tourism strategy for the State of Western Australia. He is also one of Australia's most successful major event administrators and marketers. Shane is a graduate from the University of Western Australia and is a board member of Tourism Council Australia, Aviation Policy Committee, Capital City Commerce, Curtin University's Board of Advisors for the Asia-Pacific Masters Program I Hotel and Resort Management as well as the Committee for Economic Development of Australia.

Fiona Gilmore is Chief Executive Officer (CEO) and one of the two founding partners at Springpoint, a brand positioning and corporate identity consultancy based in London, with associates in Milan, Riyadh, Hong Kong and the USA. Fiona gained an MA in Russian and French at Cambridge University before spending seven years in advertising. Since then she has directed a number of brand positioning and corporate identity programmes, which most recently have included a positioning for all Wales, a positioning strategy for Hong Kong, a global positioning, architecture and identity programme for Vodafone and a repositioning of the Britain brand for the British Tourist Authority. Fiona is a regular speaker on corporate brand positioning, migration strategies and corporate identity, and has presented papers on the subject in Beijing, Cairo, Moscow, Istanbul, New York and Hong Kong. She is a regular speaker on television and radio, and has judged the British Broadcasting Corporation (BBC) design awards. Her first book, *Brand Warriors*, was published by HarperCollins in 1997 and her second book, *Warriors on the High Wire*, was published in July 2001. Fiona is a Trustee of Wateraid and a Fellow of the Royal Society of Arts.

Derek Hall is Professor and Head of the Leisure and Tourism Management Department at the Scottish Agricultural College. He has a particular interest in national identity in tourism and development processes in south-eastern Europe and his several books include *Reconstructing the Balkans* (Wiley, 1993, with Darrick Danta).

Leo Jago is an Associate Professor and the Director of the Centre for Hospitality and Tourism Research at Victoria University, Australia and Coordinator of the Tourism Discipline within the School of Hospitality, Tourism and Marketing. He is the Chair of the Council of Australian University Tourism and Hospitality Education and the Coordinator of the Events Tourism Sub-program in the CRC for Sustainable Tourism. Coupled with his role as a tourism educator, Dr Jago has substantial operational experience, having continuously owned and operated tourism facilities over the past fifteen years. He is Associate Editor for the journal *Tourism, Culture and Communication* and on the editorial board of *Festival Management* and *Event Tourism*. He is a board member of the Country Victorian Tourism Council, a member of the Tourism and Leisure Policy Committee of the Victorian Employer Chamber of Commerce and Industry, and an executive member of the Western Region Tourism Task Force. His research interests include tourism marketing, special events, tourist behaviour, tourism planning and development, tourism impacts, wine tourism and volunteer management.

Nigel Morgan is Director of Graduate Studies in the Welsh School of Hospitality, Tourism and Leisure Management, at the University of Wales Institute, Cardiff. Dr Morgan's research interests embrace destination marketing, seaside resort development, tourism sociology and tourism advertising and branding. He has co-authored three books and over fifty papers and book chapters, and is an editorial board member for the *Journal of Vacation Marketing*. His latest book, *Constructing Tourism Identities*, is co-authored with Annette Pritchard and will be published by Channel View in 2002.

Trevor Mules is a Professor at the University of Canberra, Co-ordinator ACT node of CRC for Sustainable Tourism and Director of the Centre for Tourism Research. His research interests focus on the economic and social impacts of tourism, modelling the economics of tourism, the economics of special events and tourism demand forecasting. He has written a number of papers on the approaches to measuring the economic impact of tourism, especially the economic impact of special events. His research projects include: studies on the economic impacts of special events such as the Adelaide Grand Prix, Canberra's Floriade Festival, the projected impact of the Sydney Olympics, and the Commonwealth Games. He has also researched the Adelaide Festival, the Brisbane Festival, the Wintersun (Gold Coast) Festival, and the International Melbourne Flower Show. He has led a consultancy for the Commonwealth Government on modelling the economic impacts of major sporting events in Australia and for the Victorian State Government on the economic evaluation of major events.

Adrian Palmer is Professor of Services Marketing in the Gloucestershire Business School, Cheltenham. His previous management experience before joining academia was in the travel and transport sector. He is the author of five books and over forty refereed journal papers, which are listed at http://www.apalmer.com. He is a member of the editorial advisory board for the *European Journal of Marketing*, the *Journal of Marketing Management* and the *Journal of Vacation Marketing* and was elected a Fellow of the Chartered Institute of Marketing in 1996. Previous research and consultancy work has focused on tourism destination marketing; customer loyalty and service quality. Current research and consultancy work in electronic commerce is integrating and building upon this previous research.

Roger Pride graduated in Business Studies before beginning his career in the travel/ tourism industry with Pickfords Travel. He then moved to Avis Rent-A-Car in a sales territory management position, initially covering south-west Britain before progressing to the important 'city' territory in London. Roger then had a brief spell outside the travel industry with Golley Slater and Partners, one of Wales' leading advertising agencies, before joining the Wales Tourist Board (WTB) as Travel Trade Officer in 1985. Since then, Roger has undertaken several roles within the WTB and is now Director of Marketing. He is responsible for developing all aspects of the WTB's marketing strategy. He has a particular interest in destination branding and developed a branding strategy for the WTB which led to the award-winning 'Wales Two Hours and a Million Miles Away' campaign.

Annette Pritchard is Director of the Welsh Centre for Tourism Research in the Welsh School of Hospitality, Tourism and Leisure Management at the University of Wales Institute, Cardiff. Dr Pritchard's interests include critical tourism studies, destination marketing, tourism advertising and branding, and tourism in Wales. She has written over forty papers, book chapters and reports, and her books include: *Tourism Promotion and Power* (Wiley, 1998), *Power and Politics at the Seaside* (University of Exeter, 1999) and *Advertising in Tourism and Leisure* (Butterworth-Heinemann, 2000).

Chris Ryan is Professor of Tourism at Waikato University, New Zealand, editor of *Tourism Management,* a member of the International Academy for the Study of Tourism and was a member of the 2000 Asia-Pacific Economic Cooperation Conference (APEC) Tourism Ministers' Advisory Committee. He is the author of over 100 papers and book chapters and five books. His latest book, *Sex Tourism: Liminalities and Marginal People* is co-authored with Mike Hall and was published by Routledge in 2001.

Jan Slater is an assistant professor of advertising at E. W. Scripps School of Journalism at Ohio University in Athens, Ohio, USA. In addition to her fourteen years of teaching experience, Dr Slater has twenty years' experience in the advertising industry, having worked in both private industry and advertising agencies. Until 1990, she owned her own agency in Omaha, Nebraska. Her primary research focus has been on branding and building brand relationships. Dr Slater earned her BA at Hastings College, Hastings, Nebraska, an MSc in advertising at the University of Illinois, Champaign-Urbana, and a PhD in mass communications at S. I. Newhouse School of Public Communications at Syracuse University.

Leiza J. Wood is the former Brand Western Australia Manager of the Western Australian Tourism Commission and has managed a range of strategic development and innovation initiatives. She has also worked with Singapore Airlines in sales and marketing, and as a travel consultant. Leiza has a Bachelor of Commerce degree from Curtin University, Western Australia.

Figures

Tables

Acknowledgements

There are many people and organizations to whom the editors are indebted for their help and support in producing this book. We would like to thank all our contributors for their efforts. First, for agreeing to be part of the project and then for speedily meeting deadlines and for allowing us to edit their hard work! We would also like to express our gratitude to our editors at Butterworth-Heinemann for their assistance and guidance throughout the project, particularly our commissioning editor, Sally North.

We are also indebted to many individuals in the tourism industry and beyond who gave of their time to assist with our requests for interviews, information and visual material. Nigel and Annette would like to recognize and thank colleagues, researchers and friends at the University of Wales Institute, Cardiff (UWIC) and beyond for exchanging ideas and opinions. They are particularly indebted to Sheena Westwood at UWIC for her ideas on branding and tourism and Candice Harris at Massey University and Rachel Piggot, Marketing Communications Manager for TNZ, for sharing their unpublished work and, in Rachel's case, for permission to reproduce the TNZ visuals. Finally, Roger would like to thank all his colleagues at the Wales Tourist Board for putting up with him when he bashes the branding bible!

Nigel Morgan and Annette Pritchard
Welsh School of Hospitality, Tourism and Leisure Management, UWIC
Roger Pride
Wales Tourist Board
October 2001

Abbreviations

APEC	Asia-Pacific Economic Cooperation Conference
ASP	application service providers
ATC	Australian Tourist Commission
BBC	British Broadcasting Corporation
BDI	brand development indexing
Brand WA	Brand Western Australia
BWA	Brand Western Australia
CEE	Central and Eastern Europe
CEO	chief executive officer
CRC	Tourism Australian Co-operative Research Centre for Sustainable Tourism
DCRT	Department of Culture, Recreation and Tourism
DTO	district tourism organization
EU	European Union
fmcg	fast-moving consumer goods
FTE	full-time employee
GDN	global distribution network
GDP	gross domestic product
GDS	global distribution system
IOC	International Olympic Committee
MBA	masters of business administration
MICE	Meetings, Incentive, Corporate and Exhibitions
MMP	mixed member proportional
MPAF	Market Potential Assessment Formula
NASA	National Aeronautics and Space Administration
NASDAQ	National Association of Securities Dealers Automated Quotations
NITB	Northern Ireland Tourist Board
NOC	National Olympic Committee
NTO	national tourist office

NZTIA	New Zealand Tourism Industry Association
RTA	regional tourism associations
RTO	regional tourism organization
SIT	special interest tourism
SOCOG	Sydney Organizing Committee for the Olympic Games
SWOTC	strengths, weaknesses, opportunities, threats and constraints
TCA	Tourism Council Australia
TNZ	Tourism New Zealand
TOP	The Olympic Program
USP	unique selling proposition
UWIC	University of Wales Institute, Cardiff
UDP	unique destination proposition
UNESCO	United Nations Educational, Scientific, and Cultural Organization
VLP	Visiting Journalists Program
WATC	Western Australian Tourism Commission
WTB	Wales Tourist Board
WTO	World Tourism Organization
WWW	World Wide Web

Part One
Perspectives on Destination
Branding

1

Introduction

Nigel Morgan, Annette Pritchard and Roger Pride

Introduction

At first glance, the value of another text on destination marketing may seem limited. However, destination branding is not just another aspect of destination marketing and its study is no mere academic bandwagon. Rather it is a belated acknowledgement of a fundamental transformation in the marketing of destinations – and beyond this – in the marketing of places. Such has been the explosion of interest in destinational branding that a collection such as this, bringing together practitioners and academics, is long overdue – the practice of place branding has far outpaced the extent to which it has been written about in the public realm. Arguably, far from actively engaging with destination branding issues, many have shied away from the topic – arguing that places are too complex to include in branding discussions since they have too many stakeholders and too little management control, have underdeveloped identities and are not perceived as brands by the general public. And yet, destination branding is one of today's 'hottest' topics among place marketers – from Switzerland and New Zealand to Hawaii and Costa Rica (Piggott, 2001).

Indeed, places are potentially the world's biggest tourism brands. Choice of holiday destination is a significant lifestyle indicator for today's aspirational consumers and the places where they choose to spend their increasingly squeezed vacation time and hard earned income have to be emotionally appealing with high conversational and celebrity value. The World Tourism Organization talks about this in terms of seeing destinations as tomorrow's fashion items, suggesting that: 'The next century will mark the emergence of tourism destinations as a fashion accessory. The choice of holiday destination will help define the identity of the traveller and, in an increasingly homogeneous world, set him [*sic*] apart from the hordes of other tourists' (Lurham, 1998: 13).

As style and status indicators, destinations can offer the same consumer benefits as other more highly branded lifestyle accoutrements such as cars, perfumes, watches and clothes. All are used to communicate, reflect and reinforce associations, statements and group memberships and, in the same way, tourists use 'their trips as expressive devices to communicate messages about themselves to peers and observers' (Clarke, 2000: 330). Travel for leisure is often a highly involving experience, extensively planned, excitedly anticipated and fondly remembered. Souvenirs and 'props' trigger and display those experiences – photographs, videos and 'wish you were here' postcards are shared with friends and relatives, and logo-emblazoned merchandise and luggage labels proclaim 'been there, done that' to any observers who care to notice (Clarke, 2000; Westwood, 2000).

Tapping into the power of such emotional appeal, tourism destination brands are also beginning to reach beyond the tourism industry. Many of those brands at the leading edge of destination marketing are seeking to position themselves as place brands, whereby whole countries, states and regions are embarking on brand-building initiatives that are inclusive of tourism and economic development. While the task is by no means easy, the rewards are enormous and, drawing on many case studies from the leading edge of destination marketing practice, the chapters in this collection evidence this view. Written by an international mixture of practitioners and academics, the subsequent chapters address a varied range of destinations, each at a different stage of development and each grappling with the challenges presented by destination branding. What is striking, however, is the commonality of their approaches to the process and the recurring themes that emerge as key to destination brand building.

The reader should not, therefore, be surprised that several of the chapters reiterate these themes. Instead, the collection reflects the fact that these are the crucial issues facing contemporary destination marketers – whether their activities are at national, regional, state or city level. The ways in which each destination seeks to tackle such issues will, of course, depend on local circumstances, finances and resources – there will always be local solutions to global challenges. However, the contributions included here suggest that there are common elements to these solutions – key issues and activities which every marketer seeking to achieve successful destination branding must address. These include: the often destructive role of politics in crafting brands; the essential role of inclusive, comprehensive and ongoing market research in identifying and creating the brand values; the need to build alliances and partnerships across all the stakeholder groups; and the value of 'brand champions' who have the vision, commitment and 'staying' power to drive the brand development. Finally, the reader is left with the clear message that the success of any destination brand depends on the extent to which it truly 'lives' for tourists. To really achieve destination branding, marketers must be in the business of delivering impactful experiences, not merely constructing a clever brand identity on paper with slick slogans and brand logos. The world's most successful destination brands have achieved this and those who seek to emulate them must follow the same principles, many of which are articulated and evidenced in the following chapters.

Destination branding in perspective

The book is divided into two parts – the first focuses on destination branding perspectives while the second presents four detailed explorations of successful destination branding initiatives, together with a discussion of on-line branding opportunities. Following this introduction, in Chapter 2, Nigel Morgan and Annette Pritchard contextualize destination branding, suggesting that it offers marketers the opportunity to counter one of the greatest dilemmas facing destinations – the sheer substitutability of their offerings. As Morgan and Pritchard discuss, however, putting destination branding into practice is no easy task and destinations face a number of challenges which each have the potential to derail the best branding initiatives. As their examples of Morocco and Israel suggest, political pressures, external environmental changes and product issues all have to be successfully combated if a destination brand is to prosper and grow. That said, successful branding brings significant rewards and the remainder of their chapter discusses how strong destination brands can be built around the concepts of 'wish you were here' appeal and celebrity value, focusing on a range of examples including Spain, New Zealand, Australia and Oregon, USA. They argue that brand winners are those places rich in emotional meaning, which have great conversational value and high anticipation for tourists, while brand losers have little meaning, status or emotional pull.

Simon Anholt, in his wide-ranging and thought-provoking exploration of 'provenance' in branding, then illustrates how successful 'nation' brands provide trust, quality and lifestyle connotations that consumers can readily purchase, explore and associate with themselves. In an eclectic discussion, Anholt demonstrates how such brand images are by no means superficial, neither are they restricted to the realm of economic exchange. Instead, a nation's brand image can profoundly shape its economic, cultural and political destiny. It is not surprising, therefore, that many nations are engaged in building and enhancing their brand identities. His suggestion that global brands could be the ultimate (re)distributor of global wealth is an intriguing thought which should stimulate wider debate. Since marketing has done much to increase the unequal distribution of wealth, it follows that it also offers opportunities to reverse the trend and Anholt suggests that even the smallest countries can benefit from nation branding and exploit the Internet-driven media revolution. He also reminds us that changing nation reputations and building brands are difficult, complex and long-term challenges which require honesty, objectivity and, above all, an empathetic understanding of the consumers' mindspace. It is only then that nation branders will be able to effectively utilize and capitalize on people's perceptions of places.

The next contribution, that of Fiona Gilmore, considers how destinations can brand for success. Central to this process is the strength of a brand's emotional relationship with the consumer – the stronger this relationship, the greater the brand's pull. In exploring branding best practice, Gilmore identifies certain key concepts which she illustrates in her examples of Ireland and Scotland. Clarity of vision and the ability to prioritize are seen to be vital in terms of the destination marketplace, destination competitors and consumer targets. As Gilmore notes, perhaps the most problematic issue in destination branding is the definition of the overall brand proposition, which must be underpinned by rigorous market research. Destinations must at all costs avoid presenting consumers with a 'shopping list' of attributes. In today's crowded marketplace, this will surely lead to failure and Gilmore argues that durable, successful brands will be built on emotional values and will develop emotional relationships with consumers.

In Chapter 5, Chris Ryan focuses specifically on the politics of branding cities and regions. Readers of this collection will by this stage be fully aware of the significance of politics in the branding process and Ryan's chapter reminds us that the branding of places must be examined in its wider context. Any collection on destination branding would be incomplete without such a discussion of the contentious arena in which such place-branding (and marketing) activities exist. While most of the contributions focus on branding per se, this chapter reinforces that branding is not merely a rational marketing activity, it is also a political act based on issues such as local pride. Tourism offers communities the potential to build both identities and viable economies – not surprisingly, therefore, it attracts significant government attention. Using New Zealand as a case study, Ryan explores the changing nature of the public–private sector relationship in the 1990s and beyond, noting that changes in government policy and personnel cannot but impact on tourism promotion and practice. As Ryan himself comments, at first glance, much of his discussion may seem to have little immediate impact on destination branding. The place-marketing issues he identifies (professionalism versus enthusiasm; short-termism versus long-term perspectives; competition versus co-operation; and the perceived significance of tourism), however, will resonate heavily with marketers currently grappling with the problems of branding places.

In the final chapter of this first part, Derek Hall explores issues of provenance and nation brand building in Central and Eastern Europe (CEE) where nation branding has been influenced by the need to portray an 'EU-style identity'. Hall takes the reader on a tour of the region, highlighting how destination branders in CEE face many of the challenges articulated in Chapter 2, including inadequate finance, lack of expertise, short-termism, and a lack of partnership approaches and networks. These emerge as major obstacles to the effective branding of the CEE nations – the importance of which cannot be underestimated in a marketing environment dominated by confused, contradictory and ill-developed destination identities. Hall paints a picture of CEE destination branding which seems very reminiscent of the activities of cities like New York and Glasgow in the 1980s – less branding initiatives and more marketing activities based on slogans and logos. Having said this, branding offers such states the opportunity to create new national identities, drawing a distinct line between past and present – although Hall leaves us in no doubt that these nations face considerable problems in their efforts to appeal to Western tourism markets.

Creating the unique destination proposition

In the first chapter of Part Two, Roger Pride explores how the Wales Tourist Board took classical branding techniques and adapted them to create an award-winning brand strategy for tourism, co-operating with other organizations within Wales to address the wider issue of Wales' image deficit. Pride notes how, too often, the creativity and ambition of marketing departments within tourist boards have been constrained by the existence of two additional 'Ps' invariably linked to destination marketing – 'politics' and 'paucity'. The case of Wales, as with many of the examples in this book, illustrates the challenges of introducing new thinking into a public sector risk-averse culture. This culture, which discourages innovation, is also widespread among many key destination stakeholders and tourism businesses, and Pride makes the point that, if the WTB had persisted in doing the same thing averagely well, while Wales' market share continued to decline, there would have been relatively little criticism of the agency. In striving to change things and perhaps taking a few risks along the way, however, its destination marketers attracted criticism for openly recognizing that the future growth would come from short breaks and additional holidays, and for constructing a branding and advertising strategy which highlighted Wales' natural environment and its potential as an off-season, short-break destination.

In Chapter 8 Shane Crockett and Leiza Wood shift the focus from nation to state branding in their detailed analysis of the Western Australian Tourism Commission's (WATC) approach. This strategy, based on intensive consumer research, government–industry partnerships and infrastructural developments, demonstrates the value not merely of developing a tourism but a state-wide brand. This chapter provides a rich source of good practice for state branders everywhere through its discussion of the challenges of the state's macroenvironment, its repositioning task, the development of Brand Western Australia (BWA) and the measures adopted to evaluate its marketing and partnership strategies. As Crockett and Wood demonstrate, successful destination branding must embrace a host of activities, including infrastructural development, product enhancement, protection against environmental degradation, changes in organizational culture, and promotional partnerships – all based on intensive market research to identify consumer desires. This case study of BWA demonstrates that, when combined with the development of a distinctive, broad visual language and strong creative promotional executions, these activities can provide the platform for a successful destination brand.

Continuing the theme of state branding, Jan Slater examines the brand-building success story of Louisiana, a state that has managed to create a powerful travel destination brand in perhaps the most demanding consumer market in the world – the USA. Such success is no mean task in a country where annual state government tourism promotional spending exceeds half a billion dollars in an effort to attract a domestic audience accounting for over a billion tourism trips. As Slater explains, the travel industry, once known for its 'wallpaper' advertising is wholeheartedly embracing 'branding to order' to communicate and emphasize the 'feel' and 'personality' of a place. Destinations are thus seeking to become experiences as opposed to merely a place to spend time. Louisiana (like many other destinations), with its colourful multicultural history, has many attractions to recommend itself to the would-be visitor. It is its successful brand identity, however, which has positioned Louisiana as one of the fastest growing tourism destinations in the USA. Significantly, the process has been underpinned by the development of a strong advertising agency–government tourism office partnership. The former, through their insightful 'mining' of existing consumer research, were able to develop a strong, differentiating, brand proposition and identity for the state which has remained largely unchanged since its conception in 1993. As Slater highlights, however, brand propositions need to be matched by efficient and effective media exposure and strong budgets if they are to succeed.

This is a point made abundantly clear in the penultimate chapter, written by Graham Brown, Laurence Chalip, Leo Jago and Trevor Mules, which considers the relationship between events and destination branding from a number of perspectives. After discussing the growing importance of event tourism, the authors examine the nature of destination image in the context of conceptual and applied frameworks before evaluating the status of the relationship between event management and tourism by reporting recent insight gained in Australia. The chapter reports findings from a research project that is focusing exclusively on the role of events in destination branding before considering the implications of the Sydney Olympic Games on Brand Australia. Brown, Chalip, Jago and Mules provide a richly researched insight into how Australia's destination marketers shrewdly harnessed the global appeal of the Olympic Games to promote not only Sydney's, but the whole of Australia's tourism image to the world. The case study clearly demonstrates how the 'best ever games' was used to strategically advance Brand Australia and leaves the reader in no doubt as to the value of hosting *the* global event.

The collection concludes with an examination of the opportunities and challenges that the Internet offers destination branders. Such is the significance of the Web in this area that most of the earlier contributions, discussed above, also draw attention to the role of the Internet and some of the featured destinations are building brands which heavily feature the Internet. In Chapter 11, Adrian Palmer thus focuses on the impacts emerging high-speed data transmission technologies such as the Web, e-commerce and m-commerce will have on destination branding. Significantly, he shows that the Internet facilitates both the creation of strong, highly branded sites and a much stronger presence for individual tourism suppliers. Such a synergy should go some way to bridging the gap between destination branding and an industry which sometimes fails to see the value and impact such umbrella activities have on their businesses. In fact, Internet proliferation, audience splintering and an increasingly techno-literate society are combining to make Web-based destination branding increasingly critical. While the Web creates challenges it also opens up opportunities – of interactive adverisements, smart web sites and e-consumers seeking engagement and engaging promotions (Morgan, Pritchard and Abbott, 2001).

Given that the Web offers each individual tourism supplier the opportunity to directly position themselves and communicate interactively with potential con-sumers, challenges to destination-branding initiatives (and to the role of the destination-marketing organizations themselves) will only increase without partner-ship, communication and co-operation. As we ease our way into the twenty-first century, it cannot be denied that the role of destination branding is critical and will become ever more so. In a world dominated by change and celebrity, in which the virtual world will become the focus of much marketing activity, those destinations which can successfully 'brand' the gap between suppliers and consumers will be today's, and particularly tomorrow's, brand winners. One inescapable conclusion from this collection is that there must be much more detailed case-study-based investigations into destination branding – especially those evaluating the long-term success of such activities. Indeed, this is also true of tourism and branding in general – we need much more detailed knowledge of just how consumers interact with brands in the world's fastest growing industry.

References

Clarke, J. (2000). Tourism brands: an exploratory study of the brands box model. *Journal of Vacation Marketing*, **6**(4), 329–345.

Lurham, D. (1998). World tourism: crystal ball gazing. *Tourism, the Journal of the Tourism Society*, **96**, 13.

Morgan, N. J., Pritchard, A. and Abbot, S. (2001). Consumers, travel and technology: a bright future for the Web or television shopping? *Journal of Vacation Marketing*, **7**(2), April, 110–124.

Piggott, R. (2001). Building a brand for a country. Can commercial marketing practices achieve this in a government-funded environment? Unpublished University of Hull MBA dissertation.

Westwood, S. (2000). The holiday brand, what does it mean? An exploratory study of brand equity in the context of the package holiday experience. In *Management, Marketing and the Political Economy of Travel and Tourism, Reflections on International Tourism* (M. Robinson, N. Evans, P. Long, R. Sharpley and J. Swarbrooke, eds) pp. 517–536, Business Education.

2

Contextualizing destination branding

Nigel Morgan and Annette Pritchard

Introduction

Branding is perhaps the most powerful marketing weapon available to contemporary destination marketers confronted by increasing product parity, substitutability and competition. Today most destinations have superb five-star resorts, hotels and attractions, every country claims a unique culture and heritage, each place describes itself as having the friendliest people and the most customer-focused tourism industry and service, and facilities are no longer differentiators. Such is the substitutability of tourism destinations that, for example, UK tourists in search of a moderately priced sun and sand experience will accept a range of alternatives – from resorts in Cyprus, to those in Turkey, Spain or Greece. As a result, the need for destinations to create a unique identity – to differentiate themselves from their competitors – is more critical than ever. Indeed, it has become *the* basis for survival within a globally competitive marketplace where, for instance, a destination such as New Zealand competes with approximately ninety other destinations for only

30 per cent of the worldwide tourism market (Piggott, 2001: 79). Yet, despite this aggressive marketplace, how many country advertisements do you see which portray blue seas, cloudless skies and endless golden beaches with a less than memorable tag line? Yet what does differentiate one Caribbean or Mediterranean island from its nearest neighbour? Rarely sun and sand. In this marketplace what persuades potential tourists to visit (and revisit) one place instead of another is whether they have empathy with the destination and its values. The battle for customers in tomorrow's destination marketplace will be fought not over price but over hearts and minds – and this is where we move into the realm of branding.

In marketing terms a brand represents a unique combination of product characteristics and added values, both functional and non-functional, which have taken on a relevant meaning which is inextricably linked to that brand, awareness of which might be conscious or intuitive (Macrae, Parkinson and Sheerman, 1995). Brand advantage is secured through communication which highlights the specific benefits of a product, culminating in an overall impression of a superior brand. The image the product creates in the consumer's mind, how it is *positioned*, however, is of more importance to its ultimate success than its actual characteristics. Brand managers position their brands so that they are perceived by the consumer to occupy a niche in the marketplace occupied by no other brand – thus, for marketers, the value of a successful brand lies in its potential to reduce substitutability. Brand managers differentiate their product by stressing attributes they claim will match their target markets' needs more closely than other brands and then they create a product image consistent with the perceived self-image of the targeted consumer segment (Schiffman and Kanuk, 2000). When consumers make brand choices about products – including destinations – they are making lifestyle statements since they are buying into not only an image but also an emotional relationship (Sheth, Mittal and Newman, 1999; Urdde, 1999). Consumers have their own 'brand wardrobes'[1] from which they make selections to communicate, reflect and reinforce associations, statements and memberships; in effect, 'consumers enrobe themselves with brands, partly for what they do, but more for what they help express about their emotions, personalities and roles' (de Chernatony, 1993: 178).

Given the nature of this brand–consumer relationship, there is increased focus among marketers on differentiation through loyalty and the emotional appeal of brands, rather than through discernible, tangible benefits (Westwood et al., 1999). As Lury (1998: 4) says 'it is our perceptions – our beliefs and our feelings about a brand that are most important'. However, mere emotion is not enough, the key is to develop a strong brand which holds some *unique* associations for the consumer – 'while emotion has always been an important component of branding, emotion in the absence of a point of difference that can be articulated and firmly seated in the memory is arguably a recipe for consumer confusion' (Hallberg, 1995). Such is the importance of this product positioning that it has been described as the essence of marketing and, since it conveys how the product will satisfy a consumer need, different consumer meanings can be assigned to the same product via different positioning strategies, depending on the audience and stage in the brand life cycle.

The challenges of destination branding

No matter where destinations are in the life cycle, they all face a number of marketing challenges. Most national tourism organizations have limited budgets and yet they have to market globally, competing not just with other destinations, but also with other global brands. Procter & Gamble, the world's biggest advertiser, may spend millions each year promoting their various brands but countries such as Spain, France and Thailand still have to vie with them for consumer mindshare in a crowded environment characterized by spiralling media costs. While one corporate giant such as Sony would spend in excess of US$300 million on its annual advertising globally, the World Tourism Organization (WTO) estimates that the world's governments are currently spending around US$350 million each year on destination advertising – accounting for around half of the promotional budgets of national tourism organizations. Table 2.1 illustrates the biggest advertising spenders at the end of the 1990s (other significant spenders included Greece, Turkey, Egypt and Canada) – not, of course, including private sector spending. It is worth pointing out here that this table only illustrates *national* advertising spend – where available. It does not, for instance, include countries which have no national tourism organization. In the USA, for example, state promotion is undertaken by a variety of convention bureaux and state travel offices – whose budgets often exceed those of some countries. The Illinois state

Table 2.1 **Top national tourism organizations' advertising spend, 1997**

Country	Advertising spend (US$ millions)
Australia	30
Thailand	26
Cyprus	17
Spain	17
France	16
Puerto Rico	16
Brazil	15
Portugal	13

Source: WTO (figures to nearest million).

travel office budget in 1997 topped US$35 million, that of Texas was US$25 million and Pennsylvania almost US$20 million. Compare these figures with the national tourism budgets of Germany (US$27 million), Hungary (US$21 million) and Morocco (US$18 million) (Lurman, 1998). A recent CNN research survey (March 2000) showed that some US$538 million was spent on destination marketing alone in the USA during 1999 (Piggott, 2001: 10).

Thus, the first challenge facing destination marketers is their extremely limited budgets by comparison with the marketers of many consumer goods and services. Combine this with evidence that tourism promotion does not *persuade* uncommitted potential vacationers (but rather acts to *confirm* the intentions of those already predisposed to visit), and destination managers and their advertising agencies have genuine problems. So how can destination marketers compete with the mega-consumer brands and penetrate the fog of advertising overload? Clearly they have to *outsmart* rather than *outspend* the competition – and that means creating innovative, attention-grabbing advertising on a budget *and* maximizing the media spend. This is a simple, self-evident truth but in destination advertising it is extremely difficult to achieve. This is not to say that destination marketers are not good at their jobs, but that effective place branding is often compromised by the *politics* of destination advertising.

The challenge of politics

Successful destination branding is about achieving a balance between applying cutting-edge advertising and public relations approaches to a marketing problem and the realpolitik of managing local, regional and national politics. This is the second challenge for destination marketers and the real success stories reflect destination brands which have been able to resist the political dynamic (which is exerted at all levels of the political scene). These are brands which have strong advertising heritages, are consistent but at the same time which evolve, move with the times and appear continually contemporary and fresh. This is easy to write but difficult to achieve and that is why the same destinations are constantly cited as classic examples of cohesive, long-term branding – because they are a rare breed and they succeed against the odds. Thus, Ireland has been running the same basic proposition in its various campaigns for decades and while marketing directors and executives change the message remains constant – currently encapsulated in the *'Live a different life'* strap line.

Certainly, nowhere is the paradox of public policy and market forces more sharply defined than in destination branding. For instance, there is considerable debate among destination marketers and destination stakeholders over the use of clichés and stereotypes in marketing and advertising. Often consumers have very clichéd images about countries, yet those clichés are frequently disliked in the countries themselves. One view is if the consumer connects with a cliché about a country, then its marketers should use it since it has recognition and therefore advertising value. That, however, is an agency view – not one tempered by the experience of seeing the media fallout of an advertising campaign perceived by residents as perpetuating stereotypes which are (by definition) outdated caricatures of places and peoples. The answer – which is both politically acceptable and which makes marketing sense – is to craft images which use the cliché as a hook on which to hang more detail; the narrow, clichéd identity can then be reshaped and given greater complexity and richness through effective and consistent marketing.

Beyond such issues, public sector destination marketers are also hugely hampered by a variety of political pressures – they have to reconcile a range of local and regional interests and promote an identity acceptable to a range of constituencies (Buhalis, 2000). Some of the reasons why Brand Oregon, designed to be inclusive of tourism and economic development, began to fall apart in the late 1980s included: the tourism sector's resistance to direction from the top; the failure by some economic development organizations to see the connections between Oregon's lifestyle and business opportunities; and the tourism regions' reluctance to produce advertising and publications consistent with the state's branded campaign (Curtis, 2001: 76–7). In addition to such compromising of the creative process of marketing destinations, destination brand building is also frequently undermined by the short-termism of the tourism organizations' political masters. A destination brand's lifespan is a longer-term proposition than the careers of most politicians and Julie Curtis of the Oregon Tourism Commission urges destination marketers to 'stay the course', and resist making changes too quickly since 'it takes many years to establish a brand image, establish name recognition and develop strong awareness of a destination or product' (Curtis, 2001: 81).

Bureaucratic red tape can also confound effective advertising – the marketers of Valencia, Spain's third city, for instance, are obliged to issue new advertising contracts every year – a practice which can do little to ensure consistency of message. Frequently, political considerations within a local state can even dictate the range of photographs which are included in a campaign. Many a creative execution has had to be amended so that brochures, commercials or posters can include photographs to illustrate *all* the key areas, towns or resorts within a region or country. While this has its political advantages in that it appeases local pressure groups and local residents – and politicians are vulnerable to bad press and unrest in the trade – it will seriously compromise the impact of the branding campaign. As Bob Garfield, editor of *Advertising Age* and long-time advertising critic, has said of destination advertising: 'When you look at the ads . . .you can see transcripts of the arguments at the tourist boards . . .the membership of which all wanted their own interests served . . .you can see the destruction of the advertising message as a result of the politics' (Garfield, 1998).

Even when all the internal stakeholders are satisfied with a campaign, destination branding can run into political problems as a result of external pressures. Perhaps one of the most depressing examples of this was the 'Feast for the Senses' brand created by Publicis for the Morocco Tourist Board in the mid-1990s. The campaign was an attempt to craft a homogeneous brand identity for the country in all its generating markets – each of which had previously commissioned quite separate advertising on the reasonable premise that consumers in the UK, Germany, France, Italy, etc. all sought different experiences from a holiday to Morocco. Yet this disparate approach had created a blurred and confused image of the country. Working with the Morocco Tourist Board – whose total annual tourism budget was approximately US$18 million (Lurham, 1998) – the agency therefore decided to create a new logo and produced a number of stunning visuals in a series of ten posters and in the main brochure, followed through in television commercials – all based around the strap line 'Morocco – A Feast for the Senses'. All the advertising was produced in the key markets' languages, so while consistency of brand image was achieved, the local Morocco marketing office in each of the markets was to some extent free to choose the visual it thought would best reflect the country's most marketable brand values in that particular country.

Each of Morocco's main tourism regions was featured in the campaign, and such was the positive reaction in Morocco itself when the visuals were seen that in the next phase the agency even created posters for those areas where there was little or no tourism infrastructure. Yet, while the brand-building exercise was warmly welcomed in Morocco – and actually began to change regional policy-makers' attitudes to the potential of tourism – it proved extremely difficult to sell the idea to external stakeholders. Travel agents and tour operators had to be persuaded to embrace it and a considerable effort was put into trade promotional packs, including displays, maps and a new trade magazine. Ultimately the campaign hit problems because German tour operators lobbied the Morocco Tourist Board, concerned that the brand was promoting the country as a cultural destination and not as the sun and sea product which their customers were seeking. While the visuals and the logo were retained in the following year, Publicis lost the contract and the dilution of the strong brand values of the original concept began (Vial, 1997).

The challenge of the external environment

While all products are affected by external change, destinations are particularly vulnerable to international politics, economics, terrorism and environmental disasters. The Gulf War, volcanic eruptions and hurricanes in the Caribbean, the Asian economic collapse, political instability in Fiji, oil spills off the Galapagos Islands and the UK foot and mouth outbreak are just some of the recent crises which have derailed destination promotional planning. One destination which has seen its promising branding activities undermined by political change is Israel. In the UK, Israeli marketing has fallen into three distinct phases since 1993. Phase One (1993–8) saw the launch of marketing activities designed to enable Israel to stand out from the crowd. Phase Two (1999–2000) saw Israel make maximum capital out of its links with the Judaeo-Christian Millennium celebrations. Phase Three (2000 onwards) has seen the country's branding activities seriously compromised by the breakdown of the peace process, and today images of the country are again associated with violence and sectarianism. In 1993 Israel was a poor performer in the UK – acknowledged as perhaps the world's most competitive travel market. Research in the UK among Israel's primary target market (upper- and middle-income groups aged twenty-five to sixty) revealed that Israel scored very poorly in terms of people's future (next twelve months) holiday consideration set – considerably below competitors such as Italy and Greece, and well below Spain. Perhaps of even greater concern were the perceptions held among consumers in its target market. Israel was variously seen as a third world country, a desert, a place only for religious fanatics and last (but by no means least) a war zone. The one piece of good news, however, was that these perceptions did not cause people to totally reject the possibility of holidaying in Israel – a potential further boosted by the 1993 peace accord.

Between 1993 and 1998 Israeli advertising in the UK sought to present the country in a very positive and memorable light and, significantly, the Israeli national tourist office was prepared to make additional funds available to stimulate visitor growth – working with a total promotional budget of around $24 million, just under half of which was allocated to advertising (Lurham, 1998). Targets were set to achieve a 30 per cent increase in tourism arrivals in two years, aiming to move from attracting 230 000 to 300 000 UK visitors. At that time, visitors to Israel fell into three categories – the Jewish community (30 per cent), Christian pilgrims (20 per cent) and the upscale market (50 per cent). The last group were felt to offer the greatest opportunities for the growth demanded by the national tourist office (NTO). Within this target market, the advertising would specifically target couples aged twenty-five to thirty-five, without children, followed by the fifty-plus empty-nesters. The advertising needed to communicate that Israel was not a cheap nor a young sun and sand destination; it also needed to overcome the target markets' misconceptions. Israel was therefore branded as a 'Quality beach holiday offering the texture and atmosphere of the Mediterranean but with a rich heritage and exotic overtones'. The keys to the detail of this positioning were the quality of its four- and five-star hotels and service, its varied beaches and seas (the Red, Dead, Mediterranean and Galilee Seas), its year-round sunshine and activities, and its Mediterranean quality in tone and sophistication (rather than geography). However, the positioning needed to be communicated via a strong, simple, memorable and unique brand hook.

The final destination advertising combined 'Hava Nagila' (an Israeli folk song well known in the UK) with the concept that people want a great holiday. Hence, the strap line: 'HAV'A Great Holiday in Israel' was used in all advertisements. The campaign used television, press and poster advertisements, all focusing on the London and South East region. The 'Hava Nagila' folk song was central to the executions in every medium, being used as the musical accompaniment and also the hook for each scene change in the television commercials, as well as providing the inspiration for the copy in the posters and the main brochure – for example, 'HAV'A trip to Jerusalem' and 'HAV'A great holiday'. In the poster advertisements 'HAV'A' (displayed in bold central type) linked two separate – although linked – images, for instance, gold beaches and golden Jerusalem; each execution invited tourists to submerge themselves in the country's culture and history as well as its scenery.

The campaign performed remarkably well and, in just one year, the growth target of 30 per cent was achieved and then maintained in subsequent years. While the total winter sun market in the UK grew by 7 per cent in 1993/4, Israel's grew by 18 per cent and Eilat (one of Israel's key resorts) by 34 per cent. Israel's spontaneous awareness levels increased dramatically on pre- and post-measures, and exceeded the post-awareness levels of all its competitors. The advertising itself became famous and distinctive in a market notorious for its uniformity and lack of brand differentiation, and prompted advertising recall grew from 38 per cent in 1993 to 50 per cent in 1994 and reached 57 per cent in 1996 despite a decreasing advertising budget (Rodwell, 1999).

In 1999–2000 the 'HAV'A' campaign was suspended while Israel capitalized on the opportunities created by the Millennium, with the intention that the new campaign would provide the ideal platform for further branding opportunities based on its positioning of Israel as a Mediterranean destination with culturally exotic overtones. In the Judaeo-Christian world, no country had a stronger link with or claim to the Millennium than Israel and central to this positioning was the need to communicate with Israel's ethnic and religious market, as well as its mainstream holiday market. The destination advertising needed to speak to all people who, for whatever reason, were thinking about the Millennium in an *emotional* way. It needed to show why Israel should be considered as a destination, its inherent magic and, of course, its relevance to the Millennium.

Central to the proposition created by Israel's advertising agency (Court Burkitt and Company of London) was 'the best Millennium experience is surely where it all began'. A series of poster advertisements were produced for the UK market which invited the tourist to Israel while juxtaposing Israel's claims with those of other less 'worthy' destinations in which to celebrate the new Millennium. One execution headlined, 'In the year 2000 do you really want to say you went to Florida?', against a shot of three camels silhouetted against a glorious sunset. In a similar vein, another poster featured a beautifully shot scene of divers in the Red Sea with the copy: 'The

Millennium and it's not just 2000 years of history you'll want to dive into.' A further poster asked, 'Can you really experience the Millennium in SE10?' above a photograph of Jerusalem's skyline and Jerusalem's dome commemorating the place where the prophet Elijah is said to have ascended in to heaven. This poster had particular meaning in the UK market as it contrasted the Jerusalem temple dome with the Millennium Dome – located in SE10 (Rodwell, 1999).

The marketing success of this development of the Israel brand has, however, been dealt a serious, if not fatal blow by the recent collapse of the peace process. Images of conflict, unrest and sectarian violence are once again regularly featured on the world's news bulletins, and international tourist arrivals have declined as a result. Israeli tourism has, of course, recovered from a series of such setbacks in the past and it remains to be seen how it responds to this latest challenge. The lesson from this case study, however, is that even a well-funded, internally supported branding exercise cannot guarantee success, such is the unpredictability of the external marketing environment.

The challenge of the destination product

Examples of countries being influenced by external pressures to adapt and change their marketing activities, or whose marketing is seriously compromised by events outside their marketers' control, highlight the fact that destinations are not a single product but composite products consisting of a bundle of different components, including: accommodation and catering establishments; tourist attractions; arts, entertainment and cultural venues; and the natural environment (Buhalis, 2000; Ritchie and Crouch, 2000). Destination marketers have relatively little control over these different aspects of their product and a diverse range of agencies and companies are partners in the task of crafting brand identities. These could include local and national government agencies, environmental groups and agencies, chambers of commerce, trade associations and civic groups. While packaged goods normally have an obvious core – so that their advertisements can anchor themselves to product performance and attributes – with destinations the situation is much less clear (Morgan and Pritchard, 1998; 1999).

The essence of creating a successful brand is to build an emotional link between the product and the consumer, but what encapsulates the emotional brand values of a destination? Is it the atmosphere of a resort, the hotel the tourist stays in, the friendliness of the local people or some overall impression (Tapachai and Waryszak, 2000)? All of these factors can and do affect how the tourist views the vacation experience. In view of the fact that it is a composite product, can a destination ever evoke high levels of emotional commitment? Obviously, we would argue that it can as the potential to evoke an emotional attachment is even greater for tourism destinations than for fast-moving consumer goods (fmcg) or services – destinations have very strong and pervasive associations for tourists which, if skilfully orchestrated, can provide the basis for brand building (Baloglu and Brinberg, 1997). Today's tourists are not asking 'what can we do on holiday?', but 'who can we be on holiday?' – they are increasingly looking less for escape and more for discovery – and that creates the basis of an emotional connection which marketers can exploit through branding (Morgan and Pritchard, 2000: 278. The challenge beyond that is to make the destination brand live, so that visitors truly experience the promoted brand values and feel the authencity of a unique place.

The challenge of creating differentiation

While there are these added pressures in destination marketing, effective branding can still be accomplished. As Bob Garfield (1998) notes: 'Smart managers find out what is the meaning of their destination as a product to their potential consumer. They exploit that meaning in finding the value they can add to the sun and sand experience. Their advertising, when it's done well, should reflect that added value . . .that point of differentiation.'

Most destinations have something – a unique selling opportunity – that can be translated into a unique selling proposition. The US Virgin Islands, for example, are a sun, surf and sand destination which is physically identical to the British Virgin Islands which are 40 nautical miles away. Yet, because the US Virgin Islands' biggest market is the USA, they do have something on which to build a unique proposition. Marketers can advertise the concept that US visitors can have the exotic experience of a natural paradise – yet with the comfort and security of visiting somewhere where everyone speaks their language and uses their currency. For those Americans who want a beach holiday and are predisposed to try something partly exotic but mostly safe and familiar, the US Virgin Islands have a unique opportunity and hence marketers use the strap lines 'They're your islands' and 'The American Paradise in the Caribbean'. These differentiate the destination from the British Virgin Islands, which use the phrases 'Out of this world . . .not out of reach' and 'Nature's Little Secrets'. As the US Virgin Islands' brochure points out:

> As an American territory, the US Virgin Islands offers United States citizens significant advantages over other Caribbean vacation getaways. Even if you are an international traveler, you will find the American system of laws and customs under which the US Virgin Islands operates to be convenient and trouble-free . . .The US Virgin Islands. They're your islands. Come see them for yourself and you'll find yourself returning.

Countries often promote their history, their culture and their beautiful scenery in their marketing, but many destinations have these attributes and it is critical to build a brand on something which uniquely connects a destination to the consumer now or has the potential to do so in the future. It must also be a proposition which the competition wants and is maybe able to *copy* but which they cannot *surpass* or *usurp*. For example, other world cities can claim to be romantic or spiritual, but only Rome (or more strictly, the Vatican) is 'The Eternal City' – it has that epithet, it had it first and no other place can now claim it. Virginia in the USA has had phenomenal success with its 'Virginia is for Lovers' campaign but no destination can surpass Paris for its associations with romance. Whatever proposition is used it must also have the potential to last, to grow old and to evolve in a long-term branding campaign, so it is essential to get it right. However, the point of differentiation must reflect a promise which can be delivered and which matches expectations. Good destination branding is therefore original and different but its originality and difference needs to be *sustainable*, *believable* and *relevant* – not, for instance, as in the case of Philadelphia, USA, whose promise about your vacation memories of the place living with you forever probably promises too much.

One such destination marketing campaign which transcended the commodity nature of the product and which promised a unique (yet credible) experience was the 'India Changes You' campaign of 1998. There are many exotic countries which a consumer could visit and most of them have breath-taking scenery and fascinating heritage, yet such is the emotional power of the subcontinent with its poignant history and diverse cultures that the advertising promise to the consumer that 'India changes you' is sustainable. Garfield (1998) has described this campaign premise as 'among the most powerful advertising statements I have ever encountered in any category anywhere – it's not "get away from it all", it's not "escape the rat race", it's not "discover yourself" – which are all fairly familiar themes – it's better than discover yourself, it's "change yourself." It's breathtaking'. The brand proposition was only a part of the reason for this campaign's success. The other was that in this instance, the marketers of India also managed to transcend the politics of tourism advertising. Despite the fact that India is made up of a number of enormously populous regions, all competing for tourism business, the campaign promoted the whole of India as one destination and, in doing so, succeeded in preventing any dilution of the advertising message which the promotion of the individual regions would have created.

Branding destinations: making it happen

As we have seen, limited budgets, the lack of overall product control and internal and external pressures pose unique challenges for destination marketers. In such circumstances, the creation of brand saliency – the development of an emotional relationship with the consumer through highly choreographed and focused communications campaigns – holds the key to destination differentiation (see, for example, Anholt, 1999; Crockett and Wood, 1999; Hall, 1999; Nickerson and Moisey, 1999; Curtis, 2001). In the 1980s there were several highly successful marketing campaigns which centred on a consistent communications proposition. New York's 'I love NY' and the 'Glasgow's miles better' campaigns are two of the best known. In these, and in many other instances, the campaigns focused on logos and slogans but they were not truly *branding* initiatives. In building a brand for a destination the identity creation should not be confined to the visual, and this is the essence of 'mood brand marketing'. It is designed to create an emotional relationship between the destination and potential visitors – as in the current 'Amazing Thailand' and '100% New Zealand' campaigns. In both, the branding activities concentrate on conveying the essence or *the spirit* of the destination, often communicated via a few key attributes and associations.

Not to be confused with any religious connotations, this is marketing based very much on an emotional or spiritual appeal (Morgan and Pritchard, 2000). If successful, such activities do not only have an impact on how the rest of the world regards a place but also on a destination's view of itself. This has very much been the case in Australia, for instance. Here, the achievements of the Sydney 2000 Olympic Games (in sporting, marketing, operations management and facility design terms), coupled with the ongoing aggressive branding of the country as a whole, has created a new view of Australia as a cosmopolitan, outward-looking country, and many of the country's politicians see Sydney 2000 as symbolizing the modernization of the Australian economy (Morse, 2001; Tibbott, 2001). It has been estimated that the exposure gained through hosting the Games accelerated Australia's marketing by ten years and that they will generate an additional A$6.1 billion in foreign exchange earnings between 1997 and 2004. Moreover, 90 per cent of visitors who went to Sydney for the Games are anticipated to become repeat visitors (www.atc.net.au/news/olympic2.htm).

Achieving celebrity

Image is all-important and how a place is represented can inspire people to visit and revisit it (Coshall, 2000; Tapachai and Waryszak, 2000). Never was the saying 'accentuate the positive and eliminate the negative' more true than in destination branding. Destination marketing requires foresight and planning but it is not an exact science and branding offers destination marketers an opportunity to communicate key place attributes to their intended audience. Branding can help bridge any gaps between a destination's strengths and potential visitors' perceptions. Place reputations are not made in a vacuum and neither are tourist choices, so place marketers must establish how their destination's image compares with those of its key competitors. How the destination rates according to 'wish *you* were here?' appeal and celebrity value is critical. Do tourists regard it as a fashion accessory, a

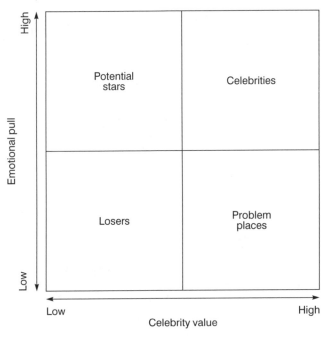

Figure 2.1 The destination celebrity matrix

must-see place on every aspirational traveller's shopping list or as a fashion faux pas – somewhere with no conversational value and even less status (Figure 2.1)? Figure 2.2 takes this celebrity matrix and illustrates a range of destination brands measured on the axes of emotional appeal and celebrity value. Obviously, how people relate to any destination brand depends on their own individual interests, opinions and experiences, and such positioning maps must be used in conjunction with pyschographic analyses of key market segments.

On any positioning map, however, brand winners emerge as those places which are rich in emotional meaning, have great conversation value and hold high anticipation for potential tourists. By comparison, brand losers are places with little meaning, even less status, virtually no conversation value and zero anticipation for tourists. Problem places are those destinations which are talked about for the wrong reasons and, far from holding an emotional appeal, actively repel potential tourists. Places which currently offer little emotional pull face an uphill task if they are ever to become destination winners. Other destinations which do have high emotional pull but currently have limited celebrity value hold huge untapped potential and could be tomorrow's winner destination brands, and currently include places such as India, Cuba, Vietnam and South Africa (Figure 2.2). The challenge for their marketers is to craft identities for these destinations which convey and build on their

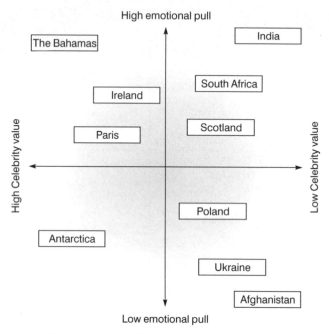

Figure 2.2 The destination brand positioning map

emotional appeal and which turn them into places with high celebrity value. The message here is that rich, strong destination brands sing a song of difference and have a sense of being somewhere worth visiting.

The destination brand fashion curve

Recognising that branding is a two-way process done *with* and not *to* the consumer, Weinreich (1999: 25–6) has suggested that instead of thinking in terms of the traditional product or brand life cycle, brand managers should be thinking of the S-curve which charts a brand's life and development through birth, growth, maturity, decay and death (although, of course, the time frames are elastic and could encompass anything from weeks to centuries). Instead of seeing the S-curve as tracking sales volume over time, managers should consider it as a series of stages in the brand's relationship with its consumers, revealing useful insights into a brand's communications requirements. Developing this concept and translating it to tourism destination brands, we can see (Figure 2.3) that at first the market is small and many places become trendy in spite of (or due to) their lack of advertising activities because the destination is new and exclusive. Here the destination brand is at the beginning of its fashionable phase and its visitors are trendsetters who,

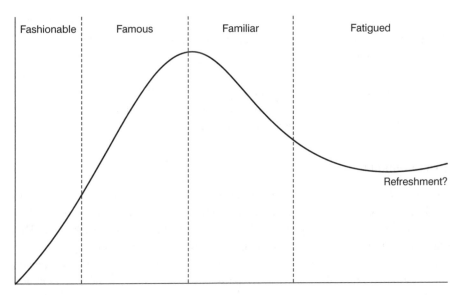

| Fashionable | Famous | Familiar | Fatigued |

Refreshment?

Figure 2.3. The destination brand fashion curve

although few in numbers, are influential opinion-formers. Yet, as the destination becomes famous and loses its cutting-edge appeal, these tourists move on to the next new place since they do not want to be seen somewhere which has become popular and rather passé. In the famous phase, a destination brand's consumers are loyal and affluent but at any time the destination's brand values may become irrelevant to them – hence the ongoing need for them to remain fresh and appealing. If the place fails to remain contemporary, it will drift into the familiar zone where everyone knows about the destination, but it has lost its appeal – it has become 'overwarm, cuddly and sentimental, the antithesis of . . .cool' (Weinreich, 1999: 28). Becoming familiar can ultimately lead a destination to fatigue – a place which finds it difficult to attract lucerative market segments. If it becomes very badly damaged, a destination brand's core values will need to be reassessed and its relevance to target markets redefined and revitalized.

For every success story such as Ireland and Spain, there are numerous destinations which have become fatally fatigued, having failed to maintain long-term marketing and advertising effort or which have been affected by external change. All brands can show signs of age, needing refreshment in the face of modern competition and even the most classic of brands need to remain contemporary. Certainly, such is the speed of change in today's market, destination brands which fail to evolve are brands which will fail. One place which once had an enviable reputation for luxury and glamour was the Côte D'Azur – Europe's dream destination which was the very essence of chic. Yet since the 1950s it has lost its cachet as the glitterati have moved to other destinations further afield and, although such places as Monte Carlo, Cannes and Nice retain their allure, the South of France as a whole has lost its strong associations with wealth and fashion. No destination brand can ever remain static, and marketers need to recognize when a place has reached a point when the brand requires refreshment. Failure to advance and develop the brand will eventually lead to stagnation and ultimately to brand decay.

Brand building

The first stage in the process of building or refreshing any destination brand is to establish the core values of the destination and its brand – these should be durable, relevant, communicable and hold saliency for potential tourists (Table 2.2). This stage should consider just how contemporary or relevant the brand is to today's tourism consumer and how it compares with its key competitors. For instance, when the Oregon Economic Development Department began its revival of Brand Oregon in the mid-1990s, it initiated a series of research projects which surveyed local businesses, regional economists, other US states with similar programmes and previous visitors – as well as visitors who had never actually been to the state (Curtis, 2001). This process (similar to recent exercises conducted by the brand developers of, among other places, Switzerland, Hawaii, Wales, Western Australia and New Zealand) assisted Oregon's brand managers to build brand value and salience with existing and potential consumers.

Once this market investigation is complete, the next phase is to develop the brand identity. Of primary importance to this phase are the concepts of the brand benefit pyramid and brand architecture (more of which below). Once the brand's core values have been established, they should underpin and imbue all subsequent marketing activity – especially in literature text and illustrations – so that the brand values are cohesively communicated. A logotype or brand signature and a design style guide, which ensures consistency of message and approach, should also reinforce the brand values. The vision (which must be shared and 'bought into' by

Table 2.2 The five phases in destination brand building

Phase One	Market investigation, analysis and strategic recommendations
Phase Two	Brand identity development
Phase Three	Brand launch and introduction – communicating the vision
Phase Four	Brand implementation
Phase Five	Monitoring, evaluation and review

all its stakeholders and potential consumers) should be clearly expressed in the brand's core values which are consistently reinforced through the product and in all marketing communications – both above and below the line – every execution in all media contributes to maintaining brand presence. To successfully create an emotional attachment a destination brand has to be:

- credible
- deliverable
- differentiating
- conveying powerful ideas
- enthusing for trade partners
- resonating with the consumer.

A destination which is currently building just such a brand proposition around its stunning natural environment is New Zealand (Harris, 2000; Piggott, 2001). A geographically disadvantaged destination, New Zealand is in the process of building a strong brand to double the country's tourism foreign exchange receipts to more than £3 billion by 2005 (Warren and Thompson, 2000). The '100% Pure New Zealand' campaign, the country's first global marketing campaign, is intended to recover some of the ground lost to Australia in the tourism marketplace (Tourism New Zealand, 2000). The campaign was launched market by market between July 1999 and February 2000 to coincide with seasonal promotional opportunities. Advertising is centred on above-the-line activity; mainly television and print (magazines) and the executions showcase New Zealand's diverse landscapes, people, culture and tourism activities. The key markets for media activity are Australia, Japan, USA, UK, Germany, Singapore and Taiwan – regions which generate the largest number of visitors to New Zealand (Piggott, 2001: 12).

The '100%' logo incorporates an image of the country's two islands – North and South – while the strap line '100% Pure New Zealand' seeks to position the destination as the ultimate backpacker and thrill-seeker paradise – what the New Zealand brochure describes as a place of 'awesome sights, breathtaking vistas, indelible experiences – that's New Zealand'. The theme of 100 per cent and purity is echoed in all the visuals and the copy of the material, with the scenery, its wines and foods, its people and its experiences being seen as being untainted, unadulterated, unaffected and undiluted (Figures 2.4, 2.5, 2.6 and 2.7). The brand is intended to position New Zealand as a place (and, indeed, an ethos) shaped by its inhabitants over time. It communicates the quality of the destination's leisure, cultural and heritage products and services, and is the latest step in a strategy to build a clear, consistent and unique identity, building on the New Zealand way and the use of the silver fern. Currently, strap lines such as '100% Pure Romance' and '100% Pure Spirit' are being used. In the long term, M&C Saatchi – the advertising

Figure 2.4 'Spa', New Zealand's 100% campaign, courtesy of Tourism New Zealand (TNZ)

Figure 2.5 'Mountain Biker', New Zealand's 100% campaign, courtesy of TNZ

Figure 2.6 'Skinny Dipping', New Zealand's 100% campaign, courtesy of TNZ

Figure 2.7 'Moeraki Boulder', New Zealand's 100% campaign, courtesy of TNZ

agency responsible for the campaign – is aiming to achieve such consumer awareness of the logo as to be able to drop the '100% New Zealand' strap line and let the '100%' logo stand for Brand New Zealand. The prime targets are so-called 'interactive travellers' – people young in body or heart who love travel, seek new experiences and enjoy the challenge of new destinations. While these consumers are a small proportion of New Zealand's overall tourism market, they are the highly influential opinion-formers who could exert significant influence and make New Zealand a fashionable or famous destination.

Such consumers are often very Web-wise and significantly, the World Wide Web (WWW) is integral to the New Zealand brand, complementing other advertising and public relations activities and media. The destination cyber scene is highly competitive and expensive, and creating and promoting an effective web site is not cheap. The current challenge is for destinations to convert e-browsers into e-buyers and, above all, to match and, where possible, exceed other e-tailer experiences (Morgan, Pritchard and Abbot, 2001). Destinations have to try to convey a sense of experiencing the place (through webcams, weather updates, music clips, oral histories, collection highlights, virtual tours, etc.) and of experiencing the brand rather than merely delivering a site encounter. The New Zealand web site (www.purenz.com) has five attractive 'zones' designed around visitor types and their needs: the wilderness zone (for nature lovers and those who always want to be alone); the thrill zone (for extreme thrill seekers); the heart zone (for visitors who want to meet and stay with real New Zealanders); the Kiwi spirit zone (for those who want to immerse themselves in New Zealand culture); and the chill out zone (offering relaxing breaks with luxurious accommodation in varied landscapes). This visually attractive site is user friendly and navigable and, above all, stimulates interest and provokes reactions. For instance, web visitors can send copies of the New Zealand adverts and photographs of natural environments as e-postcards – adding to New Zealand's conversational appeal, celebrity and anticipation value.

Brand personality and the benefit pyramid

Critical to the success of the New Zealand brand (as to any other destination brand) is the extent to which the destination's brand personality interacts with the target markets. Just like people, all brands should be complex and rich. In fact, the most powerful brands are those with the richest personalities – we all know how Nike behaves, although (just as if it were a person) we all engage with it in a slightly different way. If a destination brand manager can describe his or her brand on less than a page of A4 paper then the brand personality is nowhere near rich enough to have resonance with the consumer. Yet such complex personalities are quite rare in a world where brand attributes are often arbitrarily and superficially constructed.

Traits such as 'friendly', 'cultural', 'natural' and 'contemporary' are popular hoped-for descriptors, but they hardly help to build an engaging or aspirational brand. Destination brand building is all about developing a rich, relevant brand personality. 'Developing' is the key word here – successful brands never atrophy – instead they reflect and respond to changes in consumers' lives and while the brand's core values remain the same, its personality will continue to evolve.

A brand's personality has both a head and a heart – its head refers to the logical brand features, while its heart refers to its emotional benefits and associations. Brand propositions and communications can be based around either a brand's head or its heart: head communications convey a brand's rational values, while heart communications reveal its emotional values and associations. Brand benefit pyramids sum up consumers' relationships with a brand and are frequently established during the consumer research process where consumers are usually asked to describe what features a destination offers and what the place means to them. Using the research, it should then be relatively straightforward to ascertain what particular benefit pyramids consumers associate with the destination in question (see Figure 2.8).

The benefit pyramid can be instrumental in helping to distil the essence of a destination brand's advertising proposition. This refers to the point at which

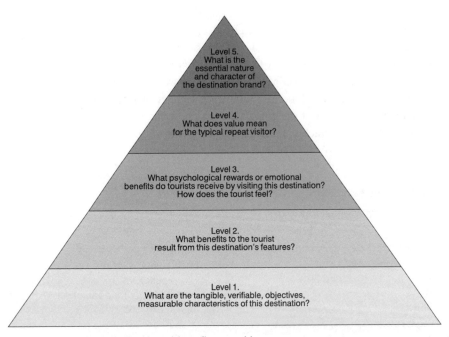

Figure 2.8 The destination brand benefit pyramid

Table 2.3   The values and personality of Brand Australia

Brand values	Brand personality
Youthful	Youthful
Energetic	Stylish
Optimistic	Vibrant
Stylish	Diverse
Unpretentious	Adventurous
Genuine	
Open	
Fun	

Source: Brand Australia, video produced by the Australian Tourism Commission, 1997.

consumers' wants and the destination's benefits and features intersect – any communication (through advertising or public relations) should then encapsulate the *spirit* of the brand. While many ideas may be suggested initially, the challenge is to develop a proposition which makes the destination brand relevant, contemporary and appealing – establishing the brand's architecture can be critical to this process. Thus, for instance, a key element of the new Brand Australia was the creation of a new trademark logo. This was intended to encapsulate the personality and the brand architecture of the destination and had to be bold, exciting, energetic, vital, adventurous and sophisticated yet friendly and fun (Table 2.3). The end result was the creation of a logo depicting a yellow kangaroo against a red sun over a background of green and a blue sea (Table 2.4). The new Australia logo was thus the culmination of a symbol of the country which conveyed the brand personality and included the colours which communicated the architecture.

Table 2.4   The heart of the Australia logo

Colours	Symbolize
Red	Earth, desert, centre, outback
Blue	Sky, sea, cool, endless
Green	Bush, rain forest, environment, clean
Yellow	Warm, nights, life, energy, sun, youth, friendly

Source: Brand Australia, video produced by the Australian Tourism Commission, 1997.

Establishing brand architecture

A brand architecture should reflect all the key components of a destination brand including its positioning, its rational (head) and emotional (heart) benefits and associations, together with its brand personality. A brand's architecture is in essence the blueprint which should guide brand building, development and marketing and is a device which can be used by all destination brand managers. More and more tourism destinations are looking to establish their brand architecture in order to put themselves ahead of competitors. Of course, when they are whole countries, destinations are often composite brands (being composed of many different places). Yet consumer research which reveals and establishes a destination's brand architecture should enable marketers to clearly see the elements and contributions of these various composite brands. It is a device critical to the development of *destination suprabrands* and *sub-brands*. Thus, Britain is a destination suprabrand and the sub-brands (England, Scotland, Wales, London) are both part of, and at the same time, distinct from it (Table 2.5). Thus the *positioning* of Scotland as a land of fire and stone is translated into the *rational benefit* of encountering rugged unspoilt wilderness, romantic history, heritage and folklore, and warm and feisty people. At a deeper, emotional or salient level these benefits offer the overseas visitor the *emotional benefits* of feeling in awe of the elements, embraced by the warmth of the people and rejuvenated by the experience of Scotland. Finally, the culmination of these brand attributes is a destination *personified* by independence, mystery and warmth. This becomes the essence of *Scotland the Brand*, with values rooted in the experience of past visitors, credible and relevant to potential visitors and, most crucially, which the product can deliver (BTA, 1997).

One of the most successful destination suprabrands, however, must be that of Spain. Once a destination with an image for poor quality service and facilities, in the early 1980s the Spanish government began what was to become one of the most consistent and successful brand-building exercises in destination marketing supported by a significant financial commitment – which is ongoing today (Table 2.6). The suprabrand of Spain is an example of an established destination which attracts 51 million visitors a year and has the world's third largest promotional budget for tourism. While España is the main brand, its cities (mainly Barcelona and Madrid) and regions (such as Andalusia and Galicia) are the second-level brands. At the country level Spain has remained remarkably constant in its advertising with each campaign promoting the diversity and variety of the country, focusing on its heritage and culture, as well as the staple sun and sand product. At the heart of the brand for almost twenty years has been Miro's logo, designed in 1983 (the year he died) by mixing elements from his own pictures and his own alphabet. As a piece of modern art, this logo symbolizes Spain's past and looks to the future, and incorporates representations of the sun (yellow and red), the stars and the bullring

Table 2.5 The brand architecture of Britain

	Positioning	Rational Benefit	Emotional Benefit	Personality
Britain	Island of traditional heritage and the unconventional	Tradition, heritage and pageantry. Landscape. Arts and culture. People	I feel stimulated by the enriching, often paradoxical experience of Britain. I feel at ease in the friendly, open culture of the British people	Great/solid yet accessible. Cold in appearance yet deeply friendly. Ordered yet quirky. Traditional yet innovative
London	City of pageantry and pop	Diverse culture, arts, pageantry, heritage, nightlife, music, glamour, shopping. Safe, cosmopolitan. Fashion leader	I feel liberated by the vibrancy of London. I feel stimulated by the wealth of heritage and culture of a great city	Open-minded. Casual. Unorthodox. Vibrant. Creative
Scotland	Land of fire and stone	Rugged, unspoilt, wilderness. Dramatic scenery. Romantic history, heritage and folklore. Warm and feisty people	I feel in awe of the elements in Scotland. I feel embraced by the warmth of the people. I feel rejuvenated by the experience of Scotland.	Independent. Warm. Mysterious. Rugged. Feisty

Table 2.5 (*Continued*)

	Positioning	Rational Benefit	Emotional Benefit	Personality
Wales	Land of nature and legend	Natural, dramatic beauty. Poetry and song. Legend and mystery	I feel inspired by the lyrical beauty of Wales. I feel uplifted by the spirituality of the natural environment.	Honest. Welcoming. Romantic. Down to earth. With passion
England	Lush, green land of discovery	Afternoon teas, quaint village pubs. Cathedrals, country houses. Rolling countryside, meandering roads, hedgerows. Rivers, canals, coastline, piers. Fêtes, morris dancing, cricket, rugged country, moorland, lakes. Industrial heritage. Bed and breakfasts, rugby	I feel fulfilled by experiencing the quaint culture and history of England. I feel relaxed by the harmonious countryside and bracing walks along the coast. I feel warmed by the hearty, down-to-earth character of England. I feel soothed by the open, unspoilt outdoors.	Conservative. Pleasant. Refined. Civilized. Eccentric. Down to earth. Approachable. Hearty. Humorous

Source: BTA (1997).

Table 2.6   Distribution of Spain's promotional budget, 1997

Promotional activities	52%
Advertising	43%
Research activities	5%
Total promotional budget	US$71 631 000

Source: WTO.

(black) to portray Spain. The shifts in the campaigns from 'Everything under the sun' (first used in 1984) to 'Passion for Life' (1992–5) to 'Bravo Spain' (introduced in 1997) have been gradual, well thought out and never compromised the brand values. The one departure from this message of passion and diversity came in 1996 when famous photographers were asked to provide their own interpretations of the essence of Spain. A series of posters were created depicting a photograph taken by each photographer with the strap line – for instance, in David Bailey's case – 'Spain by Bailey'. While the campaign won several awards for its superb photography, it was disliked by the Spanish tourism industry and proved short-lived.

The 'Bravo Spain' campaign, which replaced the unpopular 'Spain by . . .' campaign of 1996, was tested in the key markets of the UK, Germany and France where it was seen positively – the word 'Bravo' conjured up images of approval – allaying fears in Spain of any negative connotations of its association with bullfighting. Intended to communicate a different, modern Spain, this campaign uses strong, visually impactful images in its television and press and poster executions. In the print advertisements (which are the backbone of the campaign) the consistent image is of a blurred photograph with a larger, perfectly focused close-up window showing some detail of the photograph. Every region of Spain features in the advertisements, which mix well-known attractions (such as the new Bilbao museum) with less well-known sites (such as Valencia's new concert hall), and include interesting copy and a small map indicating the location of the scene in the poster.

Conclusion

The success of countries like Spain shows that destinations can become brands which are contemporary and yet timeless, and which can remain in the famous phase of their brand fashion curve over a prolonged period of time. That does not mean, however, that it is easy to build a strong place brand. It takes patience to establish brand reputations and building a powerful destination brand requires a long-term effort, which more often than not yields incremental and not exponential results. Of course, there are destination brands which have seemingly emerged from obscurity to achieve instant stardom. Such rapid elevation to celebrity status, however, often owes much to a culmination of long-term economic, political, social and cultural factors. The apparently effortless appearance of Ireland as a cool, fashionable destination, for instance, is the result of over twenty years of economic turnaround, coupled with the breakthorough of Irish culture (especially the performing arts) on to the world stage. Often such instant stardom also belies long-term marketing activity and investment built on detailed marketing research, planning and consistent positioning. Ireland has continously invested heavily in product development and in its marketing activities, and today considerably outspends all of its competitor UK destinations in the key markets.

Certainly, those destinations which have emerged as brand winners do have a number of common features – in addition to being well funded. They have all been based on a vision which is founded on intensive stakeholder, consumer and competitor research, and which is expressed with care and discipline in everything which communicates the brand's personality. Many have set out to be inclusive brands, forged through partnership and alliance, and many are spear-headed by forward-looking, innovative and commited managers. The commitment and energy of such 'brand champions' is a vital but often overlooked ingredient in any successful destination branding strategy. Such people could be influential politicians or they could be brand envisioners drawn from the destination's marketing organization. This is not to say, however, that the branding should be exclusively directed from the 'top down' and we have seen how this can be counterproductive – as in the case of Oregon in the mid-1980s. The best brands are those which are flexible and inclusive with a broad base of support. Indeed, the development of such partnerships is often a beneficial spin-off from destination brand-building activities, creating greater cohesion between tourism marketers and economic development agencies (Crockett and Wood, 1999; Curtis, 2001).

In addition to being well supported by internal stakeholders, those destination brands which have the greatest celebrity value also tend to be those who produce good advertising. The choice of advertising agency is crucial here since they must produce advertising which advances the brand and reinforces its values and personality. Successful destination brands usually have consistent, relevant, appealing and high-quality advertising, characterized by high production values – advertising which is often cutting-edge advertising and extremely creative. This is not to suggest, however, that destination brand managers must not be prepared to adjust misdirected communications. Spain showed that swift action to correct an unpopular expression of the brand's personality (the 1996 'Spain by . . .' campaign) can prevent long term-damage to the brand. Continuous monitoring and evaluation of the communications is the key here, as is open-mindedness and a willingness to embrace change on the part of the brand managers.

Figure 2.9   Reviving Brand Oregon around the 'capturing the moment' theme

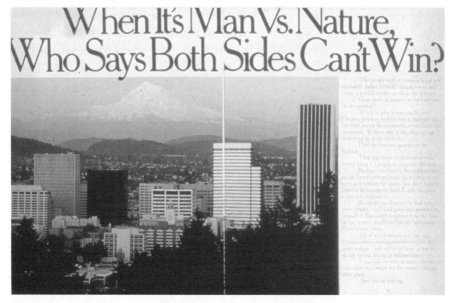

Figure 2.10   Reviving Brand Oregon: communicating the diversity of activities

Any change must be managed within the overall consistency of the brand, of course. Once the brand personality has been identified, marketers must have the courage to stay with the brand's essence – while refinements may be made to how the values are expressed in the brand architecture, the essentials of the brand personality should remain consistent. The secret is to continually evolve and enrich the original brand personality, building on the initial strengths to increase their appeal and to broaden the market. Oregon, for instance, took its established reputation as a pristine natural environment and enriched the brand's personality by including a focus on the destination's built environment and its cultural attractions (Curtis, 2001) (see Figures 2.9 and 2.10). This is similar to the strategy adopted by Spain, which wove culture, heritage and an emerging reputation for modern architecture into its original brand personality based around sun and sand. Likewise, Ireland has added culture, 'coolness' and quality to its established identity as a laid back, friendly destination and Australia has added sophistication and a cosmopolitan dimension to its youthful, fun, nature-oriented personality.

There are significant and unique problems facing destination marketers, but these should not prevent them from persevering in their aims – successful branding brings enormous rewards. Certainly, destinations cannot afford to ignore branding as it offers an innovative and effective tool by which mangers can establish emotional links with the consumer, particularly if a multiagency-driven suprabrand is constructed. Just as in the marketing of consumer goods, branding has the potential to engender consumer loyalty and position destinations to appeal to consumers' self-images and lifestyles. Moreover, while tourism is just one element of any destination's economy it should be integral to place marketing since it supports and leads the development of a place brand. The creation of celebrity and emotional appeal through a destination brand opens the way for other economic development-oriented agencies to communicate to would-be investors and residents.

Acknowledgements

The authors wish to thank Bob Garfield, the editor of *Advertising Age*, who contributed to this chapter through a personal interview and Candice Harris and Rachel Piggott for their assistance with the New Zealand 100% Pure campaign case study.

Note

1 We owe this discussion to conversations with our UWIC colleague Sheena Westwood.

References

Anholt, S. (1998). Nation-brands of the twenty-first century. *Journal of Brand Management*, **5**(6), 395–404.

Baloglu S. and Brinberg, D. (1997). Affective images of tourism destinations. *Journal of Travel Research*, **4**, Spring, 11–14.

British Tourist Authority (BTA) (1997). *Living Britain. A Guide to Understanding the Characteristics of the Geographic Brands of Britain, London, Scotland, England and Wales*. BTA.

Buhalis, D. (2000). Marketing the competitive destination of the future. *Tourism Management*, **21**(91), 97–116.

Chernatony, L. de (1993). Categorising brands: evolutionary processes underpinned by two key dimensions. *Journal of Marketing Management*, **9**(2).

Coshall, J. T. (2000). Measurement of tourists' images: the repertory grid approach. *Journal of Travel Research*, **39**(1), 85–89.

Crockett, S. R. and Wood, L. J. (1999). 'Brand Western Australia: a totally integrated approach to destination branding. *Journal of Vacation Marketing*, **5**(3), 276–289.

Curtis, J. (2001). Branding a state: the evolution of Brand Oregon. *Journal of Vacation Marketing*, **7**(1), 75–82.

Garfield, R. (1998). Personal interview.

Hall, D. (1999). Destination branding, niche marketing and national image projection in central and Eastern Europe. *Journal of Vacation Marketing*, **5**(3), 227–237.

Hallberg, G. (1995). *All Consumers Are Not Created Equal*. Wiley.

Harris, C. (2000). New Zealand's 100% Pure campaign: the UK market. Unpublished paper presented at UWIC, November 2000.

Lurman, D. (of the World Tourism Organization) (1998). Presentation at the 1998 International Travel and Tourism Awards, Valencia.

Lury, G. (1998). *Brandwatching*. Blackhall.

Macrae, C., Parkinson S. and Sheerman, J. (1995). Managing marketing's DNA: the role of branding. *Irish Marketing Review*, **18**, 13–20.

Morgan, N. J. and Pritchard, A. (1998). *Tourism Promotion and Power: Creating Images, Creating Identities*. Wiley.

Morgan, N. J. and Pritchard, A. (1999). Building destination brands: the cases of Wales and Australia. *Journal of Brand Management*, **7**(2), 102–119.

Morgan, N. J. and Pritchard, A. (2000). *Advertising in Tourism and Leisure*. Butterworth-Heinemann.

Morgan, N. J., Pritchard, A. and Abbot, S. (2001). Consumers, travel and technology: a bright future for the Web or television shopping? *Journal of Vacation Marketing*, **7**(2), April, 110–124.

Morse, J. (2001). The Sydney 2000 Olympic Games: how the Australian Tourist Commission leveraged the games for tourism', *Journal of Vacation Marketing*, **7**(2), 101–109.

Nickerson, N. P. and Moisey, N. R. (1999). Branding a state from features to positioning: making it simple? *Journal of Vacation Marketing*, **5**(3), 217–226.

Piggott, R. (2001). Building a brand for a country. Can commercial marketing practices achieve this in a government-funded environment? Unpublished University of Hull MBA dissertation.

Ritchie, B. J. R. and Crouch, G. I. (2000). The competitive destination: a sustainable prespective. *Tourism Management*, **21**(1), 1–7.

Rodwell, T. (1999). Presentation at the 1999 International Travel and Tourism Awards, Valencia.

Schiffman, L. G. and Kanuk, L. L. (2000). *Consumer Behavior*. 7th edn. Prentice Hall International.

Sheth, J. N., Mittal, B. and Newman, B. I. (1999). *Customer Behaviour: Consumer Behavior and Beyond*. Dryden Press.

Tapachai, N. and Waryszak, R. (2000). An examination of the role of beneficial image in tourist destination selection. *Journal of Travel Research*, **39**(1), August, 37–44.

Tibbott, R. (2001). Olympic economies: Sydney and the destination economy. *Locum Destination Review*, **3**, 33–34.

Tourism New Zealand (TNZ) (2000). *Growing New Zealand's Share of the UK Travel Market*. TNZ.

Urdde, M. (1999). Brand orientation: a mindset for building brands into strategic resources. *Journal of Marketing Management*, **15**(1–3), 117–133.

Vial, C. (of Publicis) (1997). Paper presented at the first International Leisure and Tourism Advertising Awards, Dubrovnik.

Warren, S. and Thompson, W. (2000). New Zealand 100% Pure. *Locum Destination Review*, **1**, 22–26.

Weinreich, L. (1999). *11 Steps to Brand Heaven: The Ultimate Guide to Buying an Advertising Campaign*. Kogan Page.

Westwood, S., Morgan, N. J., Pritchard, A. and Ineson, E. (1999). Branding the package holiday: the role and significance of brands for UK air tour operators. *Journal of Vacation Marketing*, **5**(3), July, 238–252.

www.atc.net.au/news/olympic2.htm (accessed 28 February 2001).

3

Nation brands: the value of 'provenance' in branding

Simon Anholt

Introduction

Take a look at the really successful global brands around you, and you might notice that they have something in common. Every one of them comes from a country which has a 'brand image' of its own, and the product is quite often strongly linked with that image. It is an Italian car, associated with the Italian qualities of style, speed, innovative design. It is French perfume, sold on French chic, classiness, wealth. It is a Japanese television, majoring on the Japanese virtues of high-tech expertise, miniaturization, value for money. It is American fashion, bursting with street credibility and youthful rebellion. Just like manufacturers' brands, nation brands evoke certain values, qualifications and emotional triggers in the consumer's mind about the likely values of any product that comes from that country. A nation brand can behave just like a manufacturer's brand, providing an umbrella of trust, a guarantee of quality and a set of ready-made lifestyle connotations which kick-start the entry of its new 'sub-brands' to the marketplace.

It is not surprising that most of the world's successful commercial brands come from the top ten nation brands: America, England, Scotland, France, Italy, Spain, Sweden, Japan, Switzerland and Germany. America is undoubtedly the world's leading nation brand, partly because it has been so thoroughly and expensively marketed to the rest of the world over the last century (having Hollywood as your advertising agency certainly helps, and hiring the National Aeronautics and Space Administration – NASA – as your sales promotion agency, which periodically sends a rocket into orbit in order to demonstrate the superiority of American technology to a gawping planet, is a stroke of genius). For a brand's home country to add this helpful dose of free additional equity, the only requirement is that the product should 'chime' with its country of origin in the consumer's mind, and that some kind of logic links the two.

This logic may be simple or creative: in the case of manufactured brands, it could be the straightforward logic which links Benckiser, a manufacturer of household cleaning products, with a new household cleaning product; or it could be the more lateral sort of logic which links Caterpillar, a manufacturer of bulldozers, with rugged footwear. In exactly the same way, brands from countries can range from simple national produce – pizza from Italy or soft drinks from America – to more unexpected but equally attractive pairings, like skis from Slovenia (Elan), clothing from Australia (RM Williams), or mobile phones from Finland (Nokia).

When you try to match provenance with product, there are some pairings that clearly make brand sense, and others that just do not. People might well buy Indian accountancy software (the debut of Infosys on the National Association of Securities Dealers Automated Quotations system – NASDAQ – has certainly helped this association) or a stylish Lithuanian raincoat, and although I am tempted to say that they probably would not buy Peruvian modems or Zimbabwean perfume, attitudes can and do change quickly. Fifteen years ago who would have believed that we Europeans could be happily consuming Chinese Tsingtao beer or Malaysian Proton cars, or that one of the hottest selling perfumes in Paris is Urvashi, manufactured in India by a company that previously specialized in hydraulic brake fluid? Or, indeed, who would have believed that one of the world's most successful and fastest growing manufacturers of jet aircraft would be a Brazilian company, Embraer? We do indeed live in interesting times.

The importance of nation brand equity

The idea that countries behave like brands is by now fairly familiar to most marketers, and to many economists and politicians too. Originally a rather recondite academic curiosity, the notion is gaining broader acceptance, and its value as a metaphor for how countries can position themselves in the global marketplace in order to boost exports, inward investment and tourism, is fairly well understood.

International marketers, too, are at last beginning to understand just how much equity can be added to their brands through the judicious leveraging of their real or perceived country of origin. But national brand equity goes much further than this. John Pantzalis and Carl A. Rodrigues have even proposed that the movement of international capital is influenced by perceptions of countries as brands by investors. Thus, they claim in a recent paper (Pantzalis and Rodrigues, forthcoming) that the brand positioning and brand management of a country become critical in attracting global capital to that country, as well as affecting how and when capital may flee a country in situations such as the Asian financial crisis in 1997. It is certainly a striking thought – that apparently hard-headed investors may form their view of a country's economic prospects as a result of the way in which that country's brand image has been presented to them in the media, or that they might class several countries together because of superficial brand associations (the 'Asian Tigers', for example) rather than the purely scientific appraisal that one would imagine informs such critical decision making.

Clearly, there is far more to a powerful nation brand image than simply boosting branded exports around the world – if we pursue the thought to its logical conclusion, a country's brand image can profoundly shape its economic, cultural and political destiny. What ultimately makes the European Commission decide which countries will be considered for membership of their elite club, and in which order? Their brand image, of course, and what it might or might not ultimately contribute to the brand image of the European Union itself. When complex wars erupt between countries, and even experts are hard pressed to say which is truly the victim and which the aggressor, it is surely the brand image of each country that sways world opinion towards its customary black and white view. And when suspects are tried by international courts for acts of terrorism or espionage, is the jury not swayed by their brand of origin?

The importance of the issue is not lost on the world's governments, and although the vocabulary and the methodology differ widely, many are currently looking to enhance and build their brand images. A few shining examples of countries which have successfully 'rebranded' themselves – or at least, demonstrated competent management of the way their attributes are perceived abroad – have also helped the trend to accelerate. Japan, Ireland, Germany and Scotland are often quoted cases of countries whose public perception has dramatically altered over a relatively short period, to the enormous benefit of the country's economic health and self-respect. Many others continue to work hard on the problem: New Zealand, Australia, India, Wales, Taiwan, Croatia, Slovenia, Spain, South Korea and Britain.

Then there are a handful of megabrand countries – such as America, Italy and France – whose public image seems so powerful, positive and all-pervasive, one might think they hardly need to bother managing it. These are the countries which appear effortlessly synonymous with certain valuable attributes (France for chic and quality of living, Italy for style and sexiness, America for technology, wealth, power, youth appeal and much more besides), and each time a new brand emerges from one of these countries, it seems to have a head start over all its competitors in the global marketplace. More than anything else, it is the example of such powerful nation brands which continues to stimulate other countries to follow suit, and carve out their perceptual niche on the commercial and cultural map of the world.

Emerging nations and the importance of brand image

One of the great advantages of branded products over commodities is that they are an infinitely renewable resource – that is, as long as their value is maintained through careful marketing. Their value resides primarily in the mind of the consumer, not in the factory of the producer, and, once created, that makes them surprisingly difficult to destroy. Clearly, the notion of exporting branded rather than unbranded products is a compelling one for many countries. Developing countries could especially benefit from a movement towards global brand export: it is part of a sustainable wealth-creation behaviour which could ultimately help them escape from the poverty cycle. As it stands, though, most developing countries are enmeshed in a pattern of economic behaviour that keeps them poor: selling unprocessed goods to richer nations at extremely low margins and allowing their buyers to add massive 'value' by finishing, packaging, branding and retailing to the end user. This process often helps deplete the source country's resources while keeping its foreign revenues at breakeven level or below.

Creating and selling international brands is the classic trick of industrialized nations. It is one born of necessity, perhaps, since some of the world's richest nations have precious few commodities to export, but it is one that many poorer nations would do well to emulate. For it is conceivable that if consumers in developing countries are faced with the choice between yet more brands from the G7 nations, and new brands from 'colleague countries' in the developing world with no shady colonial past, they might just feel more comfortable with the latter. Global brands as the ultimate distributor of wealth? It is an intriguing thought. The stage appears to be set for the emergence of many poorer countries as respected, even privileged provenances for successful commercial brands.

Still, many barriers must be overcome. Brazil, one of the most 'strongly branded' countries in the world, produces almost no other international commercial brands whatsoever. This is surprising, particularly because the brand print of Brazil is associated with a very homogeneous and coherent set of values. 'Brand Brazil' has much going for it – the merriment of samba dancing at carnival time; spectacular rainforests as endangered as they are exotic; sex, beaches, sport, adventure – and all of these attributes could contribute to the brand print of almost any successful youth product on the market today, especially in the food, cosmetics, fashion, music, and even automotive and industrial fields. Certainly, these are clichés that may be depressing, even insulting, to the average Brazilian, but they are undeniably a fine platform on which to build a believable global brand. It is one of the tasks of advertising and marketing to manipulate these clichés into something more creative, more substantial, more fair, more true.

The fact that there are negative associations (pollution, overpopulation, poverty, crime, corruption) within the image of Brazil is a cause for great concern, but not necessarily from the branding point of view. After all, a strong brand is a rich brand, and richness implies a complex and satisfying mix of many different elements. The brand equity of the USA also contains a significant proportion of negative elements, but this does little to diminish its attraction, especially when the audience you are dealing with is composed of younger consumers, whose prickly, contradictory nature means they demand to challenge and be challenged. Currently, however, almost all Brazil's export income derives from the sale of raw commodities (such as soy beans, tobacco, iron ore and coffee), semi-processed goods (such as cellulose, steel, soy oil and sugar) and largely unbranded manufactured goods (such as shoes, orange juice, sheet steel and automobile tyres), and many of these exports contribute directly or indirectly to the depletion of the country's natural resources. There is no question that if these bulk exports were to be enhanced or, indeed, replaced by the sale of branded goods directly to overseas consumers, then profits – at least for the owners of these brands – would rise dramatically, and the level of profit generated by the success of these brands might soon overtake the income created by the export of commodities.

The opportunity to capitalize on the positive and powerful associations which Brazil evokes in people's minds all over the world is not, by and large, being seized – at least not by Brazilian companies. It is largely through the efforts of companies in North America and Western Europe, for example, that Brazilian coffee-growers are getting fairer representation on supermarket shelves in richer countries (Café Direct in the UK and similar organizations throughout Europe were set up in order to ensure that the coffee-growers always get a fair price for their beans), and there are plenty of Western companies making great capital out of real and bogus 'rainforest' ingredients, but the real value of 'Brand Brazil' to Brazil itself is, as yet, untapped.

Not all emerging countries have Brazil's natural advantages: a strong nation brand, combined with an increasingly healthy economy, a government that actively encourages the export mentality, not to mention considerable domestic experience in brand building. After all, even though it emerged from military rule and hyperinflation only a few short years ago, Brazil enjoys a democratic climate, and this has enabled the creation of many highly successful entrepreneurs, domestic companies and domestic brands (not to mention one of the best advertising industries in the world). Nonetheless, with the right combination of marketing expertise, government support, a high-quality manufacturing base, investment and a creative brand strategy, many countries around the world have the basic potential to develop a healthy brand-based export economy. To spot the opportunities, all you need is the brand development skill, the creative flair and the grasp of global consumer psychology to make credible and attractive pairings between the country brand and the brandable products that country produces.

And the oddest things do happen. The mighty Tata Corporation of India, for example, recently acquired the Tetley Tea Company of England, the world's second largest teabag manufacturer – a spectacular reversal of the traditional arrangement, where the tea is grown in a poor country, and sold at a low price to a brand owner in a rich country, who sells it on to rich consumers at a vastly higher price. And China has proved full of nasty surprises for many Western manufacturers: more than US$270 billion has been invested in Chinese ventures, by thousands of foreign firms, since 1992, yet few Western companies have succeeded in making any money in China. Whirlpool, for example, launched enthusiastically in China in 1994, building factories to manufacture the domestic appliances it confidently expected to sell to the Chinese, only to find that it could not compete against domestic brands. (Indeed, one of these rival firms, Haier, is now beginning to market products under its own brand name, with some success, in North America.) After losing more than US$100 million and shutting down most of its factories, Whirlpool now manufactures washing machines for Guangdong Kelon, another of its Chinese competitors, which are sold to Chinese consumers under the Kelon brand. So perhaps the next great nation brand association in the making is China, soon to be recognized by consumers worldwide as a byword for quality domestic appliances. Only one example – Hong Kong businessman David Tang's retail and fashion brand Shanghai Tang – has begun to prove that Western consumers are strongly attracted by authentic, upmarket Chinese brand values, and are prepared to pay a substantial premium for them.

What it takes

Naturally, launching a global brand requires flair, confidence and chutzpah – especially if you do not come from a top ten country. It requires objectivity to an unusual degree– the ability to see yourself as others see you, and to accept that this is, at least in commercial terms, more important than the way you see yourself. It requires government support. And it requires constant investment in the country brand itself, which in turn requires commitment, collaboration and effective synergy among the main purveyors of the country's image in the global media; usually the national tourist board, the national airline and the major produce exporters, because these are the routes by which the national brand is most commonly created and exported.

Indeed, a very common problem for smaller countries is the fact that 'place branding' is an international exercise by default, yet because they are not big consumer corporations, they do not have the funds to compete in global advertising clout. Few destinations or small countries have the advertising dollars of the big marketers – the major airlines, car hire companies, hotel chains and tour operators – or, indeed, of the world's heaviest advertisers, the packaged goods companies. For, make no mistake, in competing for precious moments of the mindshare of today's message-fatigued consumer, every advertised brand is a threat, and soap powder and automobiles are as much a competitor to the small nation or region as directly-competing countries. The Slovenian Tourist Board competes with Persil and Toyota and Coca-Cola as much as it competes with the Croatian Tourist Board; the real prize is the wealthy consumer's rapidly diminishing attention span, a commodity whose price has steadily and inexorably risen during the last 100 years, as brands and their advertising messages have proliferated.

Yet there is hope even for the smallest niche players in nation branding. Until a few years ago, building a global brand invariably required substantial amounts of ready cash to buy advertising media: until the 'new media revolution' happened, this was the sine qua non of global marketing. You just could not think of building a worldwide brand for less than US$50 million or US$100 million a year; quite simply, as in all extremely mature and heavily exploited markets, every media vehicle had its own value calculated to the nth degree, and there were no bargains. But with the Internet-driven media revolution, we find ourselves in an entirely new world, in an immature and as yet very imperfectly understood market. And in immature markets, there are bargains everywhere, for anyone who knows how to recognize them – even the owners of some of the new channels of communication have yet to realize the true value of what they are offering. The Internet is, potentially, one of the most cost-effective and potent vehicles of fame creation that the commercial world has ever seen.

Until recently, it was also true to say that the biggest hurdle which emerging country manufacturers had to overcome before launching their brands boldly on to the international market was the common consumer perception of poor manufacturing quality – 'unless it comes from Europe, Japan or North America, it can't be properly made' – but, again, circumstances are conspiring to change people's minds. Paradoxically, it is, above all, big brands from rich countries which we have to thank for this change. Over the last few decades, consumers have become very familiar with those humble little stickers on the underside of their American or European-branded toys and running shoes and domestic appliances ('Made in Taiwan', 'Made in Vietnam', 'Made in Thailand', 'Made in Mexico' and many more besides), and they have quietly absorbed the fact that a great many of the products they buy are manufactured (to the high standards required by those American and European brand owners, naturally) in poor countries. The American and European brand owners could hardly have done their supplier nations a better favour. The perception only has to be enhanced a little further, and brought more explicitly to the consumer's attention, and yet another barrier preventing the development of global brands from emerging markets is removed.

One final obstacle may be purely psychological: a simple lack of self-confidence. After years of acting as mere suppliers to more commercially successful nations, many 'third world' countries suffer from what one might call Groucho Marx syndrome ('I'd never belong to a club that would have someone like me as a member'); the idea that nobody in a rich country could possibly be interested or attracted by brands coming from a country so poor and unimportant as theirs. Once again, however, circumstances appear to be conspiring to change things for the better, and that perception is probably less true now than ever before. At the start of the third millennium, there is a pronounced shift in Western tastes and fashions, towards 'Asianization' – a yearning for the values of older, wiser, more contemplative civilizations than our own. Never before has there been such a vogue for the 'ethnic', the organic, the exotic. There is World Music (currently the fastest growing part of the big record labels' catalogues, and fast overtaking the hitherto unquestioned dominance of the big American popular entertainers); World Cinema (occasionally rivalling the success of Hollywood blockbusters); World Cuisine (not long ago, a Parisian family offered to send out for some sushi when I visited their home – a phenomenon which would have been almost unthinkable a few years ago!); the phenomenal surge of interest in alternative, Eastern and pseudo-Eastern remedies (acupuncture, shiatsu, aroma-therapy); and much more besides.

The Western consumer is attracted as never before by the cultures and the products of distant lands, as the handful of examples like Shanghai Tang and Urvashi, the Indian perfume, are beginning to prove. Now, surely, is the time for the rightful owners of the truly exotic nation brands to leverage the power they hold over the imagination of the world's richest consumers. Now is the time for them to start making back some of the money which they have paid rich countries for their products over the past century, to begin to reverse the relentless flow of wealth from poor to rich, and to redress some of the imbalance between the lucky and the unlucky nations of the earth. This is one kind of aid which emerging countries could find truly valuable: the international branding expertise which can create unexpected and inspiring connections between countries and consumers, and which will enable countries to launch their products on to the global marketplace with confidence, with a big noise and, above all, with pride in their origins. Simplistic, maybe, but undeniably attractive: just add the right branding expertise to a country living on sweatshop labour and breakeven trading, and you have the beginnings of a fast-growth manufacturer economy instead of a submerging service state.

There is much simple justice in this, and a simple formula is irresistible:

- If a company in a rich country sells brands to rich consumers in rich countries, nothing really happens: money simply circulates within a more or less closed system, and there is little to criticize on moral grounds.
- If a company in a rich country sells brands to poor consumers in rich countries, there is a risk of exploitation and a further widening of the wealth gap.
- If a company in a rich country sells brands to consumers in a poor country, the risk of exploitation is far higher, partly because the cultural vulnerability of the consumers is greater: they have not yet been 'inoculated' against brands by repeated exposure to sophisticated marketing techniques.
- But if a company in a poor country sells brands to consumers in a rich country, the overall balance begins to be redressed, and justice begins to be done.

After all, marketing has done much to increase the unequal distribution of wealth during the last century, so why should not marketing be used to reverse the trend, and balance things out a little better during the next?

Changing a country's brand image

So it looks as if a healthy nation brand, linked with and driving the export of many branded products, is the remedy for every nation's economic and political ills. But, as I have said, very few countries are lucky enough to possess a powerful, distinctive international brand – and perhaps only two or three of those brands are truly positive in the areas that will most benefit the country's future development. The rest face the significant task of working out how to manage and enhance their brand images. Changing the world's perceptions of a nation is neither easy nor quick – after all, its brand image has often evolved over many centuries, shaped by wars, religion, diplomacy or the lack of it, international sporting triumphs or disasters, famous and infamous sons and daughters and, latterly, of course, by the brands it exports, as long as the brand is prepared to be explicit about its country of origin. Such deeply rooted views can seldom be changed overnight (and, it has to be said, rapid deteriorations in national image are far more commonly and simply achieved than even the most gradual improvements).

A nation brand is like the proverbial supertanker, which takes five miles to slow down and ten miles to change course. All the 'country-brand manager' can realistically hope to do is identify and isolate the positive existing perceptions of the country and calculate how to enhance whatever contributes to these in the country's external communications, while downplaying anything which does not. The logic behind this approach is standard marketing practice: as I have said, the country is competing for consumer attention alongside a million other phenomena in the media, and unless its every appearance in the public domain continually and accurately reinforces a few simple, basic, coherent truths, it is highly unlikely that a homogeneous image will ever form itself in the consumer's mind. In this respect, all brands are rather like those children's games where you have to join up the dots to draw the outline of an animal – unless the game is made pretty easy for the consumer (that is, the dots are numbered) – then he or she is unlikely ever to make out the tiger or the rabbit.

But there are exceptions to the rule, and from time to time, perceptions of countries can change far more quickly and more completely than might be expected. Perhaps the most dramatic example of how a new nation brand can be dreamed up, communicated and established across much of the world is the case of Walter Scott and Brand Scotland. Scott almost single-handedly 'invented' the image of modern Scotland, portraying a land so attractive, picturesque and compelling, it has remained rooted in the consciousness of Europe, and beyond, for centuries. It is a heartening example of how people can, if they are passionate and determined, and talented enough, sway the world's view of a nation.

The best example of 'brand turnaround' from our own times is undoubtedly that of modern Japan. Thirty years ago, 'Made in Japan' was a decidedly negative concept, as most Western consumers had based their perception of Brand Japan on their experience of shoddy, second-rate products flooding the marketplace. The products were cheap, certainly, but they were basically worthless: in many respects, the perception of Japan was much as China's is today. Yet Japan has now become enviably synonymous with advanced technology, manufacturing quality, competitive pricing, even of style and status. Japan, indeed, passes the best branding test of all: whether consumers are prepared to pay more money for functionally identical products, simply because of where they come from. It is fair to say that in the 1950s and 1960s, most Europeans and Americans would only buy Japanese products because they were significantly cheaper than a Western alternative; now, in certain very valuable market segments, such as consumer electronics, toys, high fashion, musical instruments and motor vehicles, Western consumers will consistently pay more for products manufactured by previously unknown brands, purely on the basis that they are perceived to be Japanese. Little wonder that the UK hi-fi retailer Dixons, when they launched their house brand of consumer electronics, gave it a mock-Japanese name, Matsui, in order to borrow a little of the 'public domain' equity of Brand Japan.

Such 'cuckoo brands', where a manufacturer steals its provenance from a better established cultural phenomenon in order to augment its natural brand equities, are common enough, and have been around for a very long time. The Italian confectioner, Perfetti, for example, owns a successful chewing gum brand called 'Brooklyn', a product which bears an image of the Brooklyn Bridge on its packaging, and is manufactured in Milan. This bogus provenance no doubt made perfect sense when the brand was launched in the 1950s – chewing gum was an American import, and its novelty and glamour derived principally from its provenance – but was essential to building the brand. After all, with recent memories of American soldiers in most Italian towns, no self-respecting Italian would have bought domestically produced chewing gum.

In an age where countries are beginning to invest huge sums in shaping and promoting their brand equities, one cannot help wondering how long such pilfering will be tolerated. Perhaps the Italian region of Tuscany's recent announcement that it would take steps to protect its 'natural imagery' from copyright theft (it seems that two-thirds of all car advertisements, for example, are shot in Tuscany, no matter which country the car is made in) will prove to be the first of many. How long before the chic of France, the poshness of England, the mystery of India or the precision of Switzerland are protected characteristics, and international copyright lawyers have yet another lucrative source of business?

What it takes to build a nation brand

Of all the qualities needed by those who are responsible for nurturing a country's image, objectivity is one of the most valuable, and one of the hardest to achieve. After all, marketing directors who are responsible for marketing a product are generally salaried employees, are seldom the inventor or manufacturer of the product and, so, do not find it too difficult to take a cool, objective view of the brand they are building – indeed, good ones are valued precisely because of their ability to see the brand in the same way as the consumer. But when the product does not come out of a factory, but is the very homeland of the people trying to market it – where they and their parents and grandparents were born, raised, schooled and trained – when they are public servants rather than marketing professionals, and when branding easily becomes confused with foreign policy, tourism or trade promotion, objectivity becomes an extremely elusive quality.

A lack of objectivity can be fatal to the proper branding of a country, no matter how good the intentions at the start. Typically, I find that a country branding programme will start with communications ministries and foreign office departments producing lists of their country's achievements and natural advantages – the nation's most distinguished sons and daughters, the role it has played in world events, its own major historical moments, gems of architecture and natural beauty, regional cuisine, language and folklore, all served up with pages of indigestible demographics and statistics about gross domestic product (GDP) and income per capita. The idea is that this mass of data is then distilled into a pithy slogan and a raft of quasi-tourism collateral, and thus the country is marketed to an impatient world. From the point of view of a busy consumer halfway across the world, of course, the historical achievements and natural advantages of most countries are of little interest, and seldom add up to anything which could be described as a coherent or powerful brand. Indeed, since branding programmes are most urgently needed by the smaller, poorer and newer countries, it is all the more likely that such facts will make pretty unimpressive reading to the detached observer. On more than one occasion, I have been faced with the tricky task of gently explaining to a very proud and very patriotic minister that the world will not be enthralled by the fact that the world's first all-metal suspension bridge was invented by a man whose grandfather came from his country, or that over sixty different species of wild grass grow along his eastern coastline.

I know of no more apt metaphor than this: marketing is like trying to chat up someone in a crowded bar. In effect, you walk up to somebody you have never met, and have a few seconds in which to convince them that you are worth getting to know better, and to win the chance of a longer conversation. Often, a joke will do the trick, but if the bar is in Finland or Iraq (unlikely), where making strangers laugh is both difficult and unwelcome, a different opening gambit might be preferable. Either way, there are few countries and few people who will fall in love with a stranger who kicks off the conversation with a long list of his natural advantages, impressive family tree and key historical achievements.

No, the place to start working out how to brand a country is often not with the country itself, but with the consumer and the marketplace. In the very limited amount of mindspace that each consumer has available to store perceptions of foreign countries, one must identify where there are gaps and where there are opportunities. Is there room for a country that is the ultimate youth brand? Which country could most credibly seize this opportunity? Which country is best suited to become the ultimate downshifter's paradise? Which country could position itself as the next technological minipower? Which could be the most natural source country in the world for alternative dietary and medicinal brands? Where might the best service businesses in the world be built? After all, every crowded marketplace needs definition, and a hundred or more countries all clamouring to be recognized as the ultimate combination of sun, sea and sand, or the birthplace of history, culture and cuisine, does not really make life any easier for busy and confused consumers trying to make up their minds where to visit, where to buy brands from or where to emigrate to.

The other important point to remember is that branding a country is not quite the same thing as promoting tourism. The promotion of tourism obviously occupies more common ground with nation branding than any other aspect of a country's external affairs, but it is merely a part of the whole. Although the economies of more and more countries do depend on tourism, other factors may be equally important, such as stimulating inward investment and aid, encouraging both skilled and unskilled workers to immigrate, promoting the country's branded and unbranded exports internationally, increasing the international business of the national airline, facilitating the process of integration into political and commercial organizations such as the European Union or the WTO, and a wide range of other interests. It is the sum total of these interests which compel a country to think hard about the overall image which it presents to the rest of the world, and it is often the case that the image presented by the tourist industry may be irrelevant, unhelpful or even damaging to the country's other international initiatives. A typical example of this dissonance between tourist branding and national branding was faced by both Scotland and Ireland. Both countries enjoyed an extremely valuable tourist image based around wild, empty countryside, quaint old-world charm, and a populace widely perceived as warm-hearted, uncomplicated, old-fashioned, rustic and utterly unsophisticated – hardly a useful image to have lodged in the minds of American or Japanese corporations deciding where to build their newest semiconductor plant. And yet such contrasts and even contradictions, for the very reason that they exist in the real world, can be resolved, harmonized and believably communicated in a country's branding programme. It takes creativity, objectivity, branding sense and a deep understanding of the way in which consumer logic works – or can be encouraged to work – in each target country and each target audience.

Conclusion

It is no paradox to predict that in today's global marketplace, where brands and products can come from almost literally anywhere, their 'rootedness' will surely become more and more important to consumers in their constant search for brands with trustworthiness, character and distinctiveness. For some time now, the ultimate ambition of many companies has been to turn themselves into 'global brands', and as part of the process which leads to this vague nirvana, have attempted to systematically remove every clue as to their country of origin. British Airways' decision to graduate from mere national carrier to global travel brand, drop the explicit reference to its country of origin, and bear images from many different nations on its tail fins, was one of several instances of this type. But the crucial point which they, and many other large corporations often overlook in their rush to appear global, is that a global brand is not the same thing as a brand which comes from nowhere: indeed, in many of the most successful cases, it is a brand which is sold everywhere, but *comes* from somewhere quite definite. Coca-Cola, Pepsi, McDonald's, Nike, Levis, Timberland and Marlboro, for example, would be only half the brands they are today if they were not most decidedly from America. British Airways would never have become the world's favourite airline if it had not been, first and foremost, *British* Airways: the existing perception of Brand Britain in the minds of much of the world's population (methodical, punctual, predictable, efficient, traditional, heritage obsessed, class ridden, status driven, ceremonious, boring), makes Britain the perfect, the ultimate, the supremely logical provenance for any brand in the business of air travel, hospitality and tourism. It is easy to be wise after the event, but by cutting off its connection with its provenance, British Airways simply pulled the plug on its principal brand equity.

It is the very rootedness of many global brands which gives them their power – a strength of identity, a character, which is entirely absent from many of the corporate constructs which today aspire to become the new generation of global brands. It is human nature, the first time you meet someone, to ask them where they come from. And as the likelihood of that person coming from the same place as you do becomes smaller with every year that passes, the question seems to become increasingly pertinent. Provenance is hard equity, which does not need to be built from scratch, because it already exists in the consumer's mind, and has a definite shape and form. Too many brands these days, and perhaps especially 'global' brands, because of their tendency to be large and diffuse in their activities, are rather soft in outline (typically the large international conglomerates – Vivendi, Corus, etc.). This already means that it is very hard for them to occupy a meaningful and memorable position in the mind of the consumer (I do not know what they do, I do not know where they come from), and the situation is often worsened by their attempts to rebrand themselves as 'global citizens'.

The brand names of corporations which are generated to this brief, often with the precise intention of appearing stateless, are therefore entirely culture-free and entirely uninteresting – the classic reaction to the terrifying prospect of having to communicate with millions of people in hundreds of countries (make it a name which everyone will understand, everyone can pronounce, everyone can spell and nobody can possibly object to). In reality, of course, people are not really offended at all by people (or companies) from other countries having foreign names, even hard to pronounce ones. If you think about it, nothing could be more normal and, if anything, it tends to make the person (or company) more interesting. Places like Titicaca, Timbuktu, Popocatepetl, Ouarzazate and Gstaad almost certainly owe much of their fame to their tricky names.

The point is that people do not actually mind products coming from abroad – in fact, they quite like it. There appears to be a natural tendency in most product sectors for consumers gradually to turn away from their familiar national brands, and seek the newness and stimulation of the exotic – this has already occurred in Britain with beer, cars, clothing and, more recently, even financial services. The consequence of this is that many brands may ultimately stand a better chance of survival abroad than at home. Samsung, a Korean company selling mobile phones in Sweden, the home country of mobile phones, might find this more of an opportunity than a predicament, as Swedes turn away from the almost official, state-run image of Ericsson, their national and global brand leader, towards something a little different, which helps them to stand out from the crowd. And who knows, Ericsson might ultimately find that they can do better business in Seoul than in Stockholm. These are, indeed, interesting times to be building brands, and the real significance of provenance is just beginning to emerge. In an age where a potent, distinctive and attractive brand image is of fundamental importance both to countries and to manufactured products as they compete in the global marketplace, it is time for all marketers to learn how to understand, manage and utilize the oldest brand images of all – people's perceptions of places.

Reference

Pantzalis, J. and Rodrigues, C. A. (forthcoming). Country names as brands: symbolic meaning and capital flows.

4

Branding for success

Fiona Gilmore

Introduction

There are a lot of misconceptions about branding: many people tend to think of it as something new, a product of the twentieth century and the television age. In fact the use of simple symbols to communicate is at least as old as Christianity in the Western world. The early Christians used the acronym IXTHUS (the Greek word for fish) and the fish symbol. Subsequently battle standards were used to draw soldiers into a common objective – another form of branding. Brands as we think of them today were not a product of the twentieth century but the result of the Industrial Revolution and the transformation of Western society from an agrarian and rural society to an industrial and urban one. Indeed, many of the brands we use today have been in existence for over 100 years. Certainly the arrival of television advertising transformed the practice of branding, since it offered the opportunity to use the power of moving pictures and aural communication (both words and music) to communicate more intrusively. But many great brands have not spent huge sums on advertising.

For example Marks and Spencer, still a powerful brand, positively eschewed advertising until quite recently. Branding then is not necessarily involved with slogans, clever names, advertising and public relations, although these tools may be useful.

Branding seeks to convey messages to the user or potential user of a product or service. These messages need to be simple and consistent, since we are all bombarded with messages from hundreds of products every day. They also need to be reinforced by experience – you cannot make a silk purse from a sow's ear by branding. The messages about the brand may be both rational (that is, facts or claims) and emotional. Balancing these carefully is critical and I will demonstrate this in more detail later. But it is important to note that all the greatest brands have a very powerful emotional relationship with the consumer. Sometimes this relationship is negative, when brands polarize different subsegments of the population. A young fashion brand for teenagers might well elicit very negative reaction from older consumers. This is not necessarily a bad thing and can be very powerful in destination marketing.

How do we go about branding?

There are many different ways of approaching branding a product, service or destination, which depend in part on the market, the competition and the degree of sophistication within the organization. But like the old adage, all roads lead to Rome, I shall describe only what I believe to be essential for best practice. The starting point for all branding is a clear view of the marketplace and the competitors, in particular to understand the dimensions of the market and the strength of competitor brands. Sometimes we need to examine the market definition quite carefully. If, for instance, I am Coca-Cola, is my market only cola drinks or all fizzy drinks or all cold drinks? Destination marketing often adds a complication to this process because there may be different competitors for different sorts of tourism; short breaks may pitch you up against near neighbours; longer holidays will probably give a wider geographic spread of competitors; and business conferences are yet another on the list. This process though is invaluable because it also starts you thinking about priorities because good branding does make you assess priorities. As I noted above, branded messages have to be simple, so we cannot expect to be able to include every possible positive about our brand. Equally, we rarely have the funds to appeal directly to every possible target audience, so we have to assess priorities.

Therefore the next stage is identifying our prime target audience and, if appropriate, any secondary target audiences. This used to be done by demographic indicators in terms of both social class and age. This is sometimes still useful but generally best practice is to use more detailed lifestyle descriptors and, if available, psychographic descriptors. Let me describe this in practice. If you are marketing a destination where the primary attraction is opportunities for outdoor, rural pursuits for families you might traditionally have labelled your target audience ABC1 families with children, the adults typically thirty to forty-five years old. You might nowadays describe the target as – families living in cities looking for long- and short-break holidays with a wide variety of rural pursuits. Similarly, you may well discover that while the parents are looking for a variety of rural activities and good food in the evenings, the children are primarily looking for adventurous activities. Equally, your research would reveal that in addition there is a very important subgroup of empty-nesters – those with grown up children who are looking for active short-break holidays focused on not too vigorous walking, good food and unspoilt natural beauty. Thus the process has moved from describing a broad social group to defining some real people. So any promotional activity can be tailored to their needs.

The last stage of the branding process is defining the brand and its proposition. In destination marketing, the brand is normally a city or country. In other markets there may well be the decision on the name of the brand and, increasingly, on whether or not it is a sub-brand of an existing brand or a totally new brand. As new brands are more and more expensive to launch and maintain, the use of big umbrella brands with a number of smaller sub-brands is increasingly common. This is not irrelevant to destination marketing. Take England, for example. Sub-brands, such as Shakespeare Country, Constable Country and the Garden of England can benefit from the parent brand. As destination marketing becomes more focused on the individual's needs and mood, sub-brands will have more particular products and services on offer, for example birdwatching in the Garden of England or horse trekking on Exmoor.

One specific question frequently raised in destination marketing is 'what is the destination brand – a tourism or a business investment brand?' This is often an issue because there are different purse holders for the promotional monies for each function. Far worse, it can sometimes be a turf war between the two budget-holding departments. Our experience at Springpoint is that it is enormously beneficial for there to be as much co-operation as possible between the two functions, with the intention of having a broadly common platform for promotion (albeit with the necessary nuances for the different audiences). The very things which make somewhere a good holiday destination – rapid communications, vibrant city life or unspoilt surrounding countryside – also make it attractive as a business location in terms of both business efficiency and quality of life for employees. This reveals the complexity of destination marketing since there are frequently different sources of funds for branding. For example, a city may create its own promotional budget while its surrounding hinterland also has a marketing budget, in addition to that provided by a country in which they both sit. It is important that these sub-brands are carefully co-ordinated so that they support both one another and the total country brand, rather than being small individual entities with no real clout for a share of the consumer's mind.

The most difficult area of branding is normally defining the proposition. Again there is no real substitute for rigorous market research to assess the competition, what distinguishes your brand from the rest and the extent to which you fully meet the needs of the largest audience. For example, when my company was working with the new Hong Kong government in 1998 (post-handover) on developing a clear brand proposition for Hong Kong, it was abundantly clear that the prime international competitors were London and New York, against which Hong Kong had some exciting advantages, particularly with regard to the specific culture of its people. However, it also had some drawbacks, particularly in relation to its overall provision of cultural activities – galleries, museums, music, theatre, and to its appeal to younger audiences. Hong Kong is working hard to address these needs, recognizing that people considering whether to work in Hong Kong may also be reassured to see that there is a growing choice of performing arts and entertainment programmes.

In the early days of brand promotion, particularly for packaged goods brands, there was an enormous focus on trying to discover a unique selling proposition (USP) which the competition did not or could not offer. This was often pre-emptive – seeking to occupy the ground before the competition did – but is increasingly difficult to sustain as product development cycles have shortened so dramatically. In destination marketing the search for uniqueness is important, but this normally comes from two sources: first, the culture of the destination itself, which is normally unique or a unique combination of cultures, and, second, from the combination of other benefits – convenient yet unspoilt, lively city with peaceful countryside, historic monuments and great food. For me, the importance of the discipline of searching for uniqueness is the discipline it forces on you to decide what is the core of the destination brand. In today's complex marketplace, you cannot be a shopping list of different attributes. A destination brand, like any other brand, has to have a simple, easy to understand message in order to stand out from the clutter of messages to which we are all subjected every day of our lives. Finally, the branding process needs to define the brand personality – the emotional values we want the brand to carry. These are, in my view, arguably the most important in the whole process, since it is these emotional values built up over a long period of time which will turn a name and a proposition into a durable brand with an emotional relationship with its target audience.

The research methods we employ to develop a brand proposition for a country or region are similar to those we adopt for any other brand. We may use a combination of focus groups, one-to-one interviews with business investors and the trade as well as future scenario workshops. Often it is the latter, where people's dreams for the future shed most light on the big conceptual ideas for the brand. I remember when we were running such workshops in Hong Kong among eighteen to twenty-two year old Hong Kong Chinese students, their can-do spirit, their unstoppable energy, alongside their quest for their spiritual roots reinforced one's belief and understanding about the uniqueness of Hong Kong. The notion 'whether you're here on business or for pleasure, Hong Kong liberates your mind and spirit. A power shower', sprang from those workshops.

What are the benefits of branding?

In the private sector, the economic advantages of branding are well understood by management of companies and by investors. Expressed simply, the core benefit of branding lies in its creation of customer loyalty, through both recruitment of new customers and (often of greater importance) the retention of existing customers (or share of their purchases). For example, in the confectionery market, where customers have a portfolio of favourite brands, it is the proportion of their expenditure on a brand that is the key target. The economic benefits are translated by investors into the belief that branding increases both the future income (or cash flow) and the certainty of that income (because of greater customer loyalty).

Within the public sector (where most destination marketing is undertaken) there is clearly a different set of criteria. However, it is clear that effective branding represents marketing best practice and hence it is correct for it to be adopted. Moreover, as I indicated earlier, if branding is able to co-ordinate better the individual constituent investments from different public sources – say, city, region, country for tourism and the same for inward investment – it is clearly more efficient than individual campaigns from separate organizations. Also, a well-executed branding campaign will, normally, be enthusiastically embraced by the private sector, particularly in tourism. This occurs both in the support and marketing by existing organizations such as hotels, restaurants, transport, which will assist in developing excellent communication vehicles for the brand (such as brochures, advertisements and increasingly, Internet web sites), but also in developing new products and services which enhance the overall proposition. Examples of these latter areas include provision of new holiday facilities (such as riding stables, water sports), improved quality (more gourmet restaurants, different sorts of holiday accommodation, easier car or bicycle hire) and fringe benefits (availability of local gourmet products to take home, high-quality souvenirs and local crafts).

Thus a well-executed branding campaign may be seen as a virtuous circle where the initial investment by public funds is supported by private funds in both marketing and destination 'infrastructure', which in turn enhances the destination experience bringing brand loyalty and word-of-mouth recommendation.

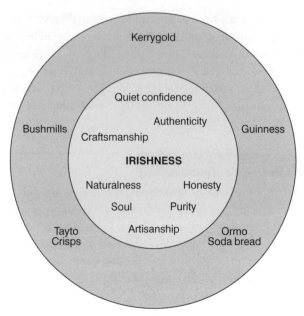

Figure 4.1 The core values of Ireland translated to brands
Source: Springpoint (1999).

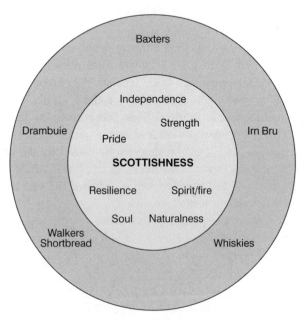

Figure 4.2 The core values of Scotland translated to brands
Source: Springpoint (1999).

Equally, an evocative destination brand with emotional roots can encourage local food, drinks and crafts brands to use these brand values and emotions as part of their promotion. For example Guinness, Scotch Whisky and Irish Whiskey all use their provenance as a key selling tool in overseas markets (Figures 4.1 and 4.2). In order to promote this approach in Wales, we are currently assisting the Welsh Development Agency in the development of a brand strategy for food from Wales.

Physical brands and service brands

As I mentioned earlier, much of the development of branding was undertaken in the fast-moving consumer goods markets. These products are characterized by having low unit value, very regular purchase cycles, widespread (if not universal) availability and a physical construction that will normally change little over time. Of course, sometimes there are improvements and new 'magic' ingredients but, in general, these products have a relatively fixed brand positioning, subject to occasional tweaks as the competitive landscape changes.

More recently there has been a significant development in the quality of branding by service companies – for example, retailers, financial institutions, travel companies and restaurants. The key characteristic of these service brands is that people deliver them and the quality of the brand experience is entirely dependent on the people involved in a given transaction. In the case of an airline, say, your experience of the service will depend on a number of people within the airline's control – check-in, boarding, flight deck, cabin service and disembarkation in a direct experience and a whole host of other people behind the scenes. As a result, the most successful airlines have invested hugely both in people training and in improving communications and customer service awareness among all their staff. More importantly, the service brand tends to have a more fluid offer to the consumer and competitive environment. As such their positionings are less fixed but their brand values and personality are clearly fixed. At Springpoint, we call this 'Brand Shifting™'.

Key issues in destination branding

The basic disciplines of branding apply to destination brands. The starting points of harnessing strengths and competitive differentiation are obvious. However, the key point about destinations is that the positioning and values have to be rooted in the fundamental truths about the destination and its culture. There can be no brand makeover for a destination (although weaknesses can be addressed over time). Clearly a destination brand has a number of target audiences, not the least important of which are the people who provide the services in the destination. This means that good destination brands create a vision that everyone in the destination can relate to.

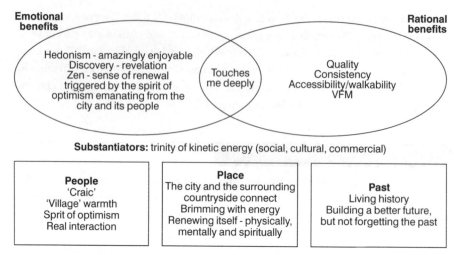

Emotional benefits

Rational benefits

Hedonism - amazingly enjoyable
Discovery - revelation
Zen - sense of renewal
triggered by the spirit of
optimism emanating from the
city and its people

Touches
me deeply

Quality
Consistency
Accessibility/walkability
VFM

Substantiators: trinity of kinetic energy (social, cultural, commercial)

People	Place	Past
'Craic' 'Village' warmth Sprit of optimism Real interaction	The city and the surrounding countryside connect Brimming with energy Renewing itself - physically, mentally and spiritually	Living history Building a better future, but not forgetting the past

Brand attitude: Warm, genuine, wry, informal, inclusive, optimistic

Figure 4.3 Belfast city brand strategy summary

This will encourage service providers to create their own training programmes for their people built around the vision.

Increasingly, when making holiday and short-break choices, people are choosing activity first, destination second. This means that you need to understand the key need states which motivate individuals, families or groups. Experience at Springpoint suggests that these needs can be summarized under three key headings: hedonism, self-improvement and spiritual. Hedonism is perhaps obvious and needs no explanation: it has been the tradition of holidays for so long – good food, good wine, sunshine, beaches, late nights, nightclubs – in short, self-indulgence. Obviously you can have a hedonistic short break in a city without the sunshine and sand. Self-improvement is about acquiring new skills or improving existing skills, typically in sport – skiing, sailing, other water sports, horse-riding – or enjoying cultural pursuits – architecture, art, music, theatre. There are some newer holiday pursuits which might combine the two – learning to paint, or even a cookery course. The spiritual needs of individuals are diverse and almost defy description and generalization since they are highly personal. However, the key issue is the individual's desire to explore himself or herself and their deepest feelings. This is most often expressed in desire for solitude and tranquillity, 'getting away from it all'. However, visits to religious buildings with great traditions in busy cities can be an equally spiritual journey.

It is also important to recognize that individuals often want satisfaction of all these needs in a single holiday: thus a skiing holiday has hedonism in its aprés-ski activity, self-improvement from developing your skiing skills and a spiritual element from the peace and tranquillity of the mountains. A short break in a major city can involve good food and wine, along with visits to art galleries, theatres or concert halls, plus the spiritual fulfilment of time spent in a cathedral or in the surrounding countryside. The key is always to assess what your customers are looking for and how you compare with competition. While destinations are selling dreams and promising pleasure, there is the need for substantiators which make this believable, not more marketing hype, and for rational benefits as well. For example, in our work on Belfast we developed the chart in Figure 4.3 to summarize our core proposition, 'Touch the spirit, feel the welcome'. In every case we have real substantiators which visitors cannot avoid experiencing which will make the promise come true.

Conclusion

Clearly, no destination can exert the same control over the deliverers of the destination promise as an employer. They are individual citizens working for diverse organizations, sometimes working anti-social hours for modest earnings – waiting and bar staff, immigration and customs officers, etc. The key requirement is that your destination brand promise must inspire them as much as the visitor, it must demonstrate their intrinsic strengths. And, since the brand must be based upon truth, you will be amplifying the existing values of the national culture, not fabricating a false promise. Moreover, a typical destination will have diverse audiences, including business investors (at home and abroad), business visitors and local businesses, holiday visitors (at home and abroad) and local day-trippers. In addition, the audience also includes students for education institutions, local people who provide services and, critically, media and opinion-formers. As noted above, we believe that a holistic approach to the destination brand which includes the business target audience as well as the more traditional leisure consumer is advantageous and makes each previous promotional pound (or dollar or whatever) go further. The precise messages for each target audience will be subtly different but the overall positioning and brand values are constant and all the messages are compatible and mutually supportive. The basis of any destination brand is a unique combination of fascination and trust – fascination being the excitement from the unique features of the destination and its culture, and trust being the confidence in the product and its delivery.

Reference

Springpoint (1999). *UK Voices of our Times: Contemporary Values, Regional and National Identity and their Impact on Communication*. February. Springpoint.

5

The politics of branding cities and regions: the case of New Zealand

Chris Ryan

Introduction

'Absolutely Positively Wellington', 'Auckland – City of Sails', 'Manaakitanga – feel the spirit – Rotorua', 'Rangitikei – the best kept secret', 'Christchurch – the Garden City' and 'Palmerston North – Knowledge City' are all examples of destination branding undertaken by local and regional tourism organizations in New Zealand. This chapter does not, however, seek the rationale behind such branding slogans, but rather tries to explain the national and local political scenarios that contextualize such exercises because the issue of 'branding' is not solely an issue of promotion. In its fullest sense marketing is about product design and service delivery beside simple promotion, and thus to divorce branding from the wider context is self-defeating if one wishes to understand the nature of the branding exercise, why it has been initiated and what it purports to do.

Take one example. Taupo's branding of 'There is more besides the Great Lake' requires not only the knowledge that there is a lake of over 600 square kilometres at Taupo, but also that there existed a sensitivity among various stakeholders in Taupo that it was perceived as having a limited portfolio of tourism attractions, and that the branding was as much a political response to the initiatives being undertaken by other local authorities as a marketing reaction. Branding destinations becomes therefore not simply a rational response to competition, but of politics based to a large part on local pride and concern. Thus, to understand the branding exercises undertaken by regional tourism organizations (RTOs), it needs to be appreciated that for the most part they are quasi-public sector bodies, in that many are primarily funded by local authorities and often have councillors present upon their executive and/or advisory boards. Additionally, in some instances, the funding local authority will effectively delegate to the RTO a number of responsibilities that de facto places the RTO in the position of possessing that authority's main source of tourism expertise, therefore becoming an important source of advice and thereby indirectly influencing policy in matters beyond promotion. Product development thus shades into a consideration of social and environmental issues. Thus the aim of this chapter is to describe, at least partially, the politics that contribute to and emerge from this situation.

This chapter requires a 'health warning', for it is based upon the author's personal experiences as a former deputy chair of a district tourism organization (DTO) in the Manawatu, and his current involvement as a chair of one of two committees that exist within the structure of an RTO in New Zealand. Thus, within this chapter will be found anecdotal, untested against empirical research, conceptualizations of what are the purposes, functions and effectiveness of an RTO. But to say that the chapter is anecdotal is not to say that the opinion expressed is without structure or reflection.

The chapter will first examine the reasons for public sector involvement in tourism. This discussion will then extend into a description of the current situation that exists in New Zealand in the last decade of the twentieth century and the first years of the new millennium, thereby providing a context from which, however, it may be possible to make generalizations that have some applicability to at least the English-speaking world. Again, it has to be explicitly stated that these generalizations are but opinion informed by observation and participation in tourism RTOs or their equivalents in the UK, Canada, Australia and New Zealand. Among the conclusions reached are, first, that RTOs are often forced to justify their existence on the premise that they are an effective investment of local government funds because they generate an economic return. Second, for all their shortcomings, RTOs represent a forum where the parochialism of local politics (and personalities) engage in a dialectic with regional and national debate in a manner not always found in local politics. Thus, RTOs are not only contributors to tourism, but also to civic action. Hence the final warning – this author believes that there exists in tourism a need for a proactive public sector in developing plans for tourism, and the means of implementing those plans. Tourism, as an industry and as a series of market transactions, consumes places and both publicly and privately owned resources. The private development of place creates public costs in terms of infrastructure, for example, roads and medical facilities, and to argue, as some political parties and politicians do in New Zealand, that neither local nor national government has a role to play in such considerations is not a view shared by the author. Inasmuch as that role, sometimes by default, falls within the regime of RTOs, the result within RTOs is a continuing tension between, on the one hand, their status as promoters of their regions and as representatives of their industry members, and, on the other, their role as, at the very least, raising awareness of the social and environmental issues associated with tourism.

The role of the public sector

Wanhill (2000) argued that in the latter part of the twentieth century, faced with the increased globalization of market power, governments responded by retreating to 'core tasks'. Among these Wanhill (2000: 224) included: 'protection of the environment to preserve public heath and well-being; the guardianship of future generations through sustainable development . . .correcting for market failure . . .In this respect, industrial policy should not be about "picking winners", but rather about providing institutional arrangements to support private entrepreneurial success'.

Such functions pertain to tourism. It has become a clichéd truism that tourism commodifies the environment, perhaps more so within New Zealand than in many other countries because it trades upon a 'clean, green' environment. Bell (1996) argued that the touristic promotion of the 'greenness' of New Zealand not only commodified the country but also became an important component of national mythology. She commented that 'In New Zealand we can see that nature and landscape have become a powerful identity "myth". "Green" is a splendid example of this; myth transforms nature into history and political expediency' (Bell, 1996: 48). Bell subsequently went on to state:

> Lost in the myth of 'beautiful New Zealand' is the ugly story of pollution . . .Short-sighted and short-term solutions to waste disposal have been driven by economic, not environmental, considerations. . . Yet the green, clean imagery survives this: first because it is restated so often and second, because a superficial glance out of the window affirms this is so – even though the lush pasture has just been drenched with chemicals, and the bush we see is just remains of a far larger forest. (Bell, 1996: 52–3)

Thus, while issues of environmental protection and intergenerational sustainability are taken as almost a given as legitimizing government intervention within tourism, one interpretation of Bell's commentary is that within a New Zealand context the issue becomes yet larger by reason of its support of a Pakeha (non-Maori/European) mythology of what constitutes the nature of New Zealand. In consequence, 'sustainability' becomes a mantra to be repeated, often, in the view of this author, without analysis of the consequences. For example, Tourism Waikato in its draft strategic planning document for 2001, speaks of its need to promote sustainable tourism in its mission statement.

One issue rarely considered when promoting intergenerational sustainability is that of intra-generational sustainability. Somehow it is assumed that all members of society have access to the natural environment; that the children of single, low-income parents in areas of urban deprivation have the same access as those of professional middle-class, dual-income families. Within New Zealand this also has racial overtones – as the urban poor disproportionately comprise Polynesian and Maori peoples. There becomes a danger that reference to intergenerational sustainability becomes a means of sustaining the status quo of current socioeconomic organization into the future. For example, the adoption of the policy that only lead-free petrol would be sold in New Zealand meant that the cost of petrol additives fell primarily on those who could least afford the newest cars with catalytic converters – namely the lower-income groups who drove the oldest cars.

In analysing the New Zealand debate about the need for a national tourism research strategy, Ryan and Simmons (1999) argued that such a strategy, and the then proposed modes of its funding, were defensible upon grounds of market failure. Like many other countries, the commercial reality of the tourism industry in New Zealand is that it is based upon large numbers of small, family owned and operated businesses, often undercapitalized and producing low rates of return upon capital. The rationale for such businesses is often not entirely economic, but either one of lifestyle, or social, in that they sustain employment in otherwise marginal (often rural) economies, and thereby help stop the drift from rural to urban regions (for example see Warren and Taylor, 1999). Tourism sustains small communities and, in doing so, may help them retain a sense of local identity, even if at times it is an invented identity. Bell provides such an example in her description of events at Ross, a former gold-mining settlement of the nineteenth century that has sought to develop a tourist attraction based upon its history. In 1995 the announcement that Ross might still have NZ$750 million of gold in its surrounding hills became a source of local concern, not pleasure. She commented:

> the reconstruction of a gold town of the past is far more highly valued than a gold town of the present. History is colourful, a form of recreation for those reconstructing it in the present; in this process of reconstruction, history can be

controlled. The historic village belongs to those who live in Ross, and who built it. A new gold mine on the same site belongs to somebody else from outside: anonymous, exploitative, capitalistic, with no sentimental links with the place and its past. (Bell, 1996: 63)

The national context of the late 1990s in New Zealand

Tourism thus represents a choice for small communities, contributing to a sense of (mythic, constructed) identity while offering a source of economic viability if not well-being. It thereby attracts the interest of government and, indeed, representatives of the industry have themselves political agendas. Wanhill argues that there are four reasons for government intervention in tourism, these being 'the complexity of the tourist product, its institutional structure, guardianship of the resource base and market failure' (Wanhill, 2000: 225). That these reasons are often accepted implies a wider legitimacy being allocated to government. Elliot (1997) argues that any rationalization of public sector management is based upon five general principles: public interest, public service, effectiveness, efficiency and accountability. However, 'public interest' is in itself a difficult area to define, and there may well be a shifting consensus or interpretation over time. As already noted, Wanhill, along with many other commentators, discerns a shift in what is deemed to be the appropriate spheres of government action in the later part of the last century. Following Hall's (1994) categorization of the role of the public sector in tourism, it becomes possible to briefly note the changing nature of the public sector–private sector relationship in the tourism industry that occurred in New Zealand in the final decade of the 1990s.

Government as a source of planning

During much of the period of the 1990s in New Zealand, conservative governments retreated from this function in the belief that the market was a better regulator of needs than was central direction. This effectively left issues of resource management to regional and local authorities, but the remit of the Resource Management Act 1991 meant that such authorities were not to develop prescriptive methods of control but to assess potential outcomes of proposals and to respond accordingly by either granting or refusing a resource consent.

Government as a source of legislation and regulation

As is evident from the above, governments at a local and national level in the 1990s became increasingly reactive rather than proactive through the legislative framework adopted in New Zealand in the 1990s. The 1990s saw tourism being assessed through a policy framed by the Resource Management Act 1991, various amendments to the 1989 Local Government Act and similar legislation. The policy direction was to free the market from constraints. Thus the Resource Management Act, while concerned about a need to protect and sustain environments, also permitted economic benefits to be weighed in the balance, and one consequence of this, as will be argued below, was to politicize at local level the whole issue of development in a way that had not previously existed. This is not to ignore the fact that development is itself a political and social action, but the legislation of the 1990s led to inconsistent policies.

Government as a co-ordinating body

Tourism is a diffuse industry or sector, and co-ordination is arguably required both vertically (i.e. between local, regional and national institutions) and horizontally (i.e. between agencies at the same level of activity). As national government retreated from this function in the 1990s, the need for co-ordination meant that local authorities and their proxies such as RTOs became the site of discourse as to the need, nature and direction of co-ordination. Pavlovich's (2000) case study of tourism entrepreneurs in the Waitomo, and her application of network theory to this location, indicates just how transient the nature of these relationships can be at the local level where personalities can become an important determinant of action. In New Zealand the paradox emerged where, as a Conservative government preached the ideology of free markets, its proxy, the New Zealand Tourism Board, started to promote marketing networks among regions which of necessity involved planning implications as to resultant flows of tourists. Even more ironic was that networks were being promulgated at a time when there were little data available as to the flows of those tourists, whether international or domestic. This situation was itself due to a 'reform' of the 1989 national government that replaced previous organizations with the New Zealand Tourism Board that had as its prime purpose the overseas marketing of New Zealand – not a data collection process of flows of tourists within New Zealand.

Government as entrepreneur

Historically, in New Zealand, the government had been a leading industrial player as the owner and operator of airlines, hotel chains and attractions. Over the latter half of the twentieth century this function had been supplanted by the private sector, with the final stage being one of privatization of a number of assets, including that of Air New Zealand in 1989.

Government as a stimulator of tourism development

Government can act as a stimulator in at least three ways. First, by operating systems of grants and tax benefits, or as a source of low interest loans, as was done by the UK under the 1969 Tourism Development Act. Second, it may seek to promote place through marketing initiatives. Thus many countries possess national tourist boards as a means of promotion and marketing, and New Zealand is no different. Tourism New Zealand receives about NZ$55 million for the marketing and promotion of the brand 'New Zealand'. Third, governments may sponsor research. In New Zealand this is undertaken at national level through the Tourism Research Council which, in 2001, seeks to co-ordinate the work of projects funded through the Foundation of Research, Science and Technology (the means by which the government directs public sector research funding), Tourism New Zealand and the Office of Tourism and Sport, and at regional and local level through various initiatives of local authorities, regional and district tourism organizations.

Government as a facilitator of economic activity

In the 1990s New Zealand's new-right governments sought to facilitate growth through the removal of what were perceived as restraints upon the market. As noted this included changing environmental legislation by removing prohibitions per se through the enforcement of policies such as zoning, and replacing them by one of awarding consents where it could be shown that overall the balance between economic, social and environmental impacts resulting from a development were beneficial. Similarly, changes in employment contract law effectively replaced collective bargaining with individual employee–employer contracts. In 1999, however, a Labour-Alliance government was elected. For those unfamiliar with New Zealand politics, the country votes in governments under a mixed member proportional (MMP) voting system, and the Labour party is a centrist-left party while the Alliance is itself an alliance of parties representing a range of socialist tendencies. In consequence the government has a predisposition towards proactive planning, but does so from the perspective of facilitating entrepreneurial activity to address social problems while retaining profitability, rather than seeking to specifically direct industry. In 1999, the Finance Minister, Dr Michael Cullen, said the Budget was about 'a new start for a new century. While government says it doesn't want to pick winners, regulate, subsidise or compel', he added, it does want to help businesses find new markets, 'and become winners . . .At times it means getting the regulatory framework right so that short term optimism does not damage the wider public commercial good. At times it means ensuring the right financing options are available. At times it means taking a direct leadership role' (cited in Coventry, 2000a).

In the view of the government in 2000, tourism was seen as not only being important economically through its role as the single largest earner of foreign currency (NZ$4.6 billion in 1999), but as a means of regeneration of economic activity in otherwise economically marginal zones. Thus the then Minister for Economic Development, Jim Anderton, expressed interest in tourism as part of a regional economic development strategy, while the government supported the development of a tourism strategy.

Government as a protector of the public interest

It can be argued that the government is fulfilling the role of custodian of the 'public interest' when seeking to be a facilitator of business, while also considering the social implications of such entrepreneurial activity. As is evident however, the interpretation of public interest and means of implementing that role has been the subject of debate and changing policies in New Zealand as elsewhere. With reference to tourism, it is perhaps significant that Mark Burton, as Minister of Tourism, addressed the 2000 New Zealand Tourism Industry Association conference with reference to the emerging tourism strategy by asking: 'What can we learn from structures and processes adopted in other countries?' He also wanted to know the costs involved and what legislation or regulations might be required to implement the plan. He continued:

> How do we ensure the New Zealand public is behind the strategy? . . .The strategy will only succeed if it has wide backing. We must quickly reach out to the wider business community, to local government, to important interest groups like Forest and Bird and the Fish and Game Council, and to iwi (Maori tribal groups). To realise our tourism potential, we must enlist as broad a spectrum of support for tourism as possible . . .But, perhaps most importantly: How do we ensure that tourism growth is sustainable? For New Zealand to benefit from tourism growth we must ensure it is sustainable – not just economically but also culturally, socially and environmentally . . .Tourism growth must not come at a cost to our natural heritage and our way of life . . .When presented with the strategy, I will be very pleased if it has managed to answer these questions! I want us to have a clear direction forward and a clear identification of roles and buy into responsibilities. (Cited in Coventry, 2000b).

It is evident from this quote that the New Zealand government of 2000 has a wider perspective of a tourism strategy beyond issues of promotion, and also an extended view of who are the stakeholders within tourism.

Politics and politicking

It can be discerned from the above that 'public interest' is thus an outcome of political action, and that in New Zealand the election of a Labour government in 1999, aided by a more proactive political leadership of the New Zealand Tourism Industry Association (NZTIA) under its then CEO, Glenys Coughlan, led to the development of a tourism industry strategy. At the time of writing (December 2000) that strategy has not yet been fully determined, but already some factors are becoming clear. Whereas under the previous national government with its user-pays, market-led philosophy, elements of statistical data generation were only to be funded for a limited period, until either the industry took over such funding or chose to let such statistical series fade as not being required by the tourism industry (Office of Tourism and Sport et al., 1998: 17) it now appears that such statistical collection is to be sustained by the government, in consultation with industry through the newly established Tourism Research Council, in the public interest. Equally, the NZTIA appears to want, from a presentation given by Glenys Coughlan at the 2000 New Zealand National Tourism and Hospitality Research Conference, for no other means of strategy implementation than moral suasion (e.g. a property developer's proposal may gain or lose credibility if seen as being consistent or inconsistent with 'the strategy') or that a proposal is consistent with the 1991 Resource Management Act. Given the view that this legislation is significantly flawed as to its implementation if not its approach (for examples and discussion pertaining to tourism see Hall, Jenkins and Kearsley, 1998; Ryan and Cheyne-Buchanan, 1996; Schöllmann, 2000), one interpretation of the NZTIA's view means that, in spite of comments about sustainability, the NZTIA tends to a view that the industry wishes for as little government intervention as is possible, other than for supporting research needs. Whether this represents the wider social good and is consistent with the sentiments expressed by the minister may be open to argument.

The period of 1997 to 2001 (including the Murray McCully affair where a minister arguably went beyond ministerial powers by intervening in the marketing policies of the then New Zealand Tourism Board) saw a politicization of both the industry and its issues as never before. The NZTIA, as a significant pressure group, was able to secure more public sector support (and funding) for the industry and its organizations, including the Office of Tourism and Sport and TNZ, and, arguably less directly, for RTOs by making local politicians more aware of the importance of tourism as a contributor to the New Zealand economy if only through the amount of attention the news media paid to the industry and its politics. Indeed, in 2000, at its annual conference the NZTIA had the ability to attract the Prime Minister, Helen Clark, as a key speaker. Coughlan's actions ensured that the industry association obtained a political presence to refute initiatives such as a tourist tax and to sustain current public funding of border controls while voicing criticisms relating to other legislation like the Employment Contracts Act and Resource Management Act. Additionally, by publicly supporting the Office of Tourism and Sport it successfully helped to secure monies for research initiatives that were currently not funded by the industry itself, but which were nonetheless oriented towards market research needs. One example was the re-establishment of a domestic visitors monitor. Here there was a congruence of interest between the wider industry, the NZTIA, the Office of Tourism and Sport and the predisposition of a Labour government to a more interventionist form of government when compared to that of its predecessor.

Thus far, since 1999, the government has adopted a hands-off approach as far as the promotion of New Zealand by TNZ has been concerned, apart from one minor criticism by the Prime Minister that there is more to the country than scenery and a green image (Hendery, 2000). This is in direct opposition to the policy adopted by Murray McCully, who, as Minister of Tourism and Sport in the previous government, sought to directly intervene in the marketing policies of the then New Zealand Tourism Board on the grounds that, in his view, it was insufficiently promoting New Zealand as the first country to see the new millennium, and was failing to grasp opportunities presented by hosting the 2000 America's Cup. As a result of his intervention, the CEO and a number of directors resigned in protest about what was seen as both an undeserved criticism of the New Zealand Tourism Board and an intervention in the daily functions of the board, thereby overstepping the functions of a minister. Incidentally, this illustrates either the ironies or pragmatism of politics, whereby a left of centre government in 2000 rejected direct intervention in overseas marketing, while a conservative, market-led government of 1999 sought to so directly interfere. While events in Wellington might be thought peripheral to the marketing of tourism at a regional level, given the small community that is New Zealand's decision makers in tourism at both regional and national level, the linkages are such that changes at 'the top' cannot but affect the regional promotion and tourism policies being undertaken.

The regional tourism organizations

Such national events and considerations have impacted upon RTOs both directly and indirectly, albeit to differing extents depending upon the nature of the region and the historical antecedents of the RTO concerned. Regional tourism organizations are not uniform within New Zealand. There were, at the outset of 2001, twenty-five RTOs, but their administrative boundaries differ from those of the twelve regional councils that exist. These councils represent a third tier of government between national and local government, but with a specific mandate for the integrated management of natural and physical environmental management (Bush, 1995). Thus, for example, under the 1991 Resource Management Act, regional councils are specifically charged with the creation of management plans for coastal areas with a view to establishing conservation and preservation policies. The regional councils are funded by both local authorities and through the ability to levy their own rate, and under Section 593(b) of the Local Government Amendment Act, can become involved with tourism promotion if all local authorities within a regional council's jurisdiction unanimously agree. Hence, in the example of the Manawatu-Whanganui Regional Council, that council stepped in to establish an RTO when differences of opinion existed between Wanganui and Palmerston North City Councils and Manawatu District Council as to the promotion of tourism. However, inasmuch as the resultant River Region RTO has a limited budget and is staffed by a part-time consultant, its ability to provide direction for better funded and, arguably, more energetic (and competing) district tourism councils is limited. A further factor that limits the ability of River Region RTO is that the administrative boundaries of the Manawatu-Whanganui Regional Council are not consistent with patterns of tourism flows or nodal points of tourism attractions. For example the region covers both the east and west sides of the Tararua Ranges, and roads and resultant traffic flows differ as to the approaches to Wellington.

On the other hand, the regional council, Environment Waikato, covers a large part of central North Island, stretching from Raglan and Kawhia on the west coast, to the east coast and the Coromandel Peninsula. In this instance there exist two RTOs, those of Tourism Waikato and Tourism Coromandel, but both of these RTOs have linked with the RTOs of Rotorua, Auckland and Taupo to establish a Central North Island Marketing Network. Yet this network also illustrates the variations that exist within RTOs. Tourism Waikato, while covering a large region that includes the tourist hotspot of Waitomo with its cluster of adventure operations and the glow worm caves, is dominated in its funding by Hamilton City Council, both in absolute terms and in funding per head of population. Hamilton City Council provides 75 per cent of the total funding (Tourism Waikato, 2001), yet, because some councillors do not perceive Hamilton as being a 'tourist attraction', while others adhere to the ideological view that the industry should pay for its own organizations, it has had difficulty in sustaining its own revenues; albeit, it must be noted, a situation not helped by a previous CEO's overspending. The nature of the debate is clearly shown by the web page sustained by local Member of Parliament, Bob Simcock. On the 22 October 1999 he wrote:

> The City Vision members oppose any expenditure on tourism promotion. They argue that the council doesn't promote plumbers, so why should it promote the tourism sector. But this is the sort of purist nonsense that gives them a bad name. The benefits from tourism are spread widely . . .The Mayor and others appear to be more interested in scoring some point over surrounding Waikato councils who they believe are not paying their fair share of the costs of Tourism Waikato . . .But the idea of promoting Hamilton in separation from the rest of the Waikato is silly. (Simcock, 1999)

This debate was not unique. Exactly the same issues arose in the case of Palmerston North City Council and the surrounding Manawatu District Council, albeit in a different format, in 1994. At that time the city council established Tourism Manawatu, funded entirely by the city council, it being aware that promotion of the city without reference to the surrounding attractions made little sense. However, some within the district council saw this as an attempt by the city to 'take over' the promotion of 'their' area and 'their' attractions, and in consequence a rival tourism promotional body was established with district council support. It was not until there was a meeting of all mayors under the auspices of the Manawatu-Whanganui Regional Council that the issue was solved. Parochialism bedevils tourism policies in New Zealand. If, as Bell contends, tourism is a means by which small communities create identities for themselves, then such identities are about matters of difference, about myths of independence from wider (and distrusted) national governments and movements of globalization. The outsider is, by definition, an 'outsider', and thereby to be opposed. But examples can be found where personalities and differences have led to intensely held views, but nonsensical outcomes. For example, both the small communities of Foxton and Waihi (each of which have populations of under 10 000) in the 1990s had, for some time, not one but two competing tourism promotional bodies. Colleagues at other universities in New Zealand could probably provide other examples of local politics inhibiting sensible actions.

Even the more successful RTOs have not been without their political battles. Tourism Rotorua is one of the larger RTOs in New Zealand in that it employs seven people (by comparison Tourism Waikato employs a CEO and two staff, as does Tourism Coromandel). Rotorua has a history of being a tourist location since the 1850s, and tourism accounts for about 20 per cent of the city's economy (Butcher, Fairweather and Simmons, 2000). Yet in the mid-1990s its then CEO resigned on a matter of what to him was an issue of principle in that he argued that the RTO's mandate was to serve all tourism businesses and organizations, and not simply the interests of the largest commercial members with the largest promotional budgets. His stand again politicized issues relating to tourism planning at a local level, and his successor has been able to build upon that to the extent that recently Tourism Rotorua has been able to initiate policies based upon Agenda 21 and cautiously advance concepts of environmental good practice.

Local government and regional tourism organizations

The relationship between RTOs, their industry memberships and their local authorities is ambiguous, to say the least. On the one hand the RTOs generally have a membership derived from the commercial stakeholders of the tourism industry, which membership will often include the accommodation and attractions sectors among others. Yet the membership fees are generally nominal, as size of membership acts as one of the validating criteria when an RTO purports to represent 'the local industry'. Hence, in many instances the major funding of an RTO is derived from local government. The same model is true for many of the DTOs. Consequently the size of budget between RTOs varies considerably. Tourism Auckland thus has a budget of about NZ$5.5 million, while Totally Wellington has a budget of about NZ$3.6 million. The contributions made by local authorities to RTOs vary considerably, both in absolute terms and in terms of rate support per head of population. Thus, in the case of Tourism Waikato, one authority, Hamilton City Council, provides 75 per cent of the total funding (about NZ$3 per head of population), while support from one other member local council is assessed at 75 cents per head of population. For the DTOs the funding can be even more disparate. Horowhenua District Council funds its DTO to a figure of over NZ$100 000, while Rangitikei District Council provides no direct funding at all to Rangitikei Tourism, which is otherwise an entirely operator-funded body. On the other hand, indirect support is provided by Rangitikei Tourism holding a contract from the district council to run two visitor information centres, a role that it was re-examining in early 2001. In other cases local authorities directly fund visitor information services (e.g. Palmerston North City Council).

It should not be thought that these funds are the sole revenues available to DTOs and RTOs. In many instances the RTOs co-ordinate specific marketing promotions, which are then funded by those stakeholders and members who have a specific interest in the promotion. For example, attraction and site operators in Northland and other regions adjacent to Auckland partook in, and financed, promotional activities aimed at those attending the defence of the America's Cup in 1999–2000 through initiatives made by the RTOs.

Probably the most successful RTO in attracting industry support has been that of Wellington. There the value of industry support in 1999–2000 was estimated as being about NZ$3.1 million (Coventry, 2000c). This is partly funded by the accommodation sector imposing a small fee on its bed rates, and then passing this fee to its RTO. The author was involved in an attempt to follow this model in another New Zealand city. First, the local motelier association was reluctant to support the initiative on the grounds that the RTO did little for them. Second, when the manager of the largest hotel promised to provide several thousand dollars to the fund, local moteliers grumbled that it 'was all right for him, it is not his own money'! Finally, the local motelier association agreed to the concept, but on the proviso that as the main beneficiary of tourism was the local retail and restaurant sector, they would participate if the local retailers and restaurants did so. As there was no one retail organization that could represent all the town's retailers (as the moteliers knew well) the initiative failed. As Rob McIntyre, CEO of Wellington's RTO stated, 'Another factor in Wellington City Council's strong investment is the significant pressure on Totally Wellington to leverage from the private sector. Last year we achieved about $2 million industry support in cash, contra and collective buying-benefit for the city' (cited in Coventry, 2000c).

The attitude of local authorities is also shown by the statements made about tourism within their local annual plans, which, under the amended Local Government Act they are required to produce. In their survey of Local Authorities in New Zealand and their attitudes towards tourism planning, Page and Thorn (1998: 183) concluded that 'This study however, is perhaps more disturbing because of the implication the findings have at the national level. Only the local and regional councils have any role at all in terms of managing tourism growth in New Zealand, and it is apparent that even there, involvement is limited.' Again, differences can be found. Whereas many city councils are practically silent on tourism issues, others make more specific mention. For example, in its *Annual Plan*, Dunedin City states: 'Tourism, along with education, is a key sector in the Dunedin economy. The role of this function is to promote Dunedin, locally and overseas, as an attractive venue for leisure, conferences and educational tourism. The main objective is to get more tourists to Dunedin and to keep them here longer and this is achieved through funding provided to Tourism Dunedin' (Dunedin City Council, 2000: 45).

This brief review indicates that the levels of funding of RTOs and DTOs and the level of concern about tourism being expressed by local authorities vary quite considerably. Why is this? A number of reasons can be suggested. First, as Page and Thorn (1998) found, there is a widespread lack of understanding of the impact being made by tourism at a regional and local level. This is in part due to past deficiencies in statistical series, but the issue is now being addressed by RTOs themselves as they seek to substantiate their existence. Certainly, as is evidenced by the case of Tourism Taranaki, which in 2000 ceased to exist for a time (see various issues of *Inside Tourism* for coverage of this debate), RTOs have no privileged right of existence. Consequently a number of RTOs commissioned research from various bodies as to the economic impact that tourism made upon their local regions. For example, Butcher, Fairweather and Simmons (2000) estimated that tourism in Rotorua was worth NZ$463 million and employed 3500 full-time employees (FTEs), thereby making it the third most important source of employment in the city. Again, Dudding and Ryan (2000) estimated that tourism was worth NZ$87 million to the Coromandel, while Hughes and Ryan (2001) estimated that tourism was contributing about 4.3 per cent to local GDP in the case of the region served by Tourism Waikato. The objective of commissioning such studies is the RTOs often use the findings to persuade councillors that tourism is an activity that is worth supporting from the public purse.

Second, attitudes will vary as to how local authorities perceive their region's standing in the national portfolio of tourist attractions, and how the regions are perceived by other key players in the industry. In this respect one cannot overlook the importance of the national carrier, Air New Zealand. It might be said that Air New Zealand has an interest in the promotion of New Zealand by TNZ and the RTOs on the premise that if New Zealand is perceived as an attractive place to visit, then demand for its services will increase. Equally, as a domestic as well as international operator, Air New Zealand would wish to serve those places that possess the ability to sustain profitable flows of visitors and which have the necessary infrastructure in place. Local authorities are very aware of that issue. For example, Queenstown sought, and gained, improvements to its airport, which included extending the runway and building new terminal facilities to not only permit direct international flights, but also to enable Air New Zealand to fly its new, larger jets on domestic flights direct into the town, thereby bypassing Dunedin. Equally, Rotorua councillors were dismayed by the news that Air New Zealand was withdrawing jet services from their city as the runway was too short, although arguably, in international terms, given that Hamilton is but an hour away and possesses a full-length runway and existing flights to Australia, opportunities exist for joint marketing initiatives between the two locations.

Geoff Burns, Manager, International Markets, for Air New Zealand, expressed the view at the 2000 New Zealand National Tourism and Hospitality Research Conference, that Air New Zealand wishes to co-operate with only about five RTOs who had the marketing clout to attract international visitors. Indeed, the then Managing Director of Air New Zealand, Jim McCrea (2000), argued that it was Air New Zealand's policy to 'leverage off major events', which major events tend to be within a limited number of locations due to the infrastructure needs required. This has been seen as preserving the status quo of airborne passengers to reconfirm what has been known as the golden triangle of tourism in New Zealand centred upon Auckland, Rotorua, Christchurch and Queenstown. This has meant that other RTOs have to compete with that perception, while the domestic market also becomes extremely important to them. Obviously local authorities that perceive themselves as being of national importance tend to better fund their RTOs.

But herein lies another issue for RTO/DTO–local authority relationship. As Page and Thorn found, rarely in local authority planning departments can there be found tourism 'specialists', and thus the expertise is more likely to be found within the RTOs. As 'tourism experts' RTOs are staffed by those who also express concerns about environmental and social aspects of tourism. Thus, the example has been given of Tourism Rotorua seeking to encourage environmental good practices, while NZTIA, to its credit, has also undertaken Agenda 21 initiatives. However, the paradox has arisen that the RTO has sometimes been less enthused by pro-development policies than have some local councillors, who therefore become critical of their RTO for not full-heartedly proclaiming a short-term promotional policy. While it is not possible here to go into all the details, the instance of Queenstown Lakes District Council and its pro-development mayor's attitudes towards issues of zoning is an interesting case study. This dispute, terminated in the Queenstown Lake Landscape Decision whereby the Environmental Court effectively renounced the piecemeal approach of the council and reinforced the protection of the environment, is a decision case study that involved tourism and its impact on the environment and the type of development to be permitted in Queenstown (see Miller, 2001; Schöllmann, 2000). Certainly the RTO and the tourism industry were not at one on these issues, some placing environmental protection before development, some arguing the economic case must have precedence, while some sought a middle way.

Finally, issues between RTOs and local authorities are sometimes made difficult because of intercouncil rivalry and distrust, as has been evidenced above. RTOs have to stand independent of their funders, even while they seek to encourage a better understanding of tourism and the needs for funding. However, Dymond (1997) found a congruence between local authorities and RTOs as to their priorities with reference to tourism. The leading three priorities for both groups were 'tourism's contribution to the economy', 'consumer satisfaction' and 'local satisfaction'. Yet this author has found examples where local councillors and operators have expressed views that seem to imply a competitive rather than strategic stance. For example, dissatisfaction has been expressed by some Waitomo operators with Tourism Waikato, arguing that it is too oriented towards Hamilton city to the detriment of the Waitomo. At another RTO's board meeting that the author attended, a councillor stated that he knew nothing about tourism other than the fact he enjoyed going on holiday. In his defence it must be stated that he was an advocate of many initiatives. On another occasion, a special meeting was convened (to which the author was invited) by a councillor who had previously shown no interest in tourism. This councillor had attended a conference where James Strong, the CEO of Qantas, had been the keynote speaker. After playing a thirty-minute tape of Mr Strong's talk, the councillor then demanded what was 'his area' doing about tourism. The remaining two hours were then taken up with an explanation of what was being done with the limited funding being made available. More seriously, some regions still feel a loss of independent political direction that followed the reforms of local government in 1989 that reduced the number of local authorities in New Zealand, and the relationship between Queenstown and its surrounding region has not always been harmonious.

Conclusion

Thus far, much of what has been written seemingly has little to do with destination marketing, but from this brief discussion of political scenarios in New Zealand as they affect tourism at national and local levels, a number of dimensions can be identified. They include those of professionalism vs enthusiasm, short-termism vs

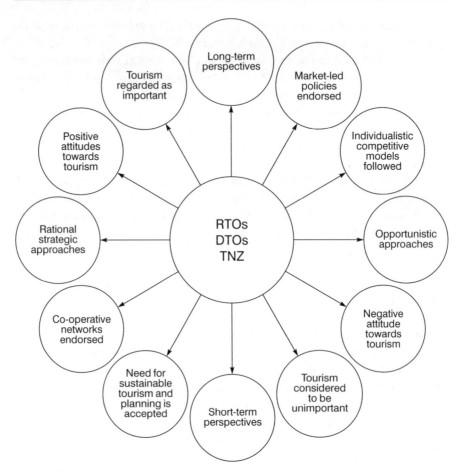

Figure 5.1 Dimensions of political perspectives

long-term perspectives, competition vs co-operation, tourism being considered not at all vs tourism being perceived as an important economic and social factor. These factors, and others, may be represented in a diagram as shown in Figure 5.1. One side of the diagram may be thought to represent the positive dimensions, the other the more chaotic if not negative.

Politics is generally assumed to be about the use of power, and the role of power structures. For an industry that is so economically significant, tourism is politically weak. It is weak because its base comprises many small concerns, not all of which are strongly economically motivated. Within New Zealand, there is no Ministry of Tourism, albeit there is a minister, who has many other portfolios including that of defence. At a local level, except for some rural areas and the urban areas of Rotorua, Queenstown and to a lesser extent Christchurch and Dunedin where tourism is well established and highly visible, the industry lacks real political influence. It has been argued that this could be addressed if more of those involved in tourism stood for local political positions. Given such a vacuum, the real sources of power in New Zealand tourism politics might be said to be Air New Zealand, a few large companies like Tourism Holdings, and public or quasi-public sector organizations like TNZ and the Office of Tourism and Sport. Much of the industry is represented by pressure groups such as the tourism industry association and its various member bodies, and thereby almost by default the NZTIA has assumed some political influence. Within this scenario it becomes possible for individuals to achieve significant levels of influence, at least within certain spheres. Among these players are the CEOs of a number of the RTOs and, to a lesser extent, DTOs. Certainly at a regional level and district level, such CEOs can possess an important ability to influence policies within the domain of tourism and those things that impinge upon it. Given the small world of New Zealand (which has a population of only 3.6 million but is larger than the UK in land area), personality and a proven record of successful ventures can go far in generating a political influence as personal networks are important (although this may be true of many societies).

Because of the high level of public funding of TNZ, RTOs and DTOs, these organizations exist within a political framework with varying degrees of ease. As was demonstrated by the McCully affair and, at least at the anecdotal level, by the interventions of councillors at the level of RTOs and DTOs, political interference can sometimes be direct. That the intervention is not more regular or often is due to the constitutional rules, understood if not written, that generally prohibit politicians from direct interference in the day-to-day running of organizations like RTOs. However, such organizations occupy an uncertain legal ground. While heavily funded by the public purse, they are not part of the 'civil service'. They possess industry members, and may engage in direct commercial activities themselves if they run visitor information centres that sell products on a commission basis. While many would perceive their essential function as being that of the promotion of a region, and as offering advisory services to their industry membership, due to their expertise they are often asked to go beyond this. They may, for example, become involved in product development through the encouragement of event and conference promotion. Although regionally based, their awareness of actual tourism flows have made the RTOs (at least in the Central North Island region) one of the biggest supporters of network marketing initiatives whereby resources are combined. Due to their awareness of social and environmental issues pertaining to tourism, they may at times be seen as inhibiting entrepreneurial activity if it is felt that such activity is dominated by short-term needs with possible negative longer-term consequences.

As was stated previously, the very ambiguity of the nature of an RTO or DTO is in part its strength. They create a forum where the public and private sectors meet, and where the needs of local authorities to create a planning regime interface with the need of operators financially to sustain themselves. By reason of their position, and the linkages that CEOs of RTOs and DTOs have with national organizations, the local interfaces with the national, and flows of information proceed in both directions. To be effective networks require density of points, communication flows, discerned directions, information and a willingness to participate. Within their own communities regional and district tourism organizations provide a key component in such networks, and thereby play an important role in information dissemination and opinion formation.

Do all of these considerations impact upon regional and destination marketing? In a direct sense the answer has to be generally 'no', in spite of the occasional example of elected politicians attempting to frame the content of marketing direction. But indirectly the answer has to be in the affirmative – for it is the political scenario that influences the level of budgets being made available to TNZ, RTOs and DTOs. In most cases budgets are tied to the annual cycle of public sector budgeting, and what elected politicians feel they can allocate from revenues derived from taxes and rates – and over which spending departmental heads engage in sometimes bitter dispute. In these considerations tourism is possibly still perceived as a frivolous source of expenditure when compared with sewage disposal, roads, medicine and health. From this arises two concerns – first, the continuing emphasis on economic performance, sometimes embroidered by expressed concern about social and environmental matters, and, second, by a search for the type of 'catch-all' slogans that were illustrated at the commence-ment of this chapter. In a world where conventional marketing wisdom dictates that relationship marketing is the way to progress, such a broad-band marketing approach as 'sloganeering' has little to recommend it. Until recently this was a practical issue for cash-strapped tourism organizations, but seemingly an answer has been provided by the Internet. Thus, TNZ's strategy is, to a large extent, web based with its theme of '100% Pure New Zealand' acting as a portal to various types of 'kiwi experiences'. At the same time, though, businesses themselves are increasingly bypassing promotional organizations for direct selling, while recog-nizing that for marketing based around special events and trade shows, where a 'public face' to a region or destination is required, the RTOs and DTOs still have an important function.

Finally it is suggested that much of what has been written above would find an echo in the tourism organizations of other English-speaking countries. One aspect of the industry that has struck the author is that it is an industry of personalities, many of whom are extrovert, many of whom like interacting with other people. Perhaps by its nature, tourism attracts enthusiasts, 'people who like people', and for many of these cool rationality would perhaps be a denial of that which can create the 'sublime tourist experience'.

References

Bell, C. (1996). *Inventing New Zealand: Everyday Myths of Pakeha Identity*. Penguin.

Bush, G. (1995). *Local Government and Politics in New Zealand*. Auckland University Press.

Butcher, G., Fairweather, J. R. and Simmons, D. (2000). *The Economic Impact of Tourism on Rotorua*. Tourism Research and Education Centre, Lincoln University, report no. 17/2000.

Coventry, N. (2000a). Paraparaumu Beach: South Pacific Media Services.

Coventry, N. (2000b). Minister ponders strategy. *Inside Tourism*, **319**, 17 August.

Coventry, N. (2000c). Retaining council support isn't easy. *Inside Tourism*, **318–2**, 11 August.

Dudding, V. and Ryan, C. (2000). The impacts of tourism on a rural retail sector: a New Zealand case study. *Tourism Economics*, in press.

Dunedin City Council (2000). *Annual Plan, 2000/1*. Dunedin City Council.

Dymond, S. (1997). Indicators of sustainable tourism in New Zealand: a local government perspective. *Journal of Sustainable Tourism*, **5**(4), 279–293.

Elliot, J. (1997). *Tourism: Politics and Public Sector Management*. Routledge.

Hall, C. M. (1994). *Tourism and Politics: Policy, Power and Place*. Wiley.

Hall, C. M., Jenkins, J. and Kearsley, G. (1998). *Tourism: Planning and Policy in Australia and New Zealand – Cases, Issues and Practice*. Irwin.

Hendery, S. (2000). 2000: Pure NZ message paying off for tourism. *New Zealand Herald*, 27 December, p. C1.

Hughes, W. and Ryan, C. (2001). Estimates of the value of tourism for Tourism Waikato. Unpublished document, Waikato Management School, University of Waikato.

McCrea, J. (2000). ANZ's industry contribution is sometimes under-appreciated. *Inside Tourism*, **296**, 9 March.

Miller, M. (2001). Court sets rules for Wakatipu. *Southland Times*, 2 January.

Office of Tourism and Sport, New Zealand Tourism Industry Association, New Zealand Tourism Board, Department of Conservation and Air New Zealand (1998). *Tourism Research and Development Strategy*. Office of Tourism and Sport.

Page, S. J. and Thorn, K. (1998). Sustainable tourism development and planning in New Zealand: local government responses. In *Sustainable Tourism* (C. M. Hall and A. A. Lew, eds) pp. 173–184, Longman.

Pavlovich, K. (2000). The organization of supply in a tourism destination: an analysis of a networked community – the Waitomo Caves Village. Unpublished PhD thesis, Waikato Management School, Waikato University.

Ryan, C. and Simmons, D. (1999). Towards a tourism research strategy for New Zealand. *Tourism Management*, **20**(3), 305–312.

Ryan, C., and Cheyne-Buchanan, J. (1996). The Resources Management Act, a bungy operation, and problems of planning. In *Pacific Rim 2000: Issues, Interrelations, Inhibitors – Conference Proceedings* (M. Oppermann, ed.) pp. 17–28, Wairiki Polytechnic.

Schöllmann, A. (2000). Local authority regulation and promotion of tourism: the management of conflict in Queenstown. Paper presented at Fourth New Zealand Tourism and Hospitality Research Conference, AUT, Auckland.

Simcock, B. (1999). *Tourism Waikato: A Victim of a Visionless Council*. http://www.bobsimcock.co.nz (22 October).

Tourism Waikato (2001). *Waikato Regional Tourism Strategy: 2000–2010: A Strategy for Sustainable Growth and Development*. Tourism Waikato.

Wanhill, S. (2000). Issues in public sector involvement. In *Tourism in the 21st Century: Lessons from Experience* (B. Faulkner, G. Moscardo and E. Laws, eds), pp. 222–242, Continuum.

Warren, J. and Taylor, N. (1999). *Developing Rural Tourism in New Zealand*. Centre for Research, Evaluation and Social Assessment.

6

Branding and national identity: the case of Central and Eastern Europe

Derek Hall

Introduction

At national and local levels, post-communist re-imaging in Central and Eastern Europe has been informed by a requirement to portray a Europeanness which conforms to requirements for European Union (EU) accession, and the projection of a safe, stable and welcoming environment to encourage foreign direct investment and international tourism. Branding of CEE destinations is taking place alongside the development and marketing of niche tourism products which represent a response to (a) changing global tourism demand, and (b) the need to raise per capita levels of tourist receipts. Recruited in the processes of national identity projection and representation, niche development has proceeded rapidly, notably in the areas of heritage and culture, nature and ideals of sustainability.

However, there is an ever-present danger of cultural tourism being exploited by regional or national governments as a means of projecting a culturally exclusive regional or national identity. Particularly for the newly independent states, and notably those countries of the former Yugoslavia, the promotion and marketing of tourism can become inextricably linked with the portrayal of self-perceived national identity. This may have both positive and negative components, with the latter acting to emphasize what the region or country wishes to indicate that it is not – e.g. not Balkan, not Yugoslav, not Russian.

Within a context of change, diversity and differentiation this chapter attempts to:

- examine ways in which national identity is employed in tourism branding and promotion in CEE
- evaluate relationships between processes of restructuring, the emergence and re-emergence of national identities and tourism marketing.

Tourism holds a significant position in the substantial political, economic and social restructuring processes which have taken place in CEE in the past decade and a half. By 1999, the impact of travel and tourism in CEE was estimated to have a GDP equivalent of €95 billion. The sector was reckoned to employ 21.3 million, representing 11.7 per cent of the region's workforce (WTTC/WEFA, 1997).

International tourism was important in the region under communism, and in many cases long before that (Hall, 1991). Until the late 1980s (except in Yugoslavia) it was usually directly managed through monopolistic state organizations – travel and tourism bureaux, hotel chains, transport companies and guide services. 'Social' domestic tourism, entailing the provision of subsidized transport and accommodation for prescribed periods, was usually available for urban workers and their families. Inbound international tourism was intended to assist the generation of convertible currency and to help provide a positive image for the country and region. Pursuit of the latter was often counterproductive because of poor levels of service and infrastructure, bureaucratic restrictions and inflexibility. With the exception of Yugoslavia, most international tourism was actually generated from other state socialist countries, whose tourists were largely inured to, and thereby unwittingly helped to perpetuate, such poor service levels. The 'brand' was ideology, and the foreign language marketing employed was often grammatically fractured and semantically ambivalent. The resulting ambience was parodied by Malcolm Bradbury (1983; 1984) and captured in the reportage of James Cameron (1967).

In the late 1980s and early 1990s tourism development became embedded within processes of economic, political and social restructuring. Embeddedness in this sense refers to the network of dynamic relationships between, and development processes of, existing and emerging tourism firms and their competitors, suppliers, other regional economic and social actors and public organizations (e.g. Grabher,

1993; Granovetter, 1985). Such relationships and processes both embraced and reflected price liberalization, privatization, deregulation, institution capacity building, changing personal mobility, infrastructural upgrading, enhanced and reoriented foreign trade and investment, and currency convertibility (Jaakson, 1996).

Those countries of post-communist Central Europe (notably Hungary, the Czech Republic and Poland) spatially and structurally best placed for EU integration and exhibiting the most explicit characteristics of global incorporation, also tended to experience the most notable growth in international tourism activity during the 1990s. By contrast, tourism and its economic impact in relatively unstable south-eastern Europe and the CIS tended to stagnate or even decline within often fluctuating annual trends. In these countries, where private sector underfunding is often a problem, a low level of infrastructure support has often persisted (Bachvarov, 1999). Further, in some, particularly former Soviet states, data accuracy remains questionable.

Transformation in CEE has taken place during a period when smaller-scale specialized niche tourism has been receiving global stimulation which has been both demand- and producer-led. Such development has provided opportunities for new or existing small indigenous companies to develop high value-added products. During the 1990s, this dimension intensified as the industry in Central Europe gained experience of responding to 'Western' market demands. However, complicating tourism development and management priorities has been a rejuvenation of the mass tourism product demand cycle both from within the region, notably from the more advanced states of Central Europe and from Russia, and from Western markets seeking relatively inexpensive beach or ski-resort holidays.

The spatial patterns arising from these processes have suggested a continued relative concentration of international tourism activity in the main cities and coastal resort locations, with domestic tourism being much more diffused across the region, albeit usually representing relatively localized activity patterns (Ivy and Copp, 1999).

Post-communist transformation

One of a growing range of conceptual frameworks employed to understand and account for the complexities of post-communism development is the path dependence approach (Stark, 1992; Stark and Bruszt, 1998). This suggests that each country has a distinctive and unique path of extrication from state socialism. Particular variables created both by diversity and by the persistence of some communist-period institutions, practices and mentalities are viewed as playing a crucial role in facilitating certain outcomes while constraining others (Meurs and Begg, 1998). Analysis of pathways cannot assume that outcomes are determined or predictable since social and technological change continuously influence choices and decisions. Recent research (Riley, 2000) has suggested that the concept of embeddedness may provide a useful analytical tool for understanding such processes, setting overtly economic activity within a framework whereby it can be seen to be shaped by social and political processes. Certainly the cultural and political impress on the marketing, representation and branding of tourism destinations and products in a number of cases can be viewed as relating closely to particular regions' and countries' post-communist development trajectories.

Tourism branding in Central and Eastern Europe?

As a symbol, slogan, name or design, or combination of these elements, a brand should comprise at least: a clear and distinct image which differentiates it from its competitors; association with quality and with a distinctive way of relating to the customer; the ability to deliver long-term competitive advantage; and, overall, something greater than a simple set of physical attributes. Such elements should produce a collection of core intangible values existing in the mind of the customer (e.g. Aaker, 1996; Kotler, Bowen and Makens, 1996).

Destination branding, with its core objective of producing a consistent, focused communication strategy (Morgan and Pritchard, 1998: 147), confronts at least three major constraints in CEE. First, a lack of adequate finance to support appropriate marketing campaigns – a common trait – has been exacerbated by limited experience of global markets and a lack of appropriate expertise. Second, tourism destination marketers may be pressured to return short-term results when long-term investment is required to build a consistent brand. Such a dilemma may be reflected in message inconsistency. Third, while centralized, relatively authoritarian regimes can impose some control and coherence over the component parts of a destination image, it is more difficult within market economies to develop a coherent brand for destinations which are composed of myriad products and environments.

At a general level, branding approaches in CEE have been faced with two sets of constraints. First, the immediate post-communist period of 1989–92 imposed new and relatively distinct images of countries and regions suddenly being open, inviting and embarking on a process of substantial transformation. Within five years, however, much of this factor had been dissipated, such that, except for the cities of Prague and Budapest, which have sustained strong identities through urban-cultural imagery, little apparent long-term competitive advantage appeared to have been gained, with often confused, contradictory or absent destination images portrayed.

Table 6.1   Central and Eastern Europe: international tourist arrivals and receipts as a proportion of the European total

Central and Eastern Europe[1]	1985	1995	1999
% of European international tourist arrivals	19.0	23.7	22.6
% of European international tourist receipts	4.6	11.0	15.1[2]

Notes: 1 Central and Eastern Europe includes all those countries falling within the WTO's 'Central/East Europe' region, together with Albania and the states of (the former) Yugoslavia which are subsumed under the WTO's 'Southern Europe' region.
2 1998 figure.

Sources: WTO, 1998: 164–5; 2000: 19–20, 26–7; author's additional calculations.

Second, CEE has tended to be associated with an image of indifferent quality and limited product ranges. Some mass marketing alludes to this in an optimistic manner, for example: 'Moscow is now a cosmopolitan city and shoppers may be surprised at the variety' (Premier Holidays, 2000: 92). Cheapness in some aspects (food, transport, attractions, shopping) is still extolled in certain mass-market brochures (e.g. Balkan Holidays, 2001: 7, 9). There is perpetuated a sense of undifferentiated destinations, with often expensive but poor quality hotel accommodation. Although the particular way of relating to the customer under state socialism – studied indifference – has largely passed from Central Europe, elements remain in areas to the east and south-east.

A requirement for brand development is clearly evident at a number of levels. Indeed, although both tourism activity and per capita levels of tourism income have significantly increased across the post-communist world, CEE still lags behind much of the rest of Europe (Table 6.1).

European economic and political convergence, and the leisure search for new experiences and products, provide a potentially wide range of opportunities for the branding and marketing of CEE tourism (Hall, 1999). At a national level, a number of marketing strap lines have been adopted to encapsulate desired brand images: uniqueness, accessibility, security and ecological friendliness (Table 6.2). At destination level, most notable branding has been pursued for urban 'cultural' destinations, with attempts to embed them within explicitly 'European' heritage and progress themes, as exemplified by *Krakow 2000: European City of Culture* (Blonski, 1998) and *Zagreb: The New European Metropolis* (Goluza, 1996).

Table 6.2 Selected examples of national destination strap line application in Central and Eastern Europe

Country	Strap line
Albania	Land of sun and hospitality
Czech Republic	In the heart of Europe
Estonia	The Baltic country with a difference
Hungary	The essence of Europe
Lithuania	Baltic hospitality at its best
Montenegro	Ecological state
Romania	Come as a tourist, leave as a friend
Serbia	Landscape painted from the heart
Slovenia	The green piece of Europe
Slovakia	A small country with a big heart

Although the conditions for destination branding across CEE differ considerably, a number of common factors suggest the importance of projecting strong brand images either sectorally or geographically based. These include the requirement to:

■ emphasize a 'Europeanness'
■ generate customer loyalty through repeat visits
■ raise per capita tourism income levels.

More specifically, although the relative importance of factors varies from country to country, branding is required to respond to:

■ new and changing market demands
■ increasing market differentiation
■ the need to disassociate from the recent past
■ the desire to (re-)create a (new) national image, which may, paradoxically, emphasize heritage factors
■ the need to disassociate from regional instability.

Although better knowledge of markets is required – relatively little market survey work on international tourists to CEE appears to have been undertaken – marketing does have a long pedigree in the region, and its resurgence is strongly evident (e.g. see Martin and Grbac, 1998; Meler, 1997). However, tourism branding and the profile of tourism are not well developed: for example, tourism is not represented among the region's 100 largest (indigenous) companies by turnover (Business Central Europe, 1998), although this is, of course, to ignore the significant role of non-indigenous companies such as transnational hotel chains.

There is also the need to respond to the new opportunities opened by technological development. Significantly, much effort is being put into producing lively and imaginative web sites, with marketing messages and logos which are emerging as branding tools in their own right.

Changing market demands

Niche products had been available in CEE for some considerable time, although not necessarily related to market segmentation. Across the region, promotion of rural heritage, for example, was characteristic of the communist period (and earlier), and was reflected in the promotion of open air 'village museums' in most countries. Under the communists, however, such heritage promotion was not necessarily intended for international tourism purposes but was often aimed to inculcate a sense of identity and pride in the country's citizens, and to act as a reminder of their rural roots. Ironically, the overall weight of ideology was heavily biased against the contemporary rural population, which was required primarily to produce cheap food for the urban-industrial proletariat.

The 1990s saw increasing diversification of niche marketing. Some segmentation, such as gastronomy (e.g. Csapo, Nagyvathy and Pakozdi, 2000; Kraus, 2000; National Authority for Tourism, 2000), has been based on local economic back-linkages, particularly with restructuring rural economies. Other segments, such as health and spa resorts (e.g. Popesku, 2000) and heritage trails (e.g. Kornecki, 2000) draw on a fund of local cultural tradition which can be traced to classical times. By contrast, the rapidly growing activity holiday segments (e.g. Stifanic, 2000; Wieczorek, 1999) represent direct responses to perceived demand, although appropriate infrastructure and quality levels may not yet be in place.

Ironically, urban cultural tourism – notably in Prague and Budapest – was transformed in the 1990s into a mass activity, exacerbating congestion and infrastructural problems (e.g. Simpson, 1999). Nonetheless, the image projection of Prague ('city of a hundred spires') in particular as 'cool', signifies the potential of CEE destinations to be marketed as 'fashion accessories'. For example, cities such as Krakow – the former national capital in southern Poland, largely untouched by wartime damage but harmed by post-war industrial pollution – and Dubrovnik – the ancient walled city of Ragusa on Croatia's Dalmatian coast targeted in the conflict with Serbia – bestowed with United Nations Educational, Scientific, and Cultural Organization (UNESCO) World Heritage Site status, are consolidating or reviving their heritage-related brand images.

While numerically, international tourism in post-communist CEE has increased substantially, in south-eastern Europe and much of the former Soviet Union, destinations have not been able to take advantage of the potentially wide range of tourist markets opened to them. This is partly due to regional instability and to characteristics which have appealed to a relatively stable and limited range of markets, the political dimensions of which may reflect certain tensions. For example, during the mid-1990s Serbia's three most important tourist markets were the culturally related (Christian Eastern Orthodox religion) and politically sympathetic Bulgaria, Greece and Russia.

Alongside change and differentiation there has been a rejuvenation of mass tourism demand from within the region, notably from the more advanced states of Central Europe and from Russia. This has been significant, for example, in assisting the rehabilitation of the post-Yugoslav war Dalmatian coast: in 1997 more than half a million arrivals were recorded from both the Czech Republic and Slovenia, although as noted below, Croatia's mass tourism marketing is now directed to entice West Europeans back to its coastal product, such that Italians and Germans led a 190 per cent increase in both international arrivals and overnight stays between 1995 and 1997 (WTO, 1998: 76–7).

Destination branding and image construction: escaping from south-eastern Europe

Positioned on the western edge of the Islamic world, the Balkans, a term loosely coterminous with south-eastern Europe, is a region which has been subject in recent history to largely pejorative image constructions in the West. Dictionary definitions of 'balkanize' tend to emphasize diversity, conflict and fractionalization (Hall and Danta, 1996; Todorova, 1994), and the recent history of south-eastern Europe has done little to persuade potential tourist markets that this subregion should be perceived otherwise. It has therefore been one role of tourism marketing for destination countries on the fringe of south-eastern Europe to distance themselves from 'Balkanness', and to employ branding to this end. The examples of Slovenia and Croatia can illustrate some of the issues raised. In both cases, as recently emergent independent states formerly of the Yugoslav federation, their use of branding has positively attempted to assist the creation of a new national image, and negatively, to distance themselves from the Yugoslav past.

Yet the two are very different. Embracing a short length of coast, a diversity of inland products and sharing borders with two EU member states, Slovenia views itself firmly within a Central Europe of mainstream European culture and economy. Croatia also sees itself as Central European, yet its long coastline was the essential ingredient of the pre-1991 Yugoslav tourism product, and as such may be many Westerners' only experience of 'Yugoslavia', an image not easy to dispel. Further, with the substantial conflict and damage inflicted on Croatian soil and the not necessarily positive political image of the late president Tudjman, Croatia has faced a number of constraints in attempts to revive the enthusiasm of its former Western tourism markets. In these efforts there is the need to emphasize change and security, but also to project a diversification of tourism products to meet the new demands from more sophisticated markets than the Croatian coast responded to in the 1970s and 1980s.

Slovenia

As one of the favoured CEE states for early EU accession, Slovenia has employed tourism as a key ingredient in its post-independence economic and political strategy and national image projection. With just 47 km of Adriatic coastline, even when part of Yugoslavia, emphasis in Slovenia was placed upon interior attractions, the development of which in many cases dates from Austro-Hungarian times: Lake Bled and the Julian Alps, Postojna and other extensive karstic cave systems, and the Lipica stud farm, famous for supplying Lippizaner horses to the Spanish Riding School in Vienna (since 1580). As such, there has been a long continuity in the image promotion of these destinations and their products, although markets have varied and changed. More recent Slovenian promotion has emphasized niche segmentation within an environmentally friendly framework. For example, the integration of gastronomy and tourism has been pursued, reinforcing a rural-cultural emphasis and efforts to increase added value to many of Slovenia's products, as encapsulated in promotions for 'wine journeys' (Fujs and Krasovec, 1996; Kveder et al., 1994).

Needing both to establish an individual national identity and a suitable vehicle for (re-)attracting both established and new Western markets, 'The sunny side of the Alps' was initially adopted as a national tourism promotion strap line, embodying positive attractions of climate, topography and contiguity with Western Europe. Following Italian objections, this was replaced in the mid-1990s with 'The green piece of Europe', symbolizing a philosophical shift in terms of emphasizing, or at least suggesting, a nature-based, environmentally aware tourism product.

In both cases, product differentiation and quality association can be seen in the way in which the country has gone to some lengths to reinforce the mental geographical imagery of Slovenia being firmly part of ('Western'/'civilized') Europe, by:

- emphasizing its Central European credentials (Habsburg heritage, Alpine associations, contiguity with Austria and Italy)
- distancing itself from any 'Balkan' association, a desire underscored by the political requirement to put the country's Yugoslav past firmly behind it.

For example, Slovenia's appearance ('Lakes and mountains of Slovenia') in a mass-tourism brochure largely devoted to Croatia, talks of 'delightful villages and warm and hospitable people, whose lives are still steeped in the traditions of centuries of Austrian rule' (Transun, 1998), thereby emphasizing a Central/ Western European heritage, untainted by more recent (communist, Yugoslav war) years and the break-up of the Austro-Hungarian empire with the outcome of the First World War. Indeed, for the purposes of the world's media, the Slovenia Tourist Board (1999: 1) bluntly states: 'Slovenia is actually situated in Central Europe not in Eastern Europe at all!'

Although the country won its independence after a short skirmish with the Yugoslav army in 1991, a Slovenia Tourist Board was not established until 1996, with the mission 'to promote Slovenia as a country with a clear and distinctive identity and clearly defined comparative and competitive advantages and thereby assist the Slovene economy by marketing Slovene tourism in a concrete manner' (Slovenia Tourist Board, 1998b: 1).

In its 1997 marketing plan the Slovenia Tourist Board began to promote the country's tourism resources in terms of five sector 'clusters': coast and karst, mountains and lakes, health resorts, cities and towns, and the countryside. A new logo was developed which incorporated four flower heads (green, yellow, red and white) breaking out of a blue square base adjacent to the name 'Slovenija' (Slovenia Tourist Board, 1998a). This has been adopted comprehensively on promotional material, including stylized brochures for each of the five sector clusters, although compared to those employed previously it is an arguably less clear and articulate brand in conveying the country's distinctive positioning.

Slovenia has found it difficult to generate the tourist numbers comparable to those before the disintegration of the Yugoslav federation, yet as a consequence of diversification, niche orientation and season extension, by the mid-1990s the country was enjoying the highest level of receipts per international tourist arrival in CEE. In 1997, at US$1219, this was almost twice the level of next highest Croatia, with US$661, and more than six times higher than the levels of Hungary (US$199) and Bulgaria (US$166). By 1999, although the gaps had narrowed somewhat, partly due to a general reduction in tourist arrivals in the wake of the Kosovo conflict, average per capita receipts for Slovenia were still $1137 compared with $727 for Croatia (WTO, 2000: 20–1, 26–7). With near neighbours Italy, Austria and Germany providing almost 60 per cent of the country's tourist arrivals, as well as generating high-spending cross-border excursionists, Slovenia's branding emphasis on natural and cultural attractions has benefited from an environmental diversity located within a relatively compact country appealing to affluent hard currency neighbours.

Croatia

Like Slovenia, Croatia was a former Austro-Hungarian, and thus Roman Catholic, constituent member of Yugoslavia. Constituting the bulk of the former Yugoslavia's coastline and thus much of its tourism industry, Croatia has not been one of the favoured countries for early EU accession. Unlike Slovenia, Croatia was enmeshed during the first half of the 1990s in continuing hostilities both on its own soil and in Bosnia, with a consequent collapse of the country's tourism industry and an undermining of much of its credible image as a post-communist democracy. Perhaps the most notable erstwhile brand image of the Yugoslav coast – the medieval walled city of Dubrovnik – was deliberately shelled by Serbs and Montenegrins during the hostilities as a means of undermining Croatia's economy.

Under these circumstances, it was vital, following the cessation of conflict, that Croatia should establish a national tourism marketing policy which, closely allied to national image rebuilding, would, as a brand, convey a distinct image in order to:

- clearly differentiate the country from its neighbours
- reassure former markets that quality and value had been restored, and which, through the country's major tourism attributes, could secure long-term competitive advantage.

Involving an appeal to previous mass-tourism markets on a destination basis while seeking to develop sector-based niche specialisms within a national framework, Croatia's attempt at destination branding was complemented by the adoption in the mid-1990s of a tourism marketing logo: a half-circle of multicoloured balls radiating from a half-orange half-red sun-like ball, with the word 'CROATIA' below, symbolizing the conjunction of sun and sea as well as a new dawn for Croatian tourism. But name apart, this visual cliché was little different from those adopted by several other tourism destinations. Indicating this weakness, some marketing material subsequently adopted a supplementary slogan below the 'CROATIA': 'Small country for a great holiday'.

From 1997, more concerted efforts were made to (re-)establish a national destination brand: a new national brand logo was launched – the word 'CROATIA' with the horizontal line through the two 'A's made wavy to symbolize the sea. The first 'A' is placed in a blue square (dark blue above the wave, light blue below) which is complemented by another, red, square immediately above the preceding 'O': 'the logotype is interwoven with the symbol . . .[which] . . .is actually the visual code of the Republic of Croatia' (Ljubicic, 1997: 27). This is the chequerboard coat of arms as adopted for the national flag with strong historical associations. This 'visual code' is also to function as a brand on crockery, food items and souvenirs. In addition, three international tourism-related conferences were hosted in

Dubrovnik in September 1997. These were intended to help relaunch both Croatia and Dubrovnik on to the West European tourism agenda, following the physical and symbolic assaults of the Yugoslav wars. Their purpose was to project a strong renewed brand image of Dubrovnik as a cherished World Heritage Site symbolizing not just the phoenix-like restoration of the city, but also of (eastern) Adriatic tourism and of Croatia itself. Through the platform provided by the conferences, particular groups of opinion-formers and representatives of upper-income niche markets were specifically targeted for the projection of this message.

Complementing the country's reappearance in mass tourism brochures has been marketing copy reinforcing the need for Croatia to recapture previous markets: 'If you have been to Croatia before – and many hundreds of thousands of British holidaymakers have – you will know already the delights that await you there in 1999' (Transun, 1998: i).

During 1998 national newspaper advertising (in the UK at least), saw the CROATIA logo promoted alongside the slogan 'A New Welcome. An Old Friend'. This mirrored glossier mass-market promotion material: 'Croatia – welcome back old friend . . .An old friend with a new name . . .The population is 90% Roman Catholic. So many aspects of Croatia will remind you of Italy, Spain and France, where strong family values remain and churches are always full on Sundays' (Holiday Options, 1998: 4). The message was clear – Croatia as a destination brand is familiar, 'like us', safe, pious, trustworthy: comfortably European and a natural component part of the successful Mediterranean tourism product. Whether this is the appropriate brand image for the markets being targeted – in some of which at least, churches are unlikely to be full on Sundays – is contestable.

Meler and Ruzic (1999: 643) have argued that 'It is possible to empirically establish that the Republic of Croatia presently does not have a determined and recognizable image resulting from an equally recognizable economic and marketing identity', and suggest that the establishment of a tourism identity must be part of a

Table 6.3 Self-perceptions of Croatia

Croatia does not belong to the Balkans – geographically, politically or historically . . .
There is no reason to put it under the same heading as Romania, Bulgaria, Albania or the other 'stuff'. Get a good geography book! (Darko Bubic, Croatia)

This is a reply to Darko Bubic's letter. The Balkans is the name of a geographical area . . . But through its ugly history of constant conflicts, the Balkans has acquired a nasty reputation in the world. I understand that calling Croatia a Balkan country upsets many people here. But as long as you call the other countries 'stuff', you only show how deeply Balkanised you are. (Marko, Croatia)

Source: Business Central Europe (2000: 10).

trinity of vehicles – the other two being exports and inward investment – which need to be appropriately positioned in relation to key markets in order to help establish a positive and coherent image for the country. However, as suggested by disagreement among Croatians (Table 6.3), the social, cultural and political dimensions of (self-)image building require substantial attention if Croatia is to prosper from promotion and branding in major economic sectors.

National identity and political change: promoting Serbia

The growth of cultural and heritage tourism has coincided with a post-communist reinvigoration of a sense of historical perspective and a heightened awareness of nationality to accompany the (re-)creation of new state systems. Images of heritage are often employed, somewhat paradoxically, as a vehicle of restructuring and modernization particularly in rural regions (e.g. Dewailly, 1998; Light, 2000). But some national and regional governments have been encouraged to recruit the heritage industry to help reinforce an exclusive national or particular ethnic identity (Hall, 1996). For example, in the tourism promotion brochure *Serbia: Landscape Painted from the Heart* (Popesku and Milojevic, 1996), 'landscape' was interpreted as both natural and cultural. In terms of heritage, however, the images of cultural 'landscape' portrayed revealed an exclusive concentration on Serbian/Orthodox tradition. One-third of the total population of Serbia was not Serbian at this time, but there was no mention of minority ethnic Hungarian or Albanian (or Romanian, Slovak, Croat or Turkish) Catholic or Muslim heritage. It appeared that minority groups had been erased from the images of this particular cultural landscape.

Following domestic political change during 2000, however, although the Saatchi and Saatchi inspired 'Landscape painted from the heart' strap line remained (Table 6.2), multiethnicity – a characteristic emphasized by the pre-Milosevic Yugoslav leadership – was brought back onto the tourism promotion agenda as an essential ingredient of Serbia's identity: 'Serbia is the meeting place of cultures, religions and languages. Although more than forty different nations live in Serbia, they do have some things in common – their homes are wide open to friends' (NTOS, 2000).

At the time of writing (early 2001) it is too early to judge the merits of Serbia's new development path. But it is clear that the country's immediate past (notwithstanding a possible rupture with Montenegro to finally lay to rest the pretence of a remnant 'Yugoslavia') places a monumental burden on national image promoters and tourism marketers to even begin to position the country in a favourable context in relation to major ('Western') tourism markets and sources of inward investment. On the other hand, diminution of the Orthodox cultural 'brand' may also lessen appeal for Serbia's hitherto political and tourism supports – Greece, Bulgaria and Russia.

Russia's constrained branding

The marketing of Russian destinations is at best constrained and fragmentary, and only partially attempts to overcome images of instability and lack of security. For example, at the 2000 World Travel Market in London, the most prominent Russian representation was expressed along two dimensions:

- organization-based – notably *Intourist,* with its corporate branding (e.g. Intourist, 2000) but offering a limited range of 'products' (Moscow, St Petersburg, Golden Ring, Cruise of the Tsars, Trans-Siberian Railway, Silk Road), or
- geographically focused, with the representation of Daghestan and Kamchatka, located at the south-western and eastern extremities of the Russian Federation, being particularly notable.

Daghestan is a Muslim republic the size of Scotland with a population of 2.1 million, within the Russian Federation. The promotion of tourism is represented exclusively through material produced by the Daghestan Tourism Ministry (1996). While adopting a motif and consistent presentational style, this is written in neo-Soviet/Malcolm Bradbury style. Although representing substantial evidence of cultural and natural heritage, Daghestan's tourism promotional material also extols the presence of manufacturing industry, and in its English language version, retains a map wholly in the Cyrillic script. Allusion is also made to the propinquity of Chechnya, whose conflict spilled over the border into Daghestan in 1999, bringing with it a major refugee problem and a very explicit constraint in tourism promotion and development.

By contrast, the isolated Kamchatka peninsula, on Siberia's Pacific rim, is being promoted by small private companies offering activity holiday products (e.g. Kamchatintour, 2000; Lena and friends, 1999; Sampo-Tour, 1999) within a land of snow, volcanoes and pure nature. Although organizationally fragmented, there is a strong sense of identity and purpose conveyed by the Kamchatka promotional material, which is written in mostly good, direct English, employing strong illustrations, emphasizing safety and security, and providing web site location follow-up. Closed to the outside world for seventy-four years, this identifiable geographic unit has rapidly become one of the more effectively branded destination areas of Russia, albeit primarily targeting Japanese and US markets rather than European. There is also strong evidence of collaboration and partnership, both between indigenous firms and between these firms and incoming operators such as those of the US west coast.

Clearly, the enormous extent and diversity of Russia lends itself to differentiation and a fragmentation of image projection. The branding of both 'traditional' (e.g. Moscow, St Petersburg, Silk Road) and 'new' (e.g. Kamchatka) destinations should be balanced with the need for product branding and more discerning market segmentation. Retention of the Intourist administrative brand may not endear, for example, Western adventure tourists looking for destinations and activities which would have been antithetical to the philosophy of the Soviet-period Intourist. This might suggest that the combination of small private companies pursuing branded niche activities is the most likely way forward to market the myriad products and regions yet to be developed for tourism within the Russian Federation. An overarching need, however, will be the continued assurance of safety and security within what is still a potentially unstable country embracing significantly volatile regional components.

Conclusion

Integration into the global economy and preparation for accession to the EU have been prime foreign-policy driving forces, especially of the more advanced economies of Central Europe. National identity and image formation have been consciously moulded towards these ends in a number of cases. International tourism has been recruited to play a significant role in this process – both in terms of image reinforcement and as an international binding agent. However, destination branding and positioning strategy is generally still poorly developed in much of the region's tourism industry, due to a combination of lack of finance, experience and expertise.

A change in emphasis from a destination to a product focus is taking place in the more advanced countries pursuing niche segmentation and in those states of south-eastern Europe wishing to shake off Balkan connotations. The value of an established brand lies not least in the perceptions of consistency and quality that it represents. Within and between the countries and regions of CEE quality is not consistent, and the marketing message – from individual destinations and countries, and collectively at a regional level – may be equally unclear. Indeed, it is questionable whether 'Eastern Europe' or 'Central and Eastern Europe' are meaningful or helpful labels with which to be associated in image-formation terms.

If CEE tourism is to further improve its level of per capita income, co-ordination between government action and tourism industry promotion would appear vital to project clear, positive national, regional and destination images which can contextualize and emphasize quality and differentiation. Across the region there is limited evidence of co-ordination of local, regional and national tourism interests. This is perhaps understandable given that over much of the region there has been a desire to reduce any form of centralized planning as a reaction to the previous half-century of state socialist impositions and the association of co-operation with collective action and thus collectivization. Yet collaboration, networks and partnerships are essential in assisting the generation of appropriate brand images if the various components of the region wish to position themselves in relation to key international tourism markets.

Yet promotion of regional destination images is further complicated by the marketing dilemmas raised by the potential conflict which exists between the development of niche markets for culturally and environmentally oriented Western tourists, and the mass market demands from tourists from within CEE, both domestic and international. With EU enlargement eastwards (Hall and Danta, 2000), the chasm between rising Central European consumption aspirations and stagnating product development in south-eastern Europe and much of the former Soviet Union is likely to widen, raising further challenges, and opportunities, for product segmentation, market positioning, quality consistency, image building and brand development.

References

Aaker, D. (1996). *Building Strong Brands*. Free Press.

Bachvarov, M. (1999). Troubled sustainability: Bulgarian seaside resorts. *Tourism Geographies*, **1**, 192–203.

Balkan Holidays (2001). *Bulgaria Croatia Slovenia Romania: Summer*. 2nd edn. Balkan Holidays.

Blonski, K. (1998). *Krakow 2000: European City of Culture*. City and Voivodship of Krakow.

Bradbury, M. (1983). *Rates of Exchange*. Secker and Warburg.

Bradbury, M. (1984). *Welcome to Slaka*. Secker and Warburg.

Business Central Europe (1998). Giants with a future? *Business Central Europe*, December, 49–53.

Business Central Europe (2000). *Business Central Europe*, September, 10.

Cameron, J. (1967). *Point of Departure*. Barker.

Csapo, K., Nagyvathy, E. and Pakozdi, J. (2000). *Hungary: Flavours of a Country*. VIVA Media Holding.

Daghestan Tourism Ministry (1996). *Discover Daghestan*. Daghestan Tourism Ministry.

Dewailly, J.-M. (1998). Images of heritage in rural regions. In *Tourism and Recreation in Rural Areas* (R. Butler, C. M. Hall and J. Jenkins, eds) pp. 123–137, Wiley.

Fujs, V. and Krasovec, M. (1996). *Wine Journeys in Slovenia*. Vas Travel Agency and Republic of Slovenia Ministry of Agriculture, Forestry and Food.

Goluza, M. (1996). *Zagreb: The New European Metropolis*. Tourist Association of the City of Zagreb.

Grabher, G. (ed.) (1993). *The Embedded Firm: On Socioeconomics of Industrial Networks*. Routledge.

Granovetter, M. (1985). Economic action and social structure: the problem of embeddedness. *American Journal of Sociology*, **91**, 481–510.

Hall, D. and Danta, D. (eds) (1996). *Reconstructing the Balkans*. Wiley.

Hall, D. and Danta, D. (eds) (2000). *Europe Goes East: EU Enlargement, Diversity and Uncertainty*. The Stationery Office.

Hall, D. R. (1996). Resources for sustainable tourism: cultural landscapes. In *Frameworks for Understanding Post-Socialist Processes* (D. Turnock, ed.) pp. 17–20, Leicester University Geography Department Occasional Paper 36.

Hall, D. R. (1999). Destination branding, niche marketing and national image projection in Central and Eastern Europe. *Journal of Vacation Marketing*, **5**, 227–237.

Hall, D. R. (ed.) (1991). *Tourism and Economic Development in Eastern Europe and the Soviet Union*. Belhaven.

Holiday Options (1998). *Dalmatian Riviera and Islands*. Holiday Options.

Ivy, R. L. and Copp, C. B. (1999). Tourism patterns and problems in East-Central Europe. *Tourism Geographies*, **1**, 425–442.

Jaakson, R. (1996). Tourism in transition in post-Soviet Estonia. *Annals of Tourism Research*, **23**, 617–634.

Kamchatintour (2000). *The Kamchatka Peninsula: Hidden Pearl at the Treasury of the Earth*. Kamchatintour.

Kornecki, M. (2000). *The Trail of Wooden Architecture*. Krakowska Agencja Rozwoju Turystyki S.A.

Kotler, P., Bowen J. and Makens, J. (1996). *Principles of Marketing: The European Edition*. Prentice Hall.

Kraus, V. (2000). *South Moravian Vineyards and Wine Cellars*. Vinarskou Akademii Valtice.

Kveder, M., Bogataj, J., Vidmar, A. and Arcon, M. (1994). *Slovenian Wine Map*. Imago.

Lena and friends (1999). *Heli-skiing/Snowboarding: Kamchatka, Russia*. Lena and friends.

Light, D. (2000). Gazing on communism: heritage tourism and post-communist identities in Germany, Hungary and Romania. *Tourism Geographies*, **2**, 157–176.

Ljubicic, B. (1997). New look Croatia. *Croatia*, Summer, 27–29.

Martin, J. H. and Grbac, B. (1998). Smaller and larger firms' marketing activities as a response to economic privatization: marketing is alive and well in Croatia. *Journal of Small Business Management*, **36**, 95–99.

Meler, M. (1997). Marketing in transition conditions: example of the Republic of Croatia. *Eastern European Economics*, **35**, 66–74.

Meler, M. and Ruzic, D. (1999). Marketing identity of the tourist product of the Republic of Croatia. *Tourism Management*, **20**, 635–643.

Meurs, M. and Begg, R. (1998). Path dependence in Bulgarian agriculture. In *Theorising transition* (J. Pickles and A. Smith, eds) pp. 243–261, Routledge.

Morgan, N. and Pritchard, A. (1998). *Tourism Promotion and Power: Creating Images, Creating Identities*. Wiley.

National Authority for Tourism (2000). *Romanian Gastronomy*. National Authority for Tourism.

National Tourism Organization of Serbia (NTOS) (2000). *Landscape Painted from the Heart*. NTOS (http://www.Serbia-info.com/ntos/inf_gen.htm).

Popesku, J. (2000). *Spas and Health Resorts in Serbia*. National Tourism Organization of Serbia.

Popesku, J. and Milojevic, L. (1996). *Serbia: Landscape Painted from the Heart*. National Tourism Organization of Serbia.

Premier Holidays (2000). *Short Breaks*. Premier Holidays.

Riley, R. C. (2000). Embeddedness and the tourism industry in the Polish Southern Uplands: social processes as an explanatory framework. *European Urban and Regional Studies*, **7**, 195–210.

Sampo-Tour (1999). *Amazing Kamchatka: Peninsula on the Edge of the World*. Sampo-Tour.

Simpson, F. R. (1999). Tourist impacts in the historic centre of Prague: resident and visitor perceptions of the historic built environment. *Geographical Journal*, **165**, 192–200.

Slovenia Tourist Board (1998a). *Marketing of Slovenia's Tourism: Corporate Image*. Slovenia Tourist Board (http://www.tourist-board.si/podoba-eng.html).

Slovenia Tourist Board (1998b). *Slovenian Tourist Board: The Role of STB*. Slovenia Tourist Board (http://www.tourist-board.si/vloga-eng.html).

Slovenia Tourist Board (1999). *Slovenia at a Glance: Some Brief Notes for Press Visitors*. Slovenia Tourist Board (http://www.slovenia-tourism.si/enews/article-01.html).

Stark, D. (1992). Path dependence and privatisation strategies in East Central Europe. *European Politics and Societies*, **6**, 17–54.

Stark, D. and Bruszt, L. (1998). *Postsocialist Pathways*. Cambridge University Press.

Stifanic, D. (2000). *Vrsar: bike eco ride*. Tourist Association of Vrsar.

Todorova, M. (1994). The Balkans: from discovery to invention. *Slavic Review*, **53**, 453–482.

Transun (1998). *Transun's Croatia*. Transun.

Wieczorek, E. (1999). *The Silesian Voivodship Invites: Active Tourism*. Silesian Voivodship Tourist and Promotion Office.

World Tourism Organization (WTO) (1998). *Tourism Market Trends: Europe.* WTO.

World Tourism Organization (WTO) (2000). *Tourism Highlights 2000.* 2nd edn. WTO.

World Travel and Tourism Council/Wharton Econometric Forecasting Associates (WTTC/WEFA) (1997). *Travel and Tourism: Jobs for the Millennium.* WTTC.

Part Two
Creating the Unique
Destination Proposition

7

Brand Wales: 'Natural revival'

Roger Pride

Introduction

For many years that venerable and respected British oracle of information and explanation, the *Encyclopaedia Britannica*, essentially denied Wales' existence. Under the entry for Wales it simply stated 'for Wales please see England' and it was not until quite recently that Wales was deemed important enough to warrant an entry in its own right. More recently still, the highly influential journal, *The Economist*, featured an article about a new country, a place called 'And Wales'. The article humorously recognized the fact that more often than not Wales, when referred to in the media, was inextricably linked to its influential and pervasive neighbour, England. More often than not, to the outside world, Wales was merely a suffix to England. England and Wales it seemed were not just joined at Offa's Dyke but also at the hip.

Both of these examples demonstrate clearly that for many years Wales, the nation, has experienced an identity problem. In marketing and commercial terms, of course, an identity problem can lead to commercial failure. This is true not just for companies and for product and service brands but for also for countries. A positive national identity can bring tangible benefits across a wide range of industry sectors. This is evidenced by a survey in which 72 per cent of Fortune 500 companies cited national identity as an important influence when purchasing goods and services. Unfortunately, there has been no identity premium for Wales. Over the last decade and a half, WTB research has consistently concluded that negative or distorted perceptions of Wales were hindering and limiting Wales' tourism performance. By the late 1990s other Welsh organizations had also recognized that these same image problems were affecting Wales' performance in other economic fields, including inward investment, export sales and advertising revenues in the Wales-based media.

The question was, how could Wales begin to address and ultimately to solve these image issues? As the newly installed Director of Marketing for the WTB, I recognized that the problem was not limited to tourism. Ultimately, improvements to Wales' image as a tourism destination would in part, require a co-ordinated effort to address the core problem. We needed to turn an identity deficit Wales into an identity premium. I believed that branding would play a critical role in addressing this problem. Thus, this chapter explains how, within the WTB, we have taken classical branding techniques and adapted them to create a brand strategy for tourism, and how we have co-operated with other organizations within Wales to attack the wider issue.

Central to this book is the question of whether a destination or a country can actually be considered a brand and whether conventional branding techniques are appropriate when one is considering a destination. It is probably true to say that destination marketers are not regarded as being at the cutting-edge of branding theory and practice. Indeed, many branding purists will still contend that it is not appropriate to consider a place as a brand and that it is impossible to brand a destination effectively. This is because, by their very nature, destinations are amorphous, delivering a wide range of products and experiences. In such an environment contends the purist, it is impossible to control the way in which people interact with or experience the destination.

Many practitioners currently responsible for marketing destinations also regard the branding process with suspicion. Too often the creativity and ambition of marketing departments within tourist boards have been constrained by the existence of two additional 'Ps' invariably linked to destination marketing: 'politics' and 'paucity'. The environment surrounding the marketing of a country is almost always political and there are pressures to satisfy the aspirations and demands of a wide range of industry sectors which can lead to compromise. As a result, the communication and advertising output from tourist boards has often been destination-led rather than market-led communications which highlight all aspects of the destination rather than showcase those elements which make the destination special. In addition, more often than not, the relatively small marketing budget available to tourist boards has also held many destinations back. Within Britain, there is no doubt that in the past tourism has been regarded as a 'candyfloss' industry. This, combined with the fact that it is sometimes difficult to directly measure the results of tourist board promotional activity, has led to underinvestment in tourism promotion by those holding the purse strings. This in turn leads to short-term thinking which militates against developing the longer-term perspective necessary for building a successful brand.

I have always believed, however, that it is possible to use branding techniques to create a focus for differentiating holiday destinations. When I was a young boy in the mining valleys of South Wales in the early 1960s, friends in the school playground would ask each other 'are you going on holidays this year?' There was certainly no assumption that all families went on holidays. Those fortunate enough to go almost invariably went on one holiday a year, and usually this would be to the same resort year after year. In our area this usually meant the seaside resort of Porthcawl on the South Wales coast and families often stayed in the same caravan and holidayed at exactly the same time each year.

With the advent of the low-cost package holidays to the Mediterranean, the annual question in the 1970s and early 1980s changed to 'where are you going on holidays this year?' The actual choice of Mediterranean resort made little difference – they were all basically offering a consistent diet of sun, sand and upset stomachs. During the late 1980s and early 1990s holiday patterns began to change again. Increased affluence and more flexible holiday arrangements led to the seemingly inexorable growth of the short break. Consumers began to ask themselves 'what do we want to do on this holiday or short break?' With the choice of holiday type and the range of available experience increasing, people now often decide on the holiday type before selecting the destination. The holiday requirement will vary with the time of year, their travelling companions and many other factors.

As we head into the new millennium we enter the age of the serial short-break taker. It is no longer unusual for people to take up to ten short breaks (including one- and two-night stays) in a year. Moreover, whether they do it consciously or not, consumers are now asking themselves 'how do we want to feel on our holiday or short break?' As the demands of modern living become ever more stressful and the pressure on time for those in work more severe, the choice of destination and selection of experience will assume even greater importance. Consumers will want more out of their holiday and will be choosing destinations which not only meet their core requirements but with which they feel an affinity. This is the territory of brands.

Despite the image problems referred to earlier, tourism has always been a vital ingredient within the Welsh economy. Tourism to Welsh resorts started with the development of the railway network in the UK, and Wales has been welcoming 'tourists' for well over 100 years. Today tourism represents about 7 per cent of Wales' GDP. It is worth more than £2 billion annually and one in ten jobs are dependent upon it. However, as a result of the factors mentioned earlier, tourism in Wales is going through structural change. Competition from other destinations is intensifying and visitor needs and aspirations are ever-changing. Wales' core business traditionally came from urban industrial regions of England such as Merseyside, Greater Manchester, the Potteries and the West Midlands. For the populations of these regions, Wales was their summer holiday playground, right on their doorstep. Families typically headed for Wales' coastal resorts and either stayed in family-run guesthouses and small hotels or, more usually, the numerous low-cost holiday parks which are speckled along Wales' 700 miles of coastline. Bill Bryson the celebrated American travel writer noted in his book *Notes from a Small Island*: 'From the train North Wales looked like holiday hell – endless ranks of prison-camp caravan parks standing in fields in the middle of a lonely wind beach nowhere' (Bryson, 1996).

Although such parks brought much needed wealth to Wales, it could be argued that in more recent times some of the lower-quality parks have made it more difficult for Wales to attract more affluent visitors. As Wales' traditional market decided to visit increasingly cheap sunshine destinations Wales' tourism industry needed to adapt to meet the needs of a new kind of tourist. The new tourists are more demanding, they require higher standards of service and quality, and they often spend two days rather than two weeks in Wales. Wales is adapting to these changing circumstances. It now offers a range of quality hotels (particularly in the countryside) and high-quality cottages and holiday parks which provide luxury family accommodation. A wide range of activity-based products has also been developed, involving everything from walking, cycling or fishing to coast-steering (an activity which is unique to the Pembrokeshire Coast which involves an extreme combination of diving and rock climbing). New golf complexes have opened to complement some of Wales' traditional links and parkland courses. The quality and variety of restaurants, pubs and visitor attractions is also improving all the time. Wales is adapting to changing circumstances and tourism remains a substantial industry, although many businesses, because of their seasonal nature, are fragile. Tourism is also one of the few industries in rural Wales which has the potential to grow further.

No doubt, one of the factors inhibiting such growth has been the afore-mentioned image problem. This was something we needed to address. We recognized that if we were going to enhance Wales' reputation as a leisure destination, we needed a single-minded, consistent, integrated and innovative communication strategy. We understood, however, that branding Wales would require a sensitive, skilled and specialist approach. When branding a country as opposed to a single product, there are a great variety of factors to consider, not least of which is the way in which the process is perceived by key influencers and by the population at large. Within the ranks of the media and traditional academia there is still an element of suspicion and scepticism regarding the branding process. These groups often view the process as being superficial and cosmetic. How often have we seen the 'and it cost X million pounds to create a new logo' type of headlines? This reaction is undoubtedly amplified when countries and places are products being marketed. Many tourism businesses in Wales (as in other destinations) also sit in the traditional and sceptical camp. One critic of the process in Wales said in a radio interview 'why don't they just say come to bloody Wales' – now there's a thought.

Introducing our new thinking into a public sector risk-averse culture presented a real challenge. This culture, which discourages innovation, is also evident among many key stakeholders and tourism businesses. If we persisted in doing the same thing averagely well, while Wales' market share continued to decline, there would be relatively little criticism of the WTB. If, however, we strove to change things and perhaps take a few risks along the way, our critics' knives would be quickly sharpened. In such an environment it can become difficult to foster creativity and innovation. Some people will find 100 reasons for not doing something rather than explore the possibilities and benefits that change might bring.

The need for a specialist and sensitive approach stems from the fundamental point that Wales the country is complex. We felt it would be wrong to believe that a single message or image could be used as a blunt instrument which would have equal success with all target audiences. Although a brand needs to be consistent, a message that will motivate a retired New York policeman to spend a week touring Wales may well be different to the message that will encourage a West Midlands factory worker to come for a weekend with his family. Ultimately, however, it will be the same country, people and landscape that they experience. The trick, it seems to me, is to ensure that all messages should be based on a core set of truths about Wales, which have been researched and agreed. Communications within individual market segments should draw upon these core values and communicate them in a credible, motivating and compelling way.

Through all of the work we had done, it was clear that it was very difficult to isolate perceptions about Wales as a tourist destination from wider ideas of Wales the country, the nation, the political entity. Consequently, among potential audiences in the UK, people found it difficult to think about Wales' positive attributes as a leisure destination because they have been influenced by a cornucopia of media messages, by stereotypical images of Welsh men and women and, in some cases, by the Welsh people that they may have known. It follows, therefore, that if the brand messages for Wales the tourist destination are to be fully effective, we must also address the issues relating to Wales the country.

Table 7.1   The key elements of the unique destination proposition framework

Domain brand	An agreed branding for the country as a whole, based on the core truths or values which then guide and influence all of the country's communications needs
Tourism brand	A motivating, credible, differentiating and deliverable position for the destination
Entry concepts	A communications idea tailored to the needs of individual market segments identified through research
Target segment	Groups of potential visitors, prioritized by scoring their potential for Wales against an agreed set of criteria
Relevant product	Offering specific products from within the destination portfolio based on the needs of individual market segments, again identified through research
Synergistic/ integrated approach	Ensuring that in terms of style and tone of voice, all messages and communications are mutually supportive

The unique destination proposition

Our solution was to devise a brand architecture and marketing framework based on a tiered or layered approach, with the country or domain brand giving direction and guidance. This was to be supported by a tourism positioning and entry concepts tailored to the needs of individual market segments (Table 7.1). We termed this brand communication framework the 'unique destination proposition' (UDP) (see Figure 7.1).

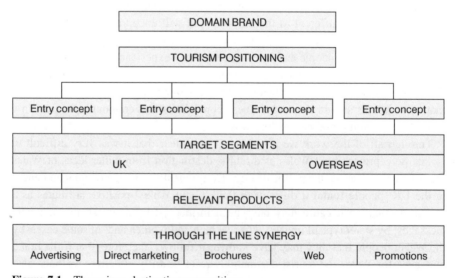

Figure 7.1   The unique destination proposition

The Wales domain brand

Determining and agreeing the overall brand proposition for Wales was without doubt the most difficult part of the whole process. There was a distinct lack of government leadership on the issue and no single organization had the responsibility or the remit to lead the process. Ultimately, a diverse group of public and private sector organizations decided to work together to agree the domain brand positioning and to create a set of brand guidelines. A specialist brand consultancy was retained to review a myriad of perceptual research previously conducted by the partner organizations and to undertake fresh qualitative work which involved opinion-formers and influencers both inside and outside Wales. It was hoped that the resulting guidelines would be adopted by all of the organizations with an interest in promoting Wales. We would all be able to speak with the same voice. Thus, all communication would contribute to creating the perception of Wales as being an important, lively, attractive and successful country.

A manual was created which defined the heart of the Wales domain brand and which suggested how Wales should be conveyed in pictures and words. It also described how the core messages and values could be applied when communicating with different audiences. The heart of this domain brand was 'In Wales you will find a passion for life – Hwyl'. Hwyl (pronounced who-ill) is a word which has no direct English translation. It is a unique Welsh feeling of passion and well-being. This core message would then be supported by tangible elements – reasons to believe the core message. Thus a campaign to encourage inward investment in Wales would be supported by communicating benefits such as Wales has a loyal, committed and flexible workforce and is a beautiful place to live. Similarly, a message to attract students to Welsh universities would be supported by communicating the benefits of a strong sense of community, the rewarding and colourful local life and high-quality education. The manual also defined the tone of voice or personality of the brand, which is lyrical, sincere, confident, inviting, down to earth and warm.

The Wales tourism brand

At the same time as WTB was involved in the creation of the domain brand guidelines we set about configuring a tourism positioning for Wales which would draw upon the domain brand but which would ensure maximum resonance with potential visitors to Wales. Considerable research was undertaken among our priority target audiences, both in the UK and overseas. Our original intention was to create a single tourism positioning, but with separate entry concepts for the different target audiences. However, during the research it became clear that the perceptions of Wales among UK consumers were vastly different to those of international audiences. Moreover, we found that the consumer needs and experiences connected with domestic holidays or short breaks were very different to holidays abroad.

As was suggested earlier, in the UK market Wales' image was often neutral or negative. However, we did have a very loyal customer base with a high percentage of repeat visitors. Unfortunately, as tastes and holiday patterns changed, many of the potential new visitors to Wales did not have strong enough reasons to come to Wales and many of them had negative ideas which would take time to change. Often Wales was perceived as being downmarket, the Welsh were sometimes perceived as being unfriendly, some thought that Wales lacked quality accommodation and that there was little to do. Others felt that Wales offered nothing special – yes it had mountains but Scotland's are higher, yes it had lakes but those in the Lake District were bigger, yes it had beaches but those in Cornwall and Devon were more familiar. It was apparent, however, that often these were problems of perception rather than reality. Visitors to Wales went away with very different views. They felt that Wales was unspoiled, that there were still traditional values in Wales and a strong sense of community, which translated into a safe holiday environment. They felt that the Welsh people were genuine and down to earth. They raved about how beautiful and green Wales is. They also confirmed that in comparison with similar destinations, Wales is much more accessible.

During the research process, we also tried to find out more about our target audiences and to establish what made them choose a particular destination. We also tried to get a better idea of what people wanted from a holiday or short break. Not surprisingly we found that for many, life is stressful. Pressure to deliver at work and at home was increasing, creating severe time pressures. Many within our target markets lived and worked in an urban environment with the resultant pressure on space – on the road, in the office and again, at home. However, although working people are often time poor, they are usually cash rich. So, whereas everyday life built up the need for regular breaks, it was often time rather than money which was the limiting factor. As we all know, people are now getting away more often than ever but for shorter periods of time. The prime motivation for the break was the need to put something back into their lives, to relax, to recharge the batteries, to rebuild relationships and to revive their spirits.

Armed with this knowledge, we decided that the brand positioning for Wales should be 'natural revival' or 'naturally reviving'. Wales would be communicated as being unspoiled, down to earth, with traditional values, genuine, green and beautiful, providing physical and spiritual revival – and all of this hidden on England's doorstep (Figure 7.2). In the communications brief developed to enable potential advertising agencies to bring this positioning to life, the shorthand for this idea was 'Wales puts back into your life what life take out – the antidote to everyday life'.

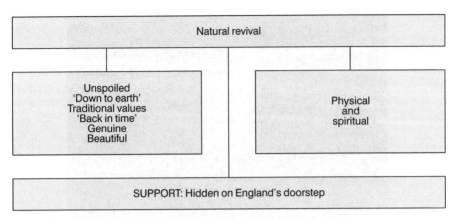

Figure 7.2 WTB UK brand positioning

After an exhaustive selection process we eventually chose London-based advertising agency, FCA!, to bring the brand to life through a creative platform and concept which would be effective in a wide range of potential media. We felt that FCA! was one of the few genuinely integrated agencies who was media neutral. Initially FCA! felt that the 'naturally reviving' positioning was not differentiating enough and so undertook additional research using its own 'Genesis' process prior to the pitch. During 'Genesis' previous visitors to Wales recalled powerful memories and images such as dolphins and seals swimming alongside boats in Cardigan Bay, snow falling over waterfalls in Snowdonia, walking along a North Wales beach while screaming at the sea on Christmas Eve and recalling simply having time for themselves as a family. On the strength of this research FCA! confirmed 'natural revival' as being the appropriate brand positioning.

The campaign that resulted developed specific creative applications for each target segment, all linked by a very distinctive creative style and supported by the strap line – 'Wales Two Hours and A Million Miles Away'. The poster, television and direct marketing executions showed black and white images of people within the target markets in stressful everyday situations and contrasted these with evocative, colourful images of the same people being 'revived' in Wales (Figure 7.5). The campaign theme tune 'A Design for Life' was provided by the successful Welsh rock band, the Manic Street Preachers. We also developed a number of innovative ideas such as dirty, grimy vans driving through London and Birmingham with the line 'Clean Air is 2 Hours Away' finger written on the back of the vans (Figure 7.4). We also distributed air fresheners to London taxi drivers emblazoned with the line 'Real Fresh Air is only 2 Hours Away' (Figure 7.3).

The campaign achieved significant stand-out from other destination campaigns and despite very challenging marketing conditions for domestic holidays, achieved

Figure 7.3 'Real Fresh Air'. Wales' Synergistic PR activities

encouraging results. Wales' share of trips and spend increased. Brochure enquiries increased from 140 000 in 1998 to 240 000 in 1999. Monitoring research revealed increases in the awareness and ranking of Wales as a holiday or short-break destination. Finally, to date, the campaign has won fifteen national and international awards including the Chartered Institute of Marketing, Travel Industry Groups and Multi Media Campaign of the Year Award in 1998 – beating off competition from such recognized brands as Virgin Atlantic, British Airways and Thomson Holidays. It is fair to say, however, that the campaign resulting from the brand positioning was not without its critics. For the first time the WTB had recognized that the future growth would come from short breaks and additional holidays. The images were not obviously high summer and there were no crowded beach scenes. The campaign highlighted Wales' natural environment rather than its built attractions. As a result, some tourism businesses which serve the traditional declining market, felt that the campaign was not for them.

Figure 7.4 Wales' Grimy Vans. Innovative PR as part of the branding approach

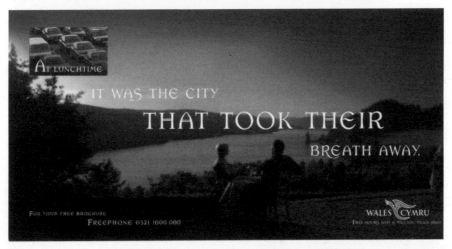

Figure 7.5 Wales. The Two Hours and a Million Miles Away Campaign

The international positioning

Despite the fact that Wales has long been recognized as a major holiday destination by people living in the rest of the UK, it has never been as successful in attracting large numbers of visitors from overseas. As was demonstrated earlier, Wales is often seen as just another part of England and has not possessed enough of the symbols of national identity like those held by our Scottish and Irish Celtic cousins. Up until 1992 the responsibility for the international marketing of Wales rested with the BTA, and the WTB was not allowed to spend any of its resources overseas. As a result the 'brand' that was promoted by the BTA was Britain. Although the BTA featured Wales within its communications, it was never treated as a separate brand and, as a result, it was never able to achieve the salience required in the market in order to significantly grow market share. For many consumers in source markets internationally, the terms 'Britain' and 'England' have become interchangeable and the lack of a clear international branding strategy for Wales only served to maintain the status quo.

On a more positive note, however, potential overseas visitors to Wales did not have the same negative perceptions of Wales as many of their UK counterparts. Fresh research conducted by the WTB in 1997 showed that overseas visitors were, in general, much more interested in messages about Wales which emphasized Wales' distinctiveness. The Welsh language, Celtic heritage and the Welsh people were all found to be motivating factors to target segments internationally which would have relatively little appeal to our core English markets. We also discovered that often the needs which have to be satisfied from a main overseas holiday were very different to those satisfied on a domestic short break. For domestic holidays intrinsic benefits such as relaxation, recharging the batteries and rest predominate. People want more, however, from holidays overseas. These can be classified as extrinsic benefits such as adventure, excitement and enrichment.

We decided, therefore, that the potentially more powerful positioning of 'Inspiring Recreation' was appropriate for and acceptable to our target markets overseas. We tested various entry concepts to this overseas positioning and eventually selected the 'Land of Nature and Legend' platform for all consumer communication and the 'Inspiring Ideas' concept for business tourism communication. Although the WTB is now allowed to market Wales internationally, resources have been very limited and, as a result, the vast majority of work is still conducted in partnership with the BTA. In those markets which we actively target, we augment the coverage of Wales by buying extra exposure for Wales within the BTA campaigns. The responsibility for the development of advertising campaigns within the BTA has been devolved to individual country managers. They have all developed communications themes with local advertising agencies which, while appropriate for each individual market, have lacked consistency across markets.

This structure and modus operandi has also made it very difficult for the WTB to develop the single-minded integrated approach that we have followed within the UK. In particular, it was impossible to achieve creative synergy between the advertising output and print fulfilment as the brochures were usually produced on a multimarket basis. To help overcome these problems, brand guidelines for the 'Nature and Legend' idea were developed in conjunction with the BTA. The following extract from these guidelines demonstrates that while the positioning is specific to the needs of overseas markets, it is compatible and complementary to the UK positioning:

> Wales is honest, welcoming and romantic. It is a country to inspire and revive.
>
> Wales holds a passion which is drawn from a heritage of poetry and song, legend and mystery. There is a spirituality about the natural and dramatic beauty of the countryside. Wales is a land of nature and legend.
>
> Wales is atmospheric and mystical but down to earth and strong. Its countryside has a compelling beauty.
>
> There is nothing trivial about the romanticism of Wales, ancient tombs lend an air of mystery while the great Welsh castles appear part of the solid natural Welsh landscape. Both are rich in the country's legend and myth.
>
> There is lyricism in the people, the Welsh language is at the heart of the country's poetic tradition. The poetry of Wales may be lyrical but it is never simply decorative. It springs from the straightforwardness, warmth and openness of the Welsh people. It is real poetry rung from the reality of everyday lives.

Conclusion

Within the WTB we now need to review and evolve our strategy and positioning. We need to learn from the lessons we have experienced over recent years and we also need to be aware of the significant change that is happening within the marketing environment. One of the key changes has been the advent of the Internet. The Internet is a very powerful tool for the promotion, selling and distribution of travel and tourism messages. However, the Internet is by its very nature anarchic. People will access the information you provide on the Web in a number of ways. To achieve consistency in the brand communication it is important that the imagery and message the Web surfer is exposed to closely reflect the off-line communication. Our current branding strategy differentiates between the UK and overseas audiences and the creative styles and messages employed are different but compatible. Although we can create gateway sites designed to target specific audiences, it is more difficult to separate the UK and overseas messages. We need to consider therefore, the implications that this will have for our brand architecture. We also need to be aware of the way in which our competitors are positioning their destinations and products. For example, shortly after we launched our UK campaign, the Jersey Tourism Board responded with a campaign with the strap line 'An Hour Away and a World Apart'. Sounds familiar?

In addition, the growth of low-cost airlines has helped to make competitor short-break destinations on the Continent appear far more accessible and affordable. We were always aware that 'naturally reviving' was not necessarily uniquely differentiating for Wales but we were concerned as to whether our English audience would find a strongly 'Welsh' positioning appealing and motivating. Should we now accelerate our plans to integrate the UK and overseas positionings? At the same time, there have also been changes within Wales. The advent of the new National Assembly for Wales has renewed political interest in the 'Welsh brand'. The National Assembly and other Welsh organizations are considering their branding strategies and this will inevitably have implications for the WTB.

Naturally, we have also been researching consumer reactions to our advertising output over recent years and considering the implications for our communications strategy. Research indicates that many of those exposed to the advertising have reformulated their views of Wales. It is now more readily considered as a short-break destination option and is perceived as a place that offers a refuge from everyday pressures. In particular, many people are ready to accept that Wales really is a beautiful country. Perhaps a decade or so earlier, many more people saw Wales as a grey rather than a green place. Images of Wales' heavy industry predominated but, for the most part, these views now appear to have changed. However, in some cases there is still consumer resistance to Wales. While they accept that Wales is green and beautiful, consumers still need reassurance that it possesses the quality infrastructure one would expect from a modern tourism destination. Consumers also need to be convinced that there are enough things to do in Wales other than simply enjoy the scenery. They want to know that after that long walk on the Pembrokeshire Coastal Path, there is a cosy pub with quality food and a lively atmosphere.

Clearly there is still much work to be done both at the domain brand level and specifically within tourism. There is little doubt, however, that considerable progress has been made within Wales in the development of an effective brand communications framework. Within the WTB we feel we have played a key role in this process. It is clear, however, that we are still at the start of that process. Wales does not enjoy the financial and economic benefits that should accompany a strong brand. We have not yet fully developed the identity premium. The core values and truths of Wales identified need to form the basis of the framework which allows communication in a wide variety of circumstances and across many industry sectors. This has to be an inclusive process and the work carried out to date provides a good starting point. We need to draw upon the tangible attributes such as our dramatic uplifting landscape, our strong sense of community, our quality education, our loyal committed workforce, our success in music and the arts, and our passion for sports, in order to create strong emotional linkages.

The successful branding of Wales will not happen automatically but it is vital that the strategy is rooted in reality and is built upon the belief of the people living and working in Wales. It is also vital that the messages communicated are relevant and motivating to the marketplace. The process needs to be carefully managed and communicated. Crucial to its success in the future, will be a commitment and leadership from the highest government levels in Wales. This has already been demonstrated with the new First Minister for Wales, Rhodri Morgan, forming a new branding group. The Welsh Assembly has realized that we are currently presented with the unique opportunity to achieve Wales' potential on a world stage.

As I have said, within the WTB we will continue to work at our tourism positioning. Perhaps the biggest challenge of all is the need to ensure that the brand promises conveyed in our communications are consistently delivered when visitors come to Wales. We have to find ways of enabling businesses in Wales to help create the 'Feel Wales Factor'. We want to ensure that the people representing the WTB, and therefore Wales, fully represent and convey the personality of Wales. We recognize that we need to give clearer guidance to our stakeholders within the tourism industry so that they, too, can fully support the brand positioning and the brand process. We need to improve our internal as well as our external communications. The UDP that we have created will, however, be the template on which we continue to build our branding strategy.

Finally, it is nice to know that some things do change for the better. The aforementioned Bill Bryson now has a very different impression of Wales. The author readily agreed to contribute a major article to our annual marketing magazine *A View of Wales*. In the 2001 edition, Bill Bryson walks along the same Offa's Dyke path that links England with Wales. He talks enthusiastically of a beautiful and still relatively undiscovered part of Britain. We have helped to convert Mr Bryson. Our commitment to branding will help us convert many more.

Reference

Bryson, B. (1996). *Notes from a Small Island*. Black Swan.

8

Brand Western Australia: 'Holidays of an entirely different nature'

Shane R. Crockett and Leiza J. Wood

Introduction

In today's cut-throat marketplace, only those destinations which have a clear market position and appealing attractions will remain at the top of consumer minds when they book their holidays. While travel agents continue to provide booking and support services, the choice of destination clearly lies with the consumer. In the highly competitive and dynamic global tourism environment, there is a need to develop a clear identity, or 'brand', based on reality while also reflecting the core strengths and 'personality' of its product. In this crowded marketplace, building and maintaining brand value is the key to business success and, as a result, brand management is quickly shifting from a peripheral marketing concern to the core business strategy. More often than not, it is the brand strategy that will determine who is successful in today's competitive business environment. This is certainly true of destinations and, according to the WTO (Jones, 1998), there is a clear contemporary trend towards highly branded destinations. As Ahmed (1991) states: 'Holiday makers of the 21st century will be looking for places with a trendy image. A strong and clear state image can increase consumer confidence in its attractions and consumer predisposition to purchase them.'

This chapter outlines the Western Australian Tourism Commission's approach to destination branding. Based on intensive consumer research, Brand Western Australia (Brand WA) resulted in an entire organizational shift and has repositioned Western Australia as a premier nature-based tourism destination in the global market. The cornerstone of the strategy was a partnership between government and industry, and this philosophy forms the platform of all policy direction, including *Partnership 21: 2000–2005 Tourism Industry Plan* (WATC, 2000) that is paving the way for tourism growth in Western Australia. To ensure delivery of the marketing promise, infrastructure development and partnerships with other key government agencies are a fundamental part of the Brand WA strategy, creating a state-wide rather than merely a tourism brand.

Essentially, Brand WA is a co-operative marketing strategy that aims to differentiate Western Australia in the global marketplace. It was developed for the state of Western Australia so that any person or organization promoting Western Australia's destination attributes, products, services, investment, etc., could market Western Australia in a unified and consistent manner. Brand WA has been built on a solid research foundation undertaken in 1996 that resulted in a set of descriptors for the personality and values of Western Australia, and an 'essence' that captures the underlying spirit of the state. Therefore, Brand WA captures the distinctive character of Western Australian people, our unique natural beauty, our wide open spaces, our pristine environment, the colours of the landscape and the free-spirited nature of the Western Australian lifestyle. The WATC has adopted a totally integrated and inclusive approach to destination branding that encompasses marketing and development strategies, and in the process is crafting a unique identity for Western Australia. This chapter will describe Western Australia's brand development and extension strategies in the context of fundamental brand-building principles. It initially outlines the macrotourism environment of Western Australia, analyses the repositioning challenge and then summarizes the development of Brand WA. Finally, it discusses and evaluates the state's fully integrated destination marketing, development and partnership strategies.

Positioning the brand

Differentiating Western Australia

Western Australia, home to 1.8 million people and offering a high standard of living, constitutes one-third of the Australian continent (with a landmass of 2.5 million square kilometres). Bounded by more than 12 000 kilometres of pristine coastline

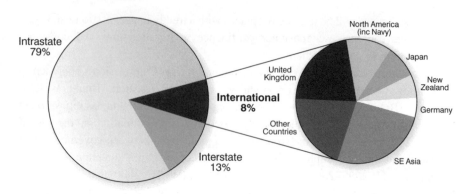

Figure 8.1 Visitors to Western Australia by origin market, 1999
Source: Bureau of Tourism Research (1999a; 1999b).

and characterized by extremes of climate ranging from tropical to desert, to warm Mediterranean and cool temperature, Western Australia offers a range of tourism experiences. Indeed, the tourism industry provides significant economic and development opportunities for Western Australia, particularly in the regional centres, which are home to many of the state's unique natural attractions. Currently tourism in Western Australia is a AUS$4.1 billion industry, attracting more than 1.46 million annual international and national visitors to the state as its fourth largest export industry (WATC, 2000). It employs some 78 000 Western Australians or 9 per cent of the state workforce, and represents approximately 4 per cent of the gross state product (WATC, 2000). Western Australia attracts 8 per cent of Australia's international and 13 per cent of its domestic tourism market (Bureau of Tourism Research, 1999a; 1999b) (see Figure 8.1).

In order to foster Western Australia's tourism industry, WATC has been given the role to accelerate the sustainable growth of the tourism industry for the long-term social and economic benefit of the state. The WATC is a state government statutory authority and by virtue of enabling legislation is charged with two core objectives:

- to promote Western Australia as an attractive tourist, event and convention destination within Australia and overseas
- to promote, foster and facilitate investment in and the development of new tourist infrastructure, services, product and the improvement of existing tourist facilities and services in Western Australia.

As can be seen from Figure 8.1, three clearly defined markets are apparent: Western Australians travelling within their own state, visitors from other parts of

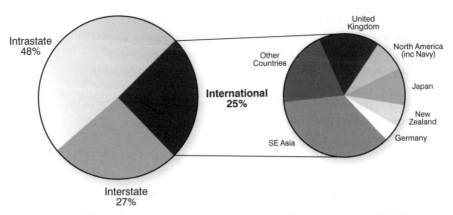

Figure 8.2 Total visitor expenditure in Western Australia by origin market, 1999
Source: Bureau of Tourism Research (1999a; 1999b).

Australia, and overseas visitors. In assessing the success of tourism, the WATC recognized that visitor expenditure or 'export income' is the critical measure of success (Figure 8.2) and that visitor numbers do not always demonstrate the real shifts in export earnings for tourism (Figure 8.1). Hence, there is a balance of marketing priorities between interstate and international markets, and the WATC encourages its contracted regional tourism associations to undertake the majority of regional marketing.

As regards its product, Western Australia offers among the finest nature-based experiences and tourist attractions in Australia. However, research undertaken in 1994 (303 Advertising, 1994) revealed that Western Australia and its capital Perth lacked a meaningful identity in the global marketplace. There was clearly a need for Western Australia to develop a strong identity that encapsulated the state's unique attributes and personality that could be marketed to those markets representing the best potential for return on investment. The vision was to produce a clear identity encompassing identified brand values. This brand would drive all marketing and development strategies. It would pervade all forms of communication and stimulate the core of the travel consumer's behaviour and decision-making process to competitively position the state of Western Australia in the global marketplace. As a result, in November 1996, the WATC launched Brand Western Australia.

The essence of branding

Kotler, Bowen and Makens (1996) suggest that the positioning task consists of three steps: identifying a set of possible competitive advantages upon which to build a position, selecting the right competitive advantages, and effectively communicating and delivering the chosen position to a carefully selected target market. Aaker's (1996) expanded model suggests that a brand encompasses many variables which all influence the brand's value proposition, credibility, brand–customer relationships and, ultimately, the brand's positioning. These include the brand as:

- a product (place) (e.g. attributes, place of origin, quality/value, etc.)
- an organization (place) (e.g. attributes, innovation, local vs global)
- a person (e.g. personality, brand–customer relationships)
- a symbol (e.g. visual imagery and metaphors; brand heritage).

Any analysis of successful brands worldwide reveals one overwhelming element – they all have a clearly defined core personality or purpose. A brand personality can be defined as the set of human characteristics associated with a given brand (Aaker, 1995) – like a human personality, it is both distinctive and enduring (Aaker, 1996). Aaker (1996) defines the core identity as being 'the central, timeless essence of the brand' which remains constant even as the brand travels to new markets and products. Depending on the target market, advertising strategies, communication tones, positioning statements and, in some cases, even the logos can all be changed, but what remains constant is the core personality or purpose. For example, in the world of sports and fashion, Nike has crafted a unique and instantly recognized identity synonymous with innovation, excitement and the pursuit of excellence in health and fitness. McDonald's, with its golden arches, conjures up images of convenience, value and consistency of product range, and extends to association with children, families and fun. Another example is found in Singapore Airlines, which instantly communicates to the public that it offers a unique, professional and somewhat exotic service. Female flight attendants (Singapore Girl) and their batik Sarong Kebaya uniforms have become an image and standard that is instantly recognized and appreciated by passengers, and competitive airlines would find it difficult to achieve significant market share using a similar approach (Kotler, Bowen and Makens, 1996). This concept of branding also extends to tourist destinations and the most successful destinations have achieved this to an extent where the mention of their name evokes mental images and perceived experiences. Thus, for examples, Bali promotes an exotic island experience, while the UK is clearly one of the world's most sought after cultural and historical destinations.

To be a famous destination brand, Western Australia needed to be more than the sum of its products, however beautifully presented, just as Nike is more than sport shoes. The destination would need to find the unique piece of information that positions its experience in potential visitors' minds differently from everywhere else in the world. The brand mission, therefore, needed to capture the very essence of the Western Australian experience and its effect on the visitor/consumer. To deliver this, Brand WA is an ambitious plan to unite the tourism industry and other business sectors to present a consistent image of Western Australia to interstate and overseas markets. It is more than just a tourism marketing campaign, and encompasses destination awareness, product awareness, consumer desire, tourism product, infrastructure and industry professional development. In addition, it was recognized that in order to be successful in 'branding', infrastructure development, promotional co-ordination, produce enhancement and protection against environmental degradation were essential to the success of the state as a tourist destination. To this end, the WATC established its tourism development strategy that included the nature-based tourism strategy to ensure Western Australia's holiday product and infrastructure would preserve its natural product and deliver its marketing promise. Underpinning the WATC's core philosophies are its partnerships with industry that ensure that the WATC's destination marketing and management is complementary to the development and promotional activities of individual tourist providers and other stakeholders.

In turn Brand WA and the tourism development strategy provided the catalyst for an entire organizational restructuring within the WATC, encompassing a new corporate culture, new direction, increased accountability, performance measurement and partnerships with industry, together with a clear customer focus. Of course, developing a strong and distinctive image calls for creativity and brilliant execution and no organization can implant an image in the public's mind overnight. To differentiate Western Australia in the marketplace and to create a strong destination image, Brand WA also needed to be an innovative long-term strategy based on the fundamental principles of brand management. This chapter, therefore, will now outline the creative and integrated approach undertaken by the WATC since its launch of Brand WA in 1996.

Brand Western Australia development

The process

The development of Brand WA was led by the WATC and involved an extensive consultative process with the possible end users of Brand WA. A brand strategy group, representing Western Australia's broader community, met regularly to co-ordinate the overall process. The composition of this group included the Premier of Western Australia, the City of Perth's Lord Mayor, the Department of Commerce and Trade, Western Australian business leaders in banking and export, and representatives from the inbound tourism industry (including the Perth Convention Bureau). The group's task was to test and endorse the foundation research and creative concepts throughout the development of Western Australia's brand. This endorsement was essential as it was to be a 'state brand' which tourism could then market. Ongoing brand development continues to employ this partnership approach.

In the development of Brand WA, it was also decided to maximize the linkage between it and the Australian Tourist Commission's (ATC) Brand Australia strategy, which markets Australia under the banner of 'Big Nature – Big City'. In many of Western Australia's target markets, Brand Australia has a very large promotional presence and, in many market segments, travellers first decide to come to Australia then, within that holiday experience, choose which particular location within Australia. Western Australia would add depth to and be a core brand of Brand Australia, reflecting the 'Big Nature' aspect of Brand Australia's core personality. At the same time, Brand WA would benefit from the promotional strength attained through synergy with Brand Australia. To this end, ATC representatives were intimately involved in the development of Brand WA.

Underpinning the Brand WA strategy (WATC, 1996) was the commitment to a partnership philosophy with industry and other key stakeholders. This is reflected in the establishment of advisory councils comprising industry representatives who provide advice and recommendations on all major marketing and industry development activities undertaken by the WATC. Additionally, ten regional tourism associations (RTAs) representing tourism regions throughout the state were formed to develop a flexible framework to produce and implement individual marketing and development plans while reflecting the broader focus of Western Australia's tourism initiatives. Destination branding is difficult since tourism (and its related industries) is a composite product consisting of many components, including accommodation, transport, catering establishments, tourist attractions, arts, entertainment and the natural environment. Through a multiagency and cross-industry approach, Brand WA ensures each stakeholder takes ownership and assumes responsibility for enhancing favourable brand images.

The foundation research

In developing Brand WA, it was vital for the core personality of the destination to be clearly defined and reflected in all marketing strategies. Marketing intelligence derived from a comprehensive qualitative research programme was used to shape all aspects of the strategy and, to establish credible and representative brand attributes, research was conducted among overseas visitors and Western Australians. There were three main components of the research programme:

- consultation with the possible end users of Brand WA
- a comprehensive market research programme in key national and international markets
- a target market selection process.

This extensive consultative process included businesses likely to export, businesses in origin international markets likely to consider investing in Western Australia, the arts, the Western Australian tourism industry, Western Australian residents, heads of government agencies, the tourist industry in source markets and visitors to the state. Further, the WATC undertook an intensive qualitative research programme conducted by Donovan Research (1996) in Western Australia's key national and international tourism markets. This research analysed global tourism trends, consumer behaviour and the decision-making processes of travel consumers, and aligned these against visitor perceptions of Western Australia, its services and attractions. The perceptual issues probed included:

- the attributes tourists ranked as high motivators for their travel
- consumer perceptions of Western Australia and Perth as a holiday destination
- what travellers imagined when they thought of Western Australia and of Perth
- consumer perceptions of the state's major strengths and weaknesses as a holiday destination.

The research revealed that Western Australia offered most of the attributes which tourists rank as high motivators of travel – such as the ability to relax and recharge, a fresh, clean environment and unspoilt natural scenery. People believed, however, that Perth (the state capital) was quiet and lacked activity. In essence, Western Australia was felt to be strong on nature-based imagery and attractions, but lacking a meaningful identity. A major reassessment of where and how the state was marketed as a destination was required.

To compete effectively in the global tourism market, any destination must be selective about which target markets represent the best return on investment. Previously, Western Australia's work in this area had been predominantly subjective with very little objective data analysis. As described earlier, in reassessing its marketing strategy, the WATC aligned visitor numbers with visitor expenditure to assist in evaluating the optimal yield return. The target market selection process was divided into two parts, being first the selection of the highest potential countries in which to market and, second, if appropriate, which target segments should be marketed to in those countries. Given that Australia as a market currently delivers 92 per cent of all visitors to Western Australia and 75 per cent of visitor expenditure, this was immediately included as a target country. The market segment results are described in the Brand WA media campaigns (see Table 8.1).

The selection of the other potential international markets was a far more complex task. An overriding philosophy was that, as a state, Western Australia has limited marketing resources and, as such, acknowledged that the state could not be in all markets at once. The Donovan research was used to determine the target market/s in each location and to select the best ways, both in terms of the messages used and the media, to reach those target markets. In addition, the WATC and the International Advisory Council simultaneously developed an objective selection model named

Table 8.1 Brand Western Australia media campaign summary

Core market	Market segment	Proposition	Strategy
National – Sydney/ Melbourne	Longer-stay holiday-makers 30–59-year-olds Higher income earners	Only Perth and Western Australia's natural environment offers an adventurous escape to the unspoilt Australia	Brand and retail – mix of 15-second and 30-second television commercials and press Timing: Apr. 1997/Oct. 1997/ Sept. 1999/Sept. 2000
International – Singapore	Short-break holiday-makers 18–35-year-olds Higher household income Extended family	Only Perth and Western Australia's natural harmony offers the opportunity to participate in Australian country and city activities	Brand – 1 × 40-second television commercial in English and Mandarin Retail – 1 × 20-second television commercial in English and Mandarin Quarter-page mono-press Timing: Jul. 1997/Mar. 1999 Chinese New Year campaign: Nov. 1998. In 1999 and 2000 the Singapore campaign consisted of 1 × 20-second brand commercial with a 10-second tactical tag. Press was used as the primary tactical medium

Table 8.1 (Continued)

Core market	Market segment	Proposition	Strategy
Indonesia	Short-break holiday-makers 25–45-year-olds Upper socioeconomic grouping	Only Perth's natural harmony offers the opportunity to see Australia's natural beauty from the comfort of a city environment	Brand – 1 × 45-second television commercial in Bahasa Indonesian Quarter-page mono-press Retail – 1 × 15-second television commercial in Bahasa Indonesian Timing: Jul. 1997 Withdrew from market in 1998 determined by MPAF
Malaysia	Upper middle-class 18–29-year-olds Ethnic Chinese and Malays Young families with children under 12 years	Only Perth's natural harmony offers the freedom to see Australian country and city activities	Brand – half-page colour press Retail – 30-second radio advertisement in English Half-page mono-press Timing: Apr./May 1997 and Mar. 1999 Press remains the major focus in this market due to the broadcast restrictions
UK	Long-haul holiday-makers 30–59-year-olds Upper income levels	Western Australia's natural harmony offers an adventurous escape to the true nature of unspoilt Australia	Brand – 3 × 20-second television commercials Retail – 1 × 10-second television commercial Timing: Sept. 1997/Mar. 1998 and Mar. 1999. The 2000 campaign consisted of a 20-second compilation of Elle/destination images with a 10-second tag. Press once again was the primary tactical medium

the Market Potential Assessment Formula (MPAF), a dynamic selection mechanism that assesses the value and potential of international markets using the criteria of:

- access – access/airline capacity; visa rejection rate
- growth – growth rate of outbound travel population; index size of outbound population; growth rate of visitation to Australia
- value – market share of visitors to Australia
- synergy – ATC activity in market; airline 'on-line' in market.

The MPAF enables the commission to set priorities and allocate resources in order to effectively work the market. Currently of the twenty markets analysed, the MPAF identified the UK, Germany, Japan, Singapore and Malaysia as core markets for Western Australia which could be pursued on the current budget allocation. This did not mean that other markets would be totally ignored. Rather, they would be continually monitored to see if their potential improves, at which time resources could be applied. To this end Italy, China, Hong Kong and South Africa were also identified as showing a strong possibility of becoming a priority market in the short to medium term. Activity in these markets is currently restricted to co-operative work with the ATC and other partners. The MPAF is reviewed twice yearly to identify shifting and emerging trends in international markets.

Once the objectives and target market have been defined, the marketing communicator must decide what response is sought (Kotler, Bowen and Makens, 1996). In the case of Western Australia, top-of-mind awareness was the initial primary indicator of success. Post-campaign research conducted in each market measured its success on two essential factors, these being 'perceived knowledge' of Perth/Western Australia as a holiday destination and 'propensity to consider' Perth/Western Australia for a holiday. Further, visitor nights and visitor expenditure targets were set and are measured yearly, although it is important to note that these targets are intended to guide the industry, rather than being definitive measures of the WATC's success. Research on perceptions, marketing strategies, positioning, and strengths, weaknesses, opportunities, threats and constraints (SWOTC) analyses are also ongoing, and are used to provide a methodical, consistent and evolving branding approach. As a result, the brand marketing strategies are constantly under review, although the brand's fundamental personality and visual interpretation remain constant.

The result

The result of the overall research was a clear brand position. Brand WA emerged as a clear, focused strategy with a defined purpose and personality. Western Australia's pristine environment made it well suited to marketing a fresh, new nature-based

Figure 8.3 Brand WA visual identity system

tourism destination with friendly, spirited people and the freedom and space to travel. As described above, the strength of a brand lies in its capacity to remain true to its core personality or purpose, irrespective of its target audiences or mode of communication. Hence, in the development and research foundation of Brand WA, it was considered vital that the core personality of the destination be clearly defined and that all marketing strategies be true to the personality. The four core personality elements of Brand WA were found to be:

- fresh
- natural
- free
- spirited.

These are the constants of Western Australia's proposition as a destination. Based on these core personality traits, an integrated visual language was prepared by the design team Cato Partners with internationally acclaimed designer Ken Cato, to ensure that all visual communications reflected the core personality. The designer's challenge was to create a distinctive style and graphic theme to present the complex, diverse and unique personality of the destination. The visual identity programme created a distinctive 'broader visual language' featuring the elements of a warm yellow sun, vast canopy of blue sky and wide horizon under which the unique attributes of the state could be featured (Figure 8.3). To reflect the diversity of Western Australia and communicate beyond the traditional tourist market, a unique colour pallet and series of graphic icons were developed to reflect the arts, business, technology, events and thematic aspects of individual regions. These integrated visual components increased the personality of Brand WA's identity. They could also be marketed to strategic partners to promote their individual objectives, thereby creating sub-brands under the overall umbrella of Brand WA. The visual language was not just a logo, in fact it was deliberately not a logo, but rather a set of design briefs which ensured the visual elements of Western Australia's marketing always reflected the core personality, adding to the strength of the brand. While a logo does exist in the visual language, it is only one of the many visual tools which can be used to impart the personality of Brand WA.

On the basis of the foundation research, the Brand WA strategy was developed as a five-year holistic package with a number of marketing and development strategies aimed at maximizing Western Australia's market exposure, servicing Western Australia's core tourism sectors, facilitating effective industry partnerships, and developing industry product and infrastructure – all of which would deliver on the marketing promise. These strategies shaped the initial development of Brand WA and have since been reviewed after further comprehensive research and consultation. The newly released tourism industry plan for 2000–5, *Partnership 21*, extends the Brand WA strategy for the tourism industry. *Partnership 21* researched and identified the latest emerging trends of the travel consumer towards experiential travel, revitalization and freedom. As travellers become more experienced, they are seeking more personalised and interactive experiences. In response, the Western Australia tourism industry is developing ways to proactively build interaction with the environment and community. As Pritchard and Morgan (1998: 216–17) have said: 'When consumers make brand choice about products – including tourism services and destinations – they are making lifestyle statements since they are trying to buy not only into an image, but also into an emotional relationship.' Through *Partnership 21*, Western Australia will continue with Brand WA's strong nature-based positioning, further enhancing it with an environmentally positive addition to the brand personality. The new dimension will be the emotional connection of being 'touched by nature'. This will provide opportunities for people to learn more about the destination and its products through interaction rather than through a passive viewing approach.

Brand Western Australia marketing strategies

The following section discusses the advertising and marketing strategies for tourism to capitalize on the brand. Strategies to establish Brand WA are discussed along with new strategies determined under *Partnership 21*. The overall marketing and promotional mix was determined as follows:

- *Price/value*: Western Australia has been positioned in its core markets as a value-for-money destination, and therefore marketing promotions are not principally price led, but rather reflect a value-added component.

- *Product*: product is principally centred around nature-based product and experiences, with a heavy focus on regional attractions.
- *Place*: marketing and promotional activities are primarily delivered through broadcast consumer media such as advertising and publicity. The tourism product is delivered through traditional and electronic distribution channels utilizing wholesale packages, retail travel agents and other travel retailers such as airlines and booking companies. The consumer web site (www.westernaustralia.net) is central to assisting visitors to conduct their information search, and its e-booking platform provides conversion via a gateway to the tourism industry. A virtual industry structure also exists, which integrates visitor servicing, retail sales and access to product knowledge through a virtual call centre, a state-wide visitor centre network, a comprehensive state-wide database of tourism product and a single entry point for all of Western Australia's tourism operators.
- *Promotion*: the Brand WA strategy relies heavily on consumer advertising, utilizing celebrity endorsement television commercials which are supported by a co-ordinated publicity campaign encouraging the publication of positive tourism stories on Western Australia. The WATC also participates in selected consumer and trade shows throughout the region and core markets.

Mass marketing and clever marketing

While word-of-mouth advertising plays an important part in the promotion of a holiday destination, it is consumer awareness created through marketing and communication campaigns, supported by appropriate collateral, which is the key to increasing awareness levels of a destination in its core markets. As the fresh and natural aspects of Western Australia were clearly seen as the state's major competitive advantage in all key markets, the core position underpinning Brand WA is the notion that Western Australia offers a holiday experience that is *fresh, natural, free and spirited*, and refreshingly different from other holiday destinations. The overriding objective was to develop a long-term campaign designed to build awareness of Western Australia as a holiday destination, in a highly competitive, dynamic and expensive global marketplace.

Celebrity endorsement was seen as an effective means of providing a point of differentiation between Western Australia and other destinations. Kotler, Bowen and Makens (1996) suggest that celebrities are likely to be effective when they personify a key product attribute. The WATC secured the services of international supermodel and actress Elle Macpherson. Ms Macpherson, an Australian, embodies the 'personality' of the state and had the ability to take this message to the world in a way no paid advertising could (see Figure 8.4). This endorsement has provided Western Australia's tourism advertising with high levels of recall and enquiry, as well as millions of dollars in free publicity. Once the initial brand campaigns were undertaken in all core markets, the next step was to convert awareness into purchase. Each of the twelve Brand WA television commercials was tagged with a packaged tourism product or a point-to-point airfare that related to the destination being advertised. Direct-response press and radio in some cases was also used. All international campaigns included a value-added component within the product offer marketed, e.g. offers and bonuses at local tourist attractions.

Brand WA was launched in November 1996 and has since involved annual campaigns in most core national and international tourism markets. Promising post-campaign international research conducted by Donovan Research revealed positive changes in attitude and belief measures in all markets, and increased awareness across the board. Although primarily intended to increase awareness, the initial six-week UK campaign in September 1997 directly resulted in 5886 visitors generating AUS$7.3 million of expenditure within Western Australia – a 500 per cent return on the advertising outlay. Following the success of the initial Brand WA commercials, Elle Macpherson was contracted for an additional four commercials which were produced in October 1998. These have been broadcast in some core markets since February 1999. The combined UK campaigns have generated in excess of AUS$25 million in direct visitor expenditure and, according to the World Tourism and Travel Council formula, this should be multiplied to three to estimate the total flow of benefits.

Over the past three years Western Australia has recorded an 11.8 per cent jump in total visitation, while interstate visitation was up 15.7 per cent on 1998, against a national average of only 0.4 per cent. In the process Perth has climbed from obscurity to become the UK's third most favoured city worldwide (Guardian Observer, 2000). The local Western Australia market currently generates some 5.35 million visitors (Bureau of Tourism Research, 2000) and represents around 45 per cent of total visitor expenditure. Like all segments, this market needs to be actively encouraged to visit Western Australia rather than vacationing in other states or overseas. The campaign reminds Western Australians of their state's great features promising a holiday that meets their expectations and includes:

- a positioning campaign to reposition the state in 'top-of-mind awareness' of local Western Australians as a destination with a wealth of nature-based attractions/ experiences
- a campaign to build on this repositioning by encouraging specific travel within Western Australia
- travel/lifestyle programmes broadcast by three Perth metropolitan commercial television stations and a commercial radio station promoting Perth and Western Australia regional destinations
- tactical initiatives to stimulate travel during low and shoulder periods (i.e. winter breaks).

Figure 8.4   Elle Macpherson: a celebrity felt to embody the spirit of Western Australia. (Courtesy of Western Australia Tourist Commission)

To date this integrated approach has achieved significant success. For example, the Winter Breaks tactical initiative in 1999 boasted high consumer awareness of 42.6 per cent (Roy Morgan Research, 1999) and returned 57 787 bed-nights, representing a 29 per cent increase over the previous year and an accumulated increase of 59 per cent since the 1996 initiative. Mass-media campaigns were conducted in co-operation with industry and these reflected and reinforced the established brand image. Mass media was also used to promote the tourism web site (www.westernaustralia.net) in combination with brand awareness campaigns.

Television commercials of 15-second duration were chosen for the national market, 40-seconds for Singapore and Malaysia and 20-second commercials for the UK market, for a number of reasons. Commercials of this length enable each to tell a unique story with a single focus. Viewer expectation is heightened through the desire to 'stay tuned for the next chapter' all of which maximizes impact. By utilizing a shorter commercial time, the advertisements can be repeated more frequently and cost-effectively, thus improving the reach and frequency among the target audience. It also provided the opportunity to include tactical tags of product and calls to action. In the national market, a reach and frequency of 97 per cent was achieved. The strategy for longer television commercials in the South East Asian market emphasizes the myriad of activities and experiences available in a holiday to remember (Table 8.1).

The global television industry is experiencing significant changes and the end-to-end conversion from analogue to digital processes, combined with interactivity, will completely transform the medium. As the television and the personal computer converge, the new television paradigm will allow for more presentations and interaction than ever before. This provides Western Australia with the perfect environment to capitalize on its highly interactive product. The WATC is currently undertaking a formal research project in conjunction with a local university, research company and creative agency to pilot interactive Brand WA television commercials in the UK in 2002.

While television is the most powerful brand-building medium, in some market categories it is not necessary or is cost-prohibitive. To this end, the WATC effectively uses media and trade familiarizations to generate extensive publicity to promote destination brand awareness. One example of this is the leveraging of the ATC's Visiting Journalists Program (VJP), which over the last three years has resulted in excess of AUS$120 million in free publicity for the state. Mass marketing will always have its place, however, in the era of one-to-one marketing, a successful marketing strategy must integrate mass marketing and one-to-one activities. The successful consumer web site (www.westernaustralia.net) and its advanced product and consumer database will facilitate future customized marketing opportunities.

Niche marketing

Niche marketing to selected groups such as adventure, trekking, diving, wild-flowers and wine tourism, and the use of electronic marketing for advertising, communicating and developing databases maximizes destination marketing opportunities. Special interest tourism (SIT) is growing on a global scale and Western Australia is well positioned to meet the demands of this broad-based market opportunity. Over the past two years, the WATC and industry partners have increased marketing activities and developed tourism products in a range of SIT strategies, including nature based, wine, dive and cultural tourism. In addition, WATC has also targeted business tourists through its Conventions and Incentives Travel Strategy – Operation Welcome Mat. Based on research that highlights the importance of making South East Asian visitors 'feel welcome' in a destination, the WATC, in partnership with the Perth Convention Bureau, embarked on a cohesive strategy to attract the top 100 Meetings, Incentive, Corporate and Exhibitions (MICE) decision makers from around the world to Perth. To date Operation Welcome Mat has hosted 124 buyers from all over the world on site inspections to Western Australia. The value of incentive business secured for Western Australia from these markets over the past three years has totalled just under AUS$6 million.

Addressing any negatives

To counter the negative perceptions of Western Australia being a little slow and lacking activity, a programme of special events was initiated. Launched in 1997, this programme, known as the 'Best on Earth in Perth', featured twelve major international sporting and cultural events over twelve months, including seven world championships, and worked to create a sense of activity and excitement. A new programme continues each year featuring a combination of regular events and events which are new to Perth and provides a global focus on Western Australia. This multidimensional campaign also gains extensive international media exposure through the broadcast of 15-second 'picture postcards' showcasing regional Western Australia, en route to commercial breaks in telecasting. The market penetration of these postcards is far greater than any advertising could achieve, particularly when they are shown in countries such as the UK or Japan. The Best on Earth in Perth in 1999–2000 featured fourteen international sporting and cultural events. The events supported by EventsCorp in the calendar generated AUS$66 million in economic impact for the state. A regional event programme 'It's Happening in WA' has also been launched as part of the new five-year plan.

Development strategies

Delivering on the promise

In establishing a brand, it is important that structures are in place to deliver on the brand's promise. In the case of Western Australia, this was primarily achieved by establishing a brand based on reality. For example, Brand WA has as one of its core personality traits the 'natural' characteristic. Western Australia offers a great array of spectacular nature and can deliver on that promise. To ensure the sustainability of this characteristic and tourism growth in Western Australia, the WATC developed a Nature-Based Tourism Strategy. In addition, commencing in 1997–8, AUS$6 million was allocated to develop tourism infrastructure projects throughout Western Australia over a four-year period. This commitment to infrastructure and product development is essential to maintain and improve quality experiences for visitors to Western Australia. As an element of Partnership 21, Western Australia's Environmental Enhancement Program (currently being piloted) will build environmental enhancement and interaction into all tourism development programmes and existing tourism product. These unique and highly interactive, interpretive, nature-based experiences add depth and diversity to the visitor experience.

Some of Brand WA's personality traits are also dependent upon community attitudes. For Western Australia, one such trait is the quality of service delivered by the tourism product and the general 'friendly and welcoming' appeal of the state. To ensure this strength is not eroded, the WATC worked in association with the state's tourism industry body, Tourism Council Australia (TCA) and implemented a quality assurance programme aimed at improving the quality of service delivered by Western Australia tourism operators. This model was subsequently adopted nationally and renamed the National Tourism Accreditation Program. As tourists become more sophisticated, so do their expectations. Delivering on expectation is very much dependent upon the quality of the service, product or experience provided.

Quality delivery is only part of the answer to exceeding tourists' expectations and many people outside the direct tourism industry, such as service station proprietors, customs officers, restaurant owners and shopkeepers, also affect visitors' experiences. Therefore, in 1996–7 the WATC introduced a Western Australian community-based campaign, Keep up the Good Work. The campaign message is, 'All Western Australians affect a visitor's satisfaction with our State and, as such, we all need to keep up the good work for our visitors, if we are to reap the rewards of tourism'. This is a long-term campaign involving mass media, community presentations and workshops. All this reinforcement becomes a vital element in creating the positive word-of-mouth promotion necessary for any destination brand to be successful. In order for the WATC and its industry to be effective an integrated partnership has been developed. Partnership 21 has formalized these relationships into a partnership model by defining and assigning the various tourism roles and responsibilities. Visitor servicing has also been enhanced through the development of a state-wide visitor servicing network. The Western Australia Tourism Network is a virtual industry structure which integrates visitor servicing, retail sales and access to product knowledge through a virtual call centre, a state-wide visitor centre network, a comprehensive state-wide database of tourism product and a single entry point for all of Western Australia's tourism operators. Assimilated at national level, the virtual structure will facilitate efficient and effective collection, distribution and promotion of tourism information and services.

Brand extension

Just as Brand WA reflects a part of Brand Australia's Big Nature – Big City, Western Australian regional brands reflect specific regional branding under the overall umbrella of Brand WA. As consumers become more familiar with the brand, they seek more detailed knowledge, and as Brand WA develops a presence and position in its target markets, it therefore needs to continually extend itself to build on its core personality. Consequently it needs to become more complex and multilayered to maintain its consumer appeal. In the case of Western Australia, the extension is achieved through a number of sub-brands, an important part of which is regional brands. Ten regional brands have been developed in conjunction with the state's ten RTAs, along with over twenty locality brands, ensuring the personality of the destination and sound marketing intelligence are employed, and are consistent with the umbrella brand. Each has its own positioning, image, target markets, competitive strengths, marketing mix, product development and tourism strategies. As Brand WA evolves, regional and locality brands are becoming more inclusive with community partnerships adding further value. The benefits to regions and localities that are being realized include the:

- highlighting of the product (e.g. tourism – attractions, facilities, infrastructure; agriculture; export)
- creation of economic opportunity
- creation of local support for local products
- promotion of a clear and consistent brand image and message
- fostering of strong community effort
- breeding of public and private sector partnerships
- creation of a marketing focus on the consumer/target market
- promotion of destinational positioning for destinational marketing purposes by broad stakeholder groups
- demonstration that product differentiation on regional brand marketing techniques works.

143

Destination ownership

Destination branding extends to combining all things associated with the 'place' (i.e. its products and services from various industries such as agriculture, tourism, sports, arts, investment, technology education, etc.) under one brand. Its aim is to capture the essence of the destination in a unified manner that can be consumed simultaneously at a symbolic and experiential level. Tourism is an industry that impacts on many aspects of the Western Australian business sector, economy and lifestyle. The Brand WA philosophy, its promise and its visual imagery must have the support of other government agencies, businesses and communities to be successful in creating a unified identity for Western Australia. For a brand to be successful in the long term, it needs to reflect the entire state's culture or personality, and residents should have ownership of the brand. It is necessary to incorporate all the elements, including individual businesses and organizations which are inextricably linked to the 'total overall product', that make up the state and its personality. A co-operative approach is essential to achieve a positive long-term image of Western Australia.

Poon (1993) originally proposed the diagonal integration concept within the ambit of tourism to include the collaborative branding and marketing of products and services that rely on tourism to survive and fringe tourism industries. Brand WA has extended diagonal integration to include all Western Australian brand associations (e.g. tourism and fringe-tourism products, activities, and associations such as taxis, leisurewear, education, investment attraction, product place of origin, regions and localities, etc.) under a single brand image (i.e. Western Australia – *fresh, natural, free and spirited*, with consistent but flexible visual branding). The WATC works closely with all key government agencies to market and manage Brand WA's image and philosophy to its audiences. Brand WA has thus also been integrated into projects with a broad community focus, including Brand WA vehicle number plates, vehicle registration stickers, driver's licences and welcome signage throughout the state and at regional gateways. A Brand WA merchandise range incorporating clothing and souvenirs has also been produced and is distributed throughout retail stores and the Internet. A particularly successful aspect of this extension has been the introduction of the Brand WA livery on taxis – as Kevin Foley, Managing Director, Swan Taxis Cooperative, has recently noted – 'taxis are often the first contact visitors have after arriving in our State, it's important they are exposed to the personality of WA – fresh, natural, free and spirited and Swan Taxis are pleased to be involved with such a successful marketing strategy'.

A brand ownership campaign was also initiated where approved licensees are able to use the visual elements of Brand WA in their own marketing and promotional efforts, thus supporting the brand identity. Brand WA thus becomes a platform on which other sub-brands can be superimposed to create uniquely Western Australian identities while still retaining a degree of individuality. The integrity of Brand WA is maintained by a clever juxtaposition of the brand with the organization's core identity. The local industry welcomed the introduction in 1996 of the distinctive Brand WA and fully supports the fresh, natural, free and spirited image it portrays. As Laurie O'Meara, President of Tourism Council Australia, has said: 'Many industry members have seized the opportunity to incorporate Brand WA into their individual marketing activities and are reaping the ongoing benefits.' So far, more than 300 organizations are approved to use Brand WA as part of their promotional activities, including advertising, promotion, stationery and corporate livery. The synergy, created by industry working with and reinforcing Brand WA's visual elements and philosophies, generates greater impact from overall marketing expenditure. Terry Bright, Executive Director, Restaurant and Catering Industry Association of Western Australia Inc., has said of the programme: 'We are a proud supporter of the philosophy of Brand WA and have benefited from the synergy created by having a common image for Western Australia business and government activities. The use of the Brand WA graphic has consolidated our position as an integral part of the State's business community.'

Commercial television stations broadcast weekly travel/lifestyle programmes throughout the year, reflecting brand attributes and imagery, and contributing to heightened destination ownership. These programmes attract extensive viewing, often ranking in the top ten of weekly viewing statistics. At the core of successful branding is a unified and consistent approach that adds value to the brand. Consistency in the messages and design, within a flexible framework, avoids proliferation of the brand, and ensures maximum leverage against a brand that has had significant investment based on fundamental brand-building techniques. This value adding will result in an extremely strong brand and tangible competitive advantages for the state of Western Australia. All of these activities represent creative ways to strengthen fundamental brand-building activities and enhance the image of Western Australia within the state, as well as nationally and internationally.

Conclusion

This chapter has presented the WATC's methodical approach to positioning Western Australia as a premier nature-based tourism destination in a worldwide market. It presents a summary of the complex process of establishing a brand for Western Australia and the complementary strategies that exist in partnership with the brand. Brand WA is a very broad strategy incorporating trade, consumer and events marketing, visual branding, convention activities, product and infrastructure development, regional marketing, place of origin product marketing, and even the way WATC and its stakeholders interact and communicate. Brand WA was launched just four years ago and has already proven successful in its core markets – in 2000, the Brand WA strategy won the Australian and State Public Sector Marketing Leadership Awards bestowed by the Australian Marketing Institute.

Partnership with industry and its stakeholders is at the core of the Western Australian Tourism Commission's philosophies. The WATC has developed a comprehensive approach to mould a unique image for Western Australia in true partnership with industry and the success of Brand WA and its associated strategies has been outstanding. Over the period 1995/6 to 1999/2000, international visitors to Western Australia increased 24.47 per cent to 590 000, interstate visitors to Western Australia jumped 64.48 per cent to 977 000 and Western Australia intrastate visitors improved 4.96 per cent to 5 541 000 visitors (Bureau of Tourism Research, 2000). Meanwhile the WATC attracted revenue of AUS$10 703 755 in 1999/2000, representing a massive 80.24 per cent increase from 1994/5. The state government contributed funding of AUS$33 812 000 in 1999/2000, being an increase of 47.14 per cent over 1995/5, thereby demonstrating the government's heightened value of the tourism industry. The holistic Brand WA strategy produced strong operational efficiency gains at the WATC and overheads were reduced by 32 per cent from AUS$10 650 000 in 1992/3 to AUS$7 242 000 in 1999/2000.

In terms of the future, Partnership 21 provides the pathway for the Western Australian tourism industry and includes greater use of innovative technology along with high quality, interpretive, participative nature experiences for the visitor, extending Brand WA's values. Further strength will be achieved through greater levels of collective marketing between government agencies and industry. Brand WA presents an innovative and totally integrated approach to destination branding and leverage opportunities for tourism industry and other organizations involved in marketing Western Australia to maximize their marketing activities. It also serves to reduce the fragmentation of the tourism industry from a marketing perspective. Of the many lessons learnt, branding requires time, flexibility, co-operation, capital and truth in brand values. Brand WA has been built on a solid platform and the results to date have been outstanding. However, the WATC and its stakeholders have only just begun to tap into the potential of Western Australia as a tourism destination. The continued success of Brand WA will provide economic and social benefits for Western Australia in terms of revenue generation and export enhancement, as well as improvements to the quality and quantity of infrastructure throughout Western Australia.

References

303 Advertising (1994). *Developing a Marketing Strategy for Western Australia.* Commissioned by the WATC – EventsCorp Division.

Aaker, D. A. (1996). *Building Strong Brands*. Free Press.

Aaker, J. L. (1995). Conceptualising and measuring brand personality: a brand personality scale. Working paper, Stanford University.

Ahmed, Z. U. (1991). The influence of the components of a state's tourist image on product positioning strategy. *Tourism Management*, December, 334–340.

Bureau of Tourism Research (1999a). *International Visitor Survey*. Bureau of Tourism Research.

Bureau of Tourism Research (1999b). *National Visitor Survey*. Bureau of Tourism Research.

Bureau of Tourism Research (2000). *National Visitor Survey*. Bureau of Tourism Research.

Donovan Research (1996). *Partnership Western Australia: Developing Brand Western Australia*. Donovan Research

Guardian Observer (2000). *Guardian Travel Awards*, Guardian.

Jones, C. B. (1998). *The New Tourism and Leisure Environment* (www.econres.com/papers).

Kotler. P., Bowen, J. and Makens, J. (1996). *Marketing for Hospitality and Tourism*. Prentice Hall.

Poon, A. (1993). *Tourism, Technology and Competitive Strategies*. CAB International, p. 215.

Pritchard, A. and Morgan, N. (1998). Mood marketing – the new destination branding strategy: a case study of Wales. *Journal of Vacation Marketing*, **4**(3), 215–229.

Roy Morgan Research (1999) *Holiday Tracking Survey*. Roy Morgan Research

Western Australian Tourism Commission (WATC) (1996). *Brand WA Strategy*. WATC.

Western Australian Tourism Commission (WATC) (2000). *Partnership 21: 2000–2005 Tourism Industry Plan*. Working strategy reviewed annually. WATC.

9

Brand Louisiana: 'Come as you are. Leave Different.®'

Jan Slater

Introduction

Branding actually evolved out of the Industrial Revolution as a means for a manufacturer to identify itself as the maker of a certain product. The brand then became the identifier for the consumer – promising consistency and quality. The basic textbook description of a brand defines it as 'a distinguishing name and/or symbol' that provides some identity to the goods or service, while providing some differentiation from the competitors (Aaker, 1991). This branding differentiation helps consumers make choices in a cluttered environment. Today, brands are not just goods or services. They have permeated every level of society. Politics, governments, charities, sports teams, utilities, media, individuals, and even cities, states and countries have endorsed branding as means of setting themselves apart amidst the clutter of competitors. In today's international marketplace, there is little doubt that 'everything and everyone is capable of becoming a brand' (Clifton and Maughan, 2000).

One industry that has embraced the branding craze is tourism bureaux and destination marketers. Once known for advertising that was considered 'wallpaper' (the same pretty scenery), the tourism industry is using branding as a means of emphasizing the feel of the place, developing a personality of the location. This differentiates the destination from the typical travelogue attraction because the branded destination is an experience, not just a place to go (Anon., 1999b). This branding mentality has been observed in recent campaigns for Australia ('Come and Say G'Day'), New Zealand's '100% Pure New Zealand', Montana's 'Big Sky Country' campaign and 'It's A Whole Other Country' for Texas. In fact, state governments in the USA spent $524.4 million in 1998–9 to promote tourism in the fifty states (Anon., 1999b).

Building a brand in today's marketplace is difficult and presents many barriers and challenges (Aaker, 1996). The key to successful brand building is identifying what the brand stands for and effectively delivering that message. This brand identity is central to the direction, purpose and meaning for the brand. Aaker (1996: 68) posits that the brand identity 'should help establish a relationship between the brand and the customer by generating a value proposition involving functional, emotional or self-expressive benefits'. While this is difficult, it is not impossible. This chapter will describe the brand-building success story of Louisiana, a powerful travel destination brand.

Background: Louisiana history

Certainly, the tourist's attraction to Louisiana is due in part to the varied and colourful history the state has endured. Its past has created a very eclectic present state of mind. The combination of its Spanish, French, Native American and African American heritage offers a unique cultural and leisure experience that is expressed in its landscape, its architecture, its food, its music, its landmarks, its waterways and its people. Louisiana was named for Louis XIV, who was the reigning monarch of France in 1682 when the French explorer, Sieur de LaSalle, took possession of the rich, bountiful country at the mouth of the Mississippi River. The area grew and developed as a French colony, building the town of New Orleans in 1718. However, the Louisiana country remained unprofitable for France and the government ceded the territories to Spain. The province was firmly under Spanish control in 1769 when Spanish Governor Alejandro O'Reilly divided the territory into twelve administrative districts, called posts, and twenty-two ecclesiastical parishes. While the system of posts was later abolished, the parishes remain intact today as the primary county-level units under state government. By 1800 Spain had returned the province to France, concerned about ongoing deficits and the possibility of fighting the Americans to retain control. On 20 April 1803, Napoleon Bonaparte sold the territory of Louisiana to the USA for $15 million. Over 900 000 square miles were included in the Louisiana Purchase. Eventually, thirteen states or parts of states would be carved out of the territory. Only one would retain the name and the influences of its founders and developers – Louisiana.

Admitted to the Union as the eighteenth state in 1812, Louisiana was to suffer great losses during the Civil War. Seceding from the Union in 1861 to join the Confederacy, Louisiana was undisturbed for a year after the war broke out. But by 1862, New Orleans had been captured due to its access to the Mississippi River. By May 1865, many of the Louisiana Confederate units had disbanded. The losses were great in terms of money, livestock, land and lives. But the South did rise again, and so did Louisiana. Today, tourists can visit the battlefields of the Civil War, watch the steamboats along the mighty Mississippi, tour the great plantations, pay tribute to Native American ceremonial mounds, skin an alligator, eat crawfish, celebrate Mardi Gras, and enjoy some of the best jazz, blues, bluegrass, zydeco or gospel music in the world. What best summarizes this most unique blend of history and culture has become the unofficial state motto – 'joie de vivre', the joy of living. In addition, that unofficial slogan translates into a successful brand identity that has positioned Louisiana as one of the fastest-growing tourism destinations in the USA.

Building the Louisiana brand

Tourism in the USA is big business. According to Dr Suzanne Cook, senior vice-president for the Travel Industry Association of America, more than 1 billion people made domestic trips in the USA during 1999 (Richard, 2000). In addition, more than 48.5 million international visitors made trips to the USA. This is a US$524.4 million investment every year as state governments promote various attractions within their borders to lure the adventurers, fun-seekers, sun-worshippers, beachcombers, mountain climbers, snowbunnies, sailors, or just the traditional family to spend time and money in the state. No matter the budget size, the challenge still remains for the state to depict the territory as a unique place, creating some point of differentiation that provides the tourist with more than just a destination spot. It provides an experience unlike any other. It is simply an issue of branding the state by creating an identity, an image, a feeling about the place and what it has to offer. The state of Louisiana did just that in developing a branding strategy.

As is typical in the USA, state governments manage the state tourism funds and development. Louisiana is no different. The Department of Culture, Recreation and Tourism (DCRT) is a cabinet agency, which is governed by the lieutenant governor of the state, an elected official. The lieutenant governor appoints the secretary to run the agency. In Louisiana, the Lt Governor is Kathleen Babineaux Blanco, and she appointed Phillip J. Jones as cabinet secretary to the DCRT. It was their combined mission to 'create a greater awareness of Louisiana's culture, history, and natural resources' to visitors as well as locals that provided the foundation for building the Louisiana brand (http://www.crt.state.la.us/crt/tourism.htm). They were helped by a New Orleans advertising agency, Peter A. Mayer Advertising. The relationship between the agency and the government tourism office would become as strong as the brand itself.

Finding a brand specialist

The DCRT has always used an advertising agency. Because tourism is a government agency, Louisiana law requires the account be reviewed every three years. The Mayer agency had pitched for the account twice, both times unsuccessfully. The agency was invited to compete for the business again in 1993, when a new lieutenant governor put the account up for review a year early. This time Peter A. Mayer Advertising would come to the bargaining table with a powerful proposition. According to Mayer president, Mark Mayer, the agency created a consortium with three other communications firms in the state. A separate entity, named Peter A. Mayer Advertising and Partners, was born out of the co-operative that includes Williams Creative Group, a public relations firm in Shreveport, G.Mc & Co., a multicultural agency in New Orleans, and the Graham Group, an advertising agency based in Lafayette.

The development of the co-operative was not because Mayer was not large enough to handle the business. The Mayer agency is the largest in the state, billing US$60 million annually. Mark Mayer asserts that 'we felt the geographic diversity would help in our understanding' of how to sell the state to tourists. The partnership provided a 'better sense of the different elements of the state in terms of regional, political and cultural differences,' Mayer continues. In fact, for those very reasons the partnership turned out to be a tremendous advantage, and the co-operative won the Louisiana tourism business in 1993. Since then, the partners have been renewed twice by the state and retain the business today.

Creating the brand identity

During the initial presentation to the state, Mayer and Partners proposed an entirely new approach to marketing Louisiana. Previously, the focus of tourism had been solely on food. There is no doubt Louisiana is known for food. It has a long history of a variety of rare cuisines that range from jambalaya, gumbo, beignets and meat pies to boiled crawfish and shrimp etouffee. Even the telephone number to gain tourist information had a food flavour: 1–800–99-GUMBO. But just like the famous gumbo, Louisiana had a lot of everything in it. Mayer and Partners thought the food focus too limiting for branding the state.

Good branding stems from good research, so the partners began by analysing existing research. While much research had been conducted regarding state tourism, it had not been used extensively. Mark Mayer asked to read the research in the hope of 'uncovering some unique element that motivated the visitor to choose Louisiana'. He was right; the answers were in the data. The research showed that Louisiana offered several unique destination elements to travellers in addition to the food attraction. A syndicated research study that uses a large consumer panel and scores individual states against national norms indicated that tourists were drawn to Louisiana because its attractions were distinctive. In addition to the food, visitors identified the state's scenery, architecture, history, culture and music among its greatest strengths. With this information, the partners did what any smart branding company would do – used this competitive differentiation to develop a strong brand position and identity.

The next step was to develop a creative strategy that incorporated the positioning with the various attractions in creative executions for a specific target group. Initially, the target audience was identified as frequent domestic out-of-state travellers, between the ages of twenty-five and fifty-four with incomes of US$30 000 plus. Six different campaigns were created and tested in focus groups against the positioning statement. Then the field was narrowed to three campaigns that were considered to be the most motivational. Those rough executions were tested against a large panel of potential visitors to determine the best campaign. The first advertisement to run was titled 'The Words,' with what would become the signature of Louisiana – the red lipstick logo and the 1–800–99-GUMBO response mechanism. According to Mark Mayer, 'We've run various versions of that campaign, but it hasn't really changed one bit. The focus is still food, culture, music, scenery, architecture, and history.' In fact, little has changed from the initial campaign developed in 1993, except that a slogan was added to the campaign in 1997. In 1996, when current Lt Governor Blanco took office and appointed Phillip J. Jones as secretary of the DCRT, more research was conducted to test the advertising and the images generated by the campaign. The research reinforced that Louisiana was unique, different from anything else. Mayer states, 'We had a monopoly. What made Louisiana different you couldn't get anywhere else.'

Jones had served as Director of Legislative and Intergovernmental Affairs for the Travel and Tourism Administration within the US Department of Commerce. In addition, he had been a spokesperson for the first-ever White House Conference on Travel and Tourism, which developed a national tourism strategy under the Clinton administration. Jones claims this time was similar to receiving a masters of business administration (MBA) in tourism, as he was able to study each state's tourism policies and determine what worked and what did not work in some cases. Jones is a Louisiana native, so it was a homecoming of sorts when he was appointed to oversee the state tourism activities. Furthermore, he wanted to use the knowledge gained in Washington and put it to work in his home state. He felt a slogan would be beneficial to the tourism campaign to leverage Louisiana even further. The research showed Louisiana was different, and basically provided 'the road map' for a slogan, as Jones recalls. Out of the research conducted in 1996, the slogan 'Louisiana. Come as you are. *Leave Different.*®' was developed and was used in all materials as the 1997 tourism campaign was launched (Peter A. Mayer Advertising and Partners, 1997). Just as the new slogan was unveiled, Key West, Florida, filed a lawsuit against Louisiana for infringing on their slogan 'Come as You Are'. Louisiana won the legal battle and because of it gained from the awareness of the slogan based on the local press coverage of the lawsuit.

As with any strong brand, every point of consumer contact must reinforce the brand image. While the brand strategy remains the same, the flexibility of the positioning allows the agency to adopt various themes – food, music, culture, history, etc. Within the current campaign, there is a special emphasis on music to take advantage of Ken Burns' documentary on jazz, and the Satchmo Summer Fest, a planned celebration of Louis Armstrong's one hundredth birthday. However, the brand image remains dominant in all the tourism communication tools. The slogan, the lipstick logo and the overall design features provide strong continuity of the image in every advertisement or promotional piece. Domestic and international advertising conveys similar design qualities (see Figure 9.1). The official tour guide

Figure 9.1 The advertisements for both domestic and international markets are similar in style and tone, reinforcing the brand

incorporates the same photography and use of the logo and slogan throughout the 300+ page book. The television commercials showcase the photography as well, and highlight a picture of the tour guide, the logo and the telephone number (see Figure 9.2). The web site and newspaper advertisements splash the signature Louisiana logo across the pages, interspersed with distinctive Louisiana photography. Trade publications targeted on travel agents, visitors' bureaux, and tour operators use similar graphics and design. Peter A. Mayer Advertising and Partners have created a strong visual and strategically positioned brand for the state of Louisiana. Furthermore, they have been able to deliver the brand message to the right people at the right time.

Figure 9.2 The consumer television advertisements for Louisiana use similar visuals as in the print ads that highlight the state. The spots are tagged with the logo and the 1–800 telephone number

The power behind the brand

Strong creative concepts, a memorable slogan and beautiful advertisements that speak to the target group are only a third of the brand battle. The creative element has to be supported by efficient and effective media exposure, and the budget has to be strong enough to support the advertising exposure as well as other tactical communication efforts such as publicity and promotion. The power behind the Louisiana brand has been a substantial advertising budget, well-targeted media placements and an effective integrated campaign that allows the image advertising to be the cornerstone, while other methods of communicating the brand's uniqueness stretch from that base.

Budget

As in most US states, tourism is funded from a portion of the state sales tax on goods and services collected by the state government. Louisiana is no different. Nevertheless, while the money may be earmarked for tourism, the secretary of DCRT must still submit and defend its budgetary requests to the governor each year. In 1996, the year Jones took his cabinet position, the Louisiana tourism budget was US$13 million. The budget for 2001 is US$17 million, with the understanding that the 2002 budget will be US$18–US$20 million. This is an average annual increase of 6 per cent, or 31 per cent in just five years. The state has been ranked among the top ten state travel budgets in recent years (Anon., 1999a). Jones states the fact of the matter, 'The more money we spend, the more visitors we get.' Furthermore, Jones spends his budget wisely. Administration is kept low at 5 per cent of the budget. Ten per cent goes to fulfilment – sending out consumer information based on enquiries. Another 10 per cent is spent on staffing and maintaining ten welcome centres throughout the state, and the remaining 75 per cent of the budget is spent on marketing and advertising efforts. With the consistent increases in the budget and the effective management of their resources, DCRT and its agency have managed to provide the power to expose a strong creative strategy and execution.

Media

Delivering the brand message is more challenging today than ever before. While the choices for media delivery have increased, the audiences for many media vehicles have become more fragmented. Intercepting the consumer at the right place at the right time means that planning the media delivery requires understanding a well-defined target and using some creativity in reaching them. The current primary target audience for the Louisiana brand is families, adults aged twenty-five to fifty-four, with children still at home and household incomes of US$40 000 plus per year (LDCRT, 2001a). In addition, secondary targets comprise the following: seniors, adults aged fifty-five plus, no children at home, with a household income of US$40 000 plus per year; and African-Americans and Hispanic-Americans, aged twenty-five to fifty-four with household income of US$30 000 plus. According to Mayer, these audiences are reached through a combination of print, television and some radio advertising. Print is the primary media choice, which receives approximately 60 per cent of the advertising dollars, with 40 per cent being allocated to spot television and radio in various regions.

Strong branding requires strong research throughout. The media plan for Louisiana tourism uses brand development indexing (BDI) to rank and index all US markets to 'determine their propensity to generate visitors to Louisiana' (LDCRT, 2001a: 17). The top twenty major markets are then analysed and the key markets are identified for spot television and radio flights for the yearly campaign. The current BDI rankings are provided in Table 9.1. *Note*: 'An index of 100 indicates that

Table 9.1   The thirteen markets for Louisiana's media campaign

Market	BDI
Beaumont/Pt Arthur, Texas	1328
Biloxi/Gulfport, Mississippi	1254
Jackson, Mississippi	1146
Tyler-Longview, Texas	1015
Laurel/Hattiesburg, Mississippi	962
Houston, Texas	781
Mobile, Alabama/Pensacola, Florida	562
Dallas, Texas	434
Greenwood/Greenville, Mississippi	417
Little Rock, Arkansas	354
Montgomery/Selma, Alabama	277
Waco/Temple, Texas	245
Corpus Christi, Texas	228
Greenville/Spartanburg, Mississippi	221
Austin, Texas	194
Memphis, Tennessee	190
Oklahoma City, Oklahoma	149
San Antonio, Texas	136
Birmingham, Alabama	135
Huntsville/Florence, Alabama	126

consumers living in a particular market are likely to visit Louisiana at the same rate as the national average. This means that an index of 200 would indicate that the market is twice as productive in generating visitors to Louisiana as the national average' (LDCRT, 2001a: 17).

For the 2000/1 campaign, thirteen markets were chosen for spot television and radio flights. These markets include Albuquerque, New Mexico; Atlanta, Georgia; Austin, Texas; Dallas, Texas; Houston, Texas; Jackson, Mississippi; Jacksonville, Florida; Little Rock, Arkansas; Memphis, Tennessee; Mobile, Alabama; Pensacola, Florida; Springfield, Illinois; Tucson, Arizona and Tyler, Texas (see Figure 9.3 for map). In addition to television and radio, consumer magazines (both regional and national), trade publications, newspapers and travel directories are used as part of the media mix. Some of the publications include: *AAA Tourbook*; *Better Homes and Gardens*; *Black Enterprise*; *Bon Appetit*; *Family Circle*; *Gourmet*; *Harpers*; *Modern Maturity*; *National Geographic Traveler*; *New Yorker*; *Parade*; *Texas Monthly*; *USA Today* and *Walking*. In total, more than fifty publications have been used in exposing the campaign (LDCRT, 2001a). All advertisements in these publications include the 1–800–99–GUMBO number for ordering the *Louisiana Tour Guide*. Travel directories run with a bound-in business reply card and a reader service listing. Each advertisement is coded so that enquiries can be tracked accordingly.

In addition to traditional media, the web site LouisianaTravel.com provides additional image support as well as serving as an efficient and effective means of generating enquiries. The web site hosts special features on current events, special

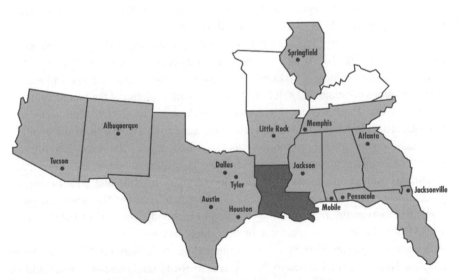

Figure 9.3 The 2000/1 Louisiana campaign targeted these regional markets determined to have the best potential

sections for travel agents, an opportunity to view all the various regions of the state and a place to make on-line reservations at hotels and restaurants throughout the state. Furthermore, international visitors to the site can download printable versions of the international brochures in country-specific languages. According to Phillip Jones, 'we embraced the web early and have seen some huge results.' Huge indeed. Seventy per cent of all enquiries come from the web site – which totals more than 1.7 million enquiries. According to the research, 37 per cent of those converted into actual visitors to the state (LDCRT, 2001a).

Promotions and public relations

To capitalize on the advertising investment in the Louisiana brand, the promotions and public relations activities are planned in conjunction with the advertising campaign exposure. The promotions and public relations work in tandem as the promotions attract the media and public relations efforts leverage the coverage. For example, Louisiana is a promotional partner with the Montreal International Jazz Festival in Quebec. During the ten-day festival, Louisiana sponsors a daily Mardi Gras parade, the 'Gumbo Louisiane' stage which hosts Louisiana musicians, and several food kiosks for sampling Louisiana fare. The promotion is a natural tie-in with the state's jazz heritage and the state attracts many visitors from Quebec. But the awareness and press coverage it generates provides a solid return on the investment in the promotion. In 1999, the state received an US$8 million return on an investment of US$250 000. This included more than 200 newspaper articles, 200 minutes of television reports and radio coverage (LDCRT, 1999a). The 2000 promotion garnered US$3.4 million in television and radio exposure and US$2 million in newspaper coverage of Louisiana's participation in this international event (LDCRT, 2000b). Another promotion, Francofete, which celebrated the 300 years of French influence in Louisiana, generated more than US$14 million in public relations coverage (LDCRT, 1999b). The state is planning the bicentennial of the Louisiana Purchase as a yearlong celebration in 2003. The web site www.LouisianaPurchase2003.com has already generated awareness of the event.

In addition to special promotions as described above, the state has formed promotional alliances with various entities in order to showcase Louisiana. Filmmaker Ken Burns debuted his *Jazz* documentary in 2001 and with Louisiana prominently featured as the birthplace of jazz, the state arranged for cards to request Louisiana tourism information to be included in each videotape, DVD and CD sold. TABASCO®, a local manufacturer of hot sauce, has agreed to promote the state with a special tourism offer on its packaging and the 1–800–99-GUMBO telephone number. Record label Putumayo has agreed to focus on Louisiana music and is running special promotions in selected Barnes and Noble bookstores showcasing events that include zydecko musicians and Cajun chefs. A special arrangement with

American Express allows the tourism department to send more than 200 000 mailers to cardholders who visited a competitive travel state. Every tactic, whether promotion, advertising or public relations conveys the same brand message – what Louisiana has, you cannot get anywhere else.

Evaluation

The final step in a strong brand strategy is to determine if the campaign has been successful in meeting its objectives. This is necessary in order to improve the campaign or to provide guidance for change. Those behind the efforts in developing and maintaining the Louisiana brand understand that research is important at the front end and the back end of the campaign. Therefore, extensive research is conducted to evaluate the effectiveness of the advertising and promotional campaigns. Conversion studies are used annually and conducted by the University of New Orleans to measure the percentages of enquiries converted to visitors. In addition, research is done by the university to determine the cost for attracting a visitor and the return on the advertising investment. The Marketing Workshop, Inc., a research firm in Atlanta, Georgia, works with the Office of Tourism to measure awareness generated from the advertising. The survey measures ad recall, image awareness and intentions to travel to Louisiana and other selected states (LDCRT, 2001a: 14). In addition to the primary research just discussed, the state also purchases an annual syndicated study from the US Travel Data Center that measures the economic impact of travel on Louisiana. The study predominantly measures how much a traveller spends in the state, and the economic effect that tourism has on employment and tax receipts by counties. It also provides a means to track the state's tourism market share.

Conclusion

When Lt Governor Blanco unveiled the 'Louisiana. Come as you are. *Leave Different.*®' campaign on 15 January 1997, she was quoted as saying, 'We are hopeful this campaign . . .will help us continue our growth in the tourism industry' (LDCRT, 1997). At that time, the 23 million visitors to the state created a US$6.6. billion economic impact on the state's economy. By 1999, 25 million tourists were visiting the state and spending on average US$120 per day per person. Tourism had grown to US$8.2 billion, the second-largest industry in the state with 118 000 jobs directly attributed to tourism. The economic impact of tourism had grown 24 per cent in just three years, showing no signs of slowing down. By 2000, the figure had grown to US$8.7 billion and it is expected to reach US$9.5 billion by 2004 (LDCRT, 2001a). Furthermore, the number of visitor enquiries (any request for information on Louisiana as a travel destination) surpassed 2.5 million, showing an increase of 150 per cent since 1996, and a 344 per cent increase since 1993. However, the cost of generating those enquiries had been reduced by more than 50 per cent in the same time period – the campaign is not only successful, it is efficient as well.

The Travel Industry Association of America claims Louisiana's tourism growth rate for the past five years has climbed 17.6 per cent compared with a national increase of less than 7.5 per cent and a regional increase of only 2.9 per cent (Salomon, 2000; LDCRT, 2000a). Furthermore, a recent study released by Plog Research on visitor satisfaction revealed that the state delivers on its brand promise. Louisiana was one of two states in the southern region of the USA named in the top twelve national destinations for traveller satisfaction. The previous study had ranked Louisiana twenty-first. Other states making the list are included with rankings (LDCRT, 2001b) in Table 9.2.

As any good brand manager knows, building a brand is only part of the battle. Maintaining the brand is just as formidable. The lieutenant governor, the secretary of DCRT and Peter Mayer Advertising and Partners are just as cognizant of the task that lies ahead of them. While enjoying successes in developing the Louisiana brand, no one is resting on their laurels. Growth is still the major tourism objective and there is the understanding that a long-term strategy is required to keep that goal in mind as well as to keep Louisiana in the minds of travellers.

In planning for future growth, the lieutenant governor assembled specialists from the US travel industry to discuss the changes and challenges the state might face in the coming years. The Louisiana Tourism Collegium 2010 was held in Baton Rouge in November 2000. In addressing concerns regarding sustaining Louisiana's travel growth, the forum drafted a long-term action plan. The plan outlines six key areas in which recommendations were made. The areas include technology, infrastructure, marketing, education, training and quality of life. Lt Governor Blanco was quoted as saying: 'To accomplish our goals, we need the full participation of every community in Louisiana. As we enhance our technology and train our hospitality professionals, we also need to strengthen the quality of life across the state through an increased sense of pride in our culture, our heritage and the unique experience Louisiana offers' (Richard, 2000). The

Table 9.2   The top twelve US states for traveller satisfaction

1	Hawaii	7	Maine
2	Florida	8	Arizona
3	California	9	New York
4	Nevada	10	Washington
5	Alaska	11	Montana
6	Colorado	12	Louisiana

brand position is evidenced even in the lieutenant governor's remarks – what Louisiana offers is not available anywhere else.

The stewards of the Louisiana brand have invested heavily in the equity of the brand. According to branding expert David Aaker (1996), the Louisiana brand involves all the factors identified with a strong brand. They are as follows:

- A strong brand identity with a competitive advantage has been developed. The brand identity drives the brand association that Louisiana is a unique, historical, cultural, musical, culinary experience.
- The brand has achieved awareness via extensive and strategic exposure to its strong, consistent message.
- The brand has perceived quality in the fact that visitors believe what they read, see and hear about the state, and those expectations are fulfilled once the visit has been made. The brand delivers on its promise of providing something that is unavailable elsewhere.
- There is brand loyalty in that there are repeat visitors and the state does an excellent job in providing visitors with a reason to return, i.e. the Louisiana Purchase Celebration and the Satchmo Summer Fest.

All these brand assets add value to the brand, in turn providing brand equity. Strong brand equity generates growth and profits. In the case of Louisiana, the brand has been successful in generating both more visitors to the state and a strong economic return on the investment. As stated in the early paragraphs of this chapter, 'everything and everyone is capable of becoming a brand'. This study of the Louisiana brand is a textbook case as to the importance of brand development and maintenance. It further underscores that branding is not just about identity; it is about differentiation from the competitors. By nature, Louisiana has that differentiation. It took a branding campaign to make the world aware of it.

Acknowledgements

The author would like to thank Mr Mark Mayer, President of Peter A. Mayer Advertising and Mr Phillip J. Jones, secretary of the Louisiana Department of Culture, Recreation and Tourism for their assistance with this chapter. Both were interviewed for this piece.

References

Aaker, D. A. (1991). *Managing Brand Equity*. Free Press.
Aaker, D. A. (1996). *Building Strong Brands*. Free Press.

Anon. (1999a). Illinois tops state tourist spending. *Hotel and Motel Management*, 17 August, 14.

Anon. (1999b). Taking the less traveled road. *Brandweek*, 4 October.

Clifton, R. and Maughan E. (2000). *The Future of Brands*. New York University Press.

Louisiana Department of Culture, Recreation and Tourism (LDCRT) (1997). Blanco unveils new advertising campaign. Press release, 14 January.

Louisiana Department of Culture, Recreation and Tourism (LDCRT) (1999a). Tourism benefits from promotional partnership. Press release, 27 August.

Louisiana Department of Culture, Recreation and Tourism (LDCRT) (1999b). Louisiana Office of Tourism recognized for Public Relations Efforts. Press release, 19 October.

Louisiana Department of Culture, Recreation and Tourism (LDCRT) (2000a). State's visitors spent over $8 billion in 1999. Press release, 2 June.

Louisiana Department of Culture, Recreation and Tourism (LDCRT) (2000b). Louisiana entertains record crowds at Montreal Jazz Festival. Press release, 22 August.

Louisiana Department of Culture, Recreation and Tourism (LDCRT) (2001a). *Louisiana Marketing Report 2000–2001*. Louisiana Department of Culture, Recreation and Tourism.

Louisiana Department of Culture, Recreation and Tourism (LDCRT) (2001b). Tourism investments pay off according to visitors' satisfaction research. Press release, 12 January.

Louisiana web site: http://www.crt.state.la.us/crt/tourism.htm

Peter A. Mayer Advertising and Partners (1997). Lt. Governor Blanco introduces new tourism advertising campaign at 1997 Travel and Tourism Summit. Press release, 15 January.

Richard, J. (2000). Ten-year action plan formed at tourism forum. Louisiana Department of Culture, Recreation and Tourism press release, 29 November.

Salomon, A. (2000). The marketing 100, *Advertising Age*, 26 June, s. 30.

10

The Sydney Olympics and Brand Australia

Graham Brown, Laurence Chalip, Leo Jago and
Trevor Mules

Introduction

According to Janiskee (1996: 100), 'this is the age of special events'. It is certainly difficult to visit a major city without being confronted by an impressive list of sport and cultural events that compete to capture the attention of tourists. The events add to the city's range of tourist attractions and they often actively seek media coverage as a promotional strategy, hoping more people will be encouraged to visit the city in the future. Thus, the relationship between events and tourism has become intrinsically linked. One significant element of this relationship is the way images associated with an event may be transferred to the destination. In this way the destination brand may be strengthened, enhanced or changed.

The aim of this chapter is to consider the relationship between events and destination branding from a number of perspectives. After discussing the growing importance of event tourism, the nature of destination image is examined in the context of conceptual and applied frameworks. An attempt is then made to determine the status of the relationship between event management and tourism by reporting recent insight gained in Australia. The findings from a research project that is focusing exclusively on the role of events in destination branding are discussed before considering the implications of the Sydney Olympic Games on Brand Australia.

The section on the Sydney Olympics provides an opportunity to assess the extent to which it is possible to manage outcomes associated with an event of this size and complexity. It serves as a valuable case study because the 2000 Olympics are widely regarded as a particularly successful event and tourism objectives were accorded a more important role in Sydney than at any previous Olympic Games. 'No other host country has taken the opportunity to use the Games to promote the whole country's tourism image as well as the host city's. No other country has worked so closely with the Olympic partners to develop mutual benefits from linking the tourism brand with their products and services' (ATC, 2001b: 5).

The emergence of event tourism

Observation and anecdotal evidence suggest that the number of special events has increased substantially over time (Getz 1991; Getz and Wicks 1994; Janiskee 1994). However, they are not a recent phenomenon. The first Olympic Games were held in 776 BC and religious events and festivals have been held throughout the ages. What is new, is the scale of event tourism with many cities seeking to specialize in the creation and hosting of special events due to the economic benefits they bring (Lynch and Veal, 1996). Event management is now regarded as a distinct field of study (Getz, 2000) but it is still at a formative stage and no definitional consensus has emerged in the literature (see, for example, Arcodia and Robb, 2000; Burns, Hatch and Mules, 1986; Getz, 1989; 1991; Hall, 1992; Jago and Shaw, 1994; 1998; Ritchie, 1984). Jago and Shaw (1998: 29) have proposed that a special event is: 'A one-time or infrequently occurring event of limited duration that provides the consumer with a leisure and social opportunity beyond everyday experience. Such events, which attract, or have the potential to attract, tourists, are often held to raise the profile, image, or awareness of a region.'

The term 'event tourism', which formalized the link between events and tourism, was coined in the 1980s (Getz, 1997) and has been defined as 'the systematic planning, development and marketing of festivals and special events as tourist attractions, catalysts, and image builders' (Getz and Wicks, 1993: 2). Much of the attention that has been accorded special events has been tourism based, as places have come to recognize the power of special events to attract visitors from outside the region. The Formula One Grand Prix held in Melbourne in 2000 attracted 14 per cent of its visitors from overseas, and 19 per cent from outside the state (National Institute of Economic and Industry Research, 2000), while the 1998 Gold Coast

Wintersun Festival attracted 2 per cent of its visitors from overseas, and 61 per cent from interstate (Fredline et al., 1999). It is important to recognize the role played by local communities in special events as they often depend heavily on the patronage of the local market for their success (Crompton and McKay, 1997; Getz, 1997). Despite this, tourist attendance at special events continues to be seen as a major objective, partly because event tourists have a higher than average daily expenditure, although the expenditure profile varies with the type of event (Getz, 1994a).

The success of special events in capturing market appeal has been attributed to the fact that they match important changes in the demand for leisure activities – namely, they are 'short-term, easily accessible, with a flexible time commitment, and offer options for all ages' (Robinson and Noel, 1991: 79). Some of the reasons for the dramatic increase in the popularity of special events also relate to demographic and psychographic changes that have occurred, such as:

- increasing levels of average disposable income
- a move to more frequent short-term holiday breaks
- increasing interest in experiential travel
- increasing interest in authenticity
- increasing interest in culture.

Special events have been used to supplement natural and existing built attractions (Burns, Hatch and Mules, 1986) as, in many cases, little additional infrastructure is required. They can be held in most locations and, in principle, can be scheduled at times and in places to reduce the impacts of seasonality or to reduce crowding and damage in more sensitive areas (Getz, 1991). The type of people that travel to special events have been classed as high 'quality tourists' (Getz, 1994c) as they are often concerned about the social and environmental impacts of their behaviour, making them well suited to sustainable development (Uysal and Gitelson, 1994). Hughes (1993a), however, has cautioned that it is still not clear that special event tourists are in fact more beneficial than other categories of tourists.

Special events can be an important motivator for travel behaviour – both day trip and overnight. As Getz (1989: 125) observed: 'Although the majority of events have probably arisen for non-tourist reasons . . .there is clearly a trend to exploit them for tourism and to create new events deliberately as tourist attractions.' Pleasure travel as a result of attendance at special events accounts for about 3 per cent of the total pleasure travel in the USA, but it is one of the fastest growing segments of the tourism industry (Backman et al., 1995). In a study conducted by Wicks and Fesenmaier (1995) that involved a survey of 2100 randomly selected households, it was found that 57 per cent of all pleasure trips in the previous year had included a special event. Of these, 55 per cent indicated that attendance at a special event resulted in an overnight stay, which demonstrated the importance of the field of special events to the tourism industry.

Governments have become interested in special events largely because of their ability to attract visitors, and hence visitor spending, as well as their ability to raise the awareness of the host region for future tourism (Mules and Faulkner, 1996). The importance of special events for Australia's tourism industry was recognized in the National Tourism Strategy (Commonwealth Department of Tourism, 1992), and most state tourism strategies, produced since 1992, have acknowledged special events as an important tourism development option (see, for example, Tourism Victoria, 1993; 1997). As a consequence of these strategies, special event divisions have been established in most of Australia's state and territory tourism organizations (Jago and Shaw, 1998). The special event divisions that have been established by many of Australia's cities also generally fall within tourism departments.

The growing importance of special events is such that they 'are starting to dominate natural or physical features in the identification of cities' (Burns, Hatch and Mules, 1986: 5). They can have very wide-ranging impacts and a given event can be staged for a large number of reasons as indicated in the following literature:

- increased visitation to a region (Getz, 1989; 1991; Hall, 1992; Kang and Perdue, 1994; Light, 1996; Ritchie, 1984; Tourism South Australia, 1990)
- positive economic impact (Burns, Hatch and Mules, 1986; Faulkner, 1993; Getz, 1991; Goeldner and Long, 1987; Hall, 1990; 1992; Kang and Perdue, 1994; Light, 1996; McCann and Thompson, 1992; Mules and Faulkner, 1996; Murphy and Carmichael, 1991; Ritchie, 1984; Ritchie, 1996; Witt, 1988)
- increased employment (Hall, 1992; Ritchie, 1984)
- improvement of a destination's image or awareness (Backman et al., 1995; Burns, Hatch and Mules, 1986; Hall, 1990; 1992; 1996; Kaspar, 1987; Ritchie, 1984; Ritchie and Smith, 1991; Roche, 1994; Travis and Croize, 1987; Wells, 1994; Witt, 1988)
- enhanced tourism development (Chacko and Schaffer, 1993; Faulkner, 1993; Getz, 1989; Hall, 1987; Pyo, Cook and Howell, 1988; Ritchie and Yangzhou, 1987; Spilling, 1996)
- ability to act as a catalyst for development (Evans, 1995; Getz, 1991; 1997; Hall, 1990; 1992; Hodges and Hall, 1996; Hughes, 1993b; Kaspar, 1987; Law, 1993; Light, 1996; Mihalik, 1994; Roche, 1994; Spilling, 1996)
- reduction of seasonal fluctuations or extension of the tourism season (Getz, 1989; 1991; 1997; Goeldner and Long, 1987; Kaspar, 1987; Ritchie and Beliveau, 1974)

- animation of static attractions (Getz, 1991)
- enhanced community pride (Getz, 1989; Hall, 1992; Light, 1996; Ritchie, 1984; Roche, 1994; Williams, Hainsworth and Dossa, 1995)
- advancement of political objectives (Getz, 1994b; Hall, 1992).

Since many events require government assistance in order to be staged, a justification is usually required in economic terms (Burgan and Mules, 2000). This helps explain the focus on economic impact of much of the research that has been conducted to date. This, however, represents a preoccupation with the short-term implications of staging events. There is substantial scope to explore further the role that events can play as catalysts for development and in helping to build an image for a region that will attract longer-term visitation.

Events and branding: a conceptual framework

Despite the growth of event tourism, little attention has been given to the psychological processes that undergird the ways that events can impact a destination's brand. In essence, the linking of a destination's brand to one or more events is a co-operative branding activity. The event's brand image is linked to that of the destination. The use of co-operative branding enjoyed a 40 per cent growth in the latter years of the twentieth century (Spethmann and Benezra, 1994), suggesting that marketers have found it to be a useful tactic for building brand equity. One result of that growth has been a parallel growth in the literature on brand alliance effects (e.g. Gwinner and Eaton, 1999; Rao and Ruekert, 1994; Simonin and Ruth, 1998; Till and Shimp, 1998). This section of the chapter considers implications of that literature for the use of events in destination branding.

Brands are typically linked in order to increase brand awareness, and/or to enhance or change brand image. The use of events as a means to enhance consumers' awareness of a destination is a common reason that destinations seek to host events (cf. Boyle, 1997; Whitson and Macintosh, 1996). Indeed, the economic value of an event to the host city or region is often predicated on the media attention that the event obtains (Mules and Faulkner, 1996). However, the use of events as a means to enhance or change a destination's image is less well understood. In order for an event to have an impact on a destination's image there must be some spillover from the event's image on to the destination's image. Although the effects of an event's image on a destination's image have not been well demonstrated, evidence from the sponsorship literature suggests that the strongest benefits to brand image from an event will accrue when consumers perceive a meaningful match between the event's image and that of the destination (Gwinner and Eaton, 1999; McDaniel,

1999; Speed and Thompson, 2000). However, from the standpoint of both theory and practice, this conclusion suffers two deficiencies. First, it fails to specify what factors render an appropriate match. Second, by mandating a strong match-up at the outset, the focus is placed on the enhancement of image, rather than on the change of an image. In many instances, destinations seek to use events to change their image (cf. Bramwell, 1997; Berg, Braun and Otgaar, 2000). In such instances, there will, at the outset, be some degree of mismatch between the event's image and that of the destination. What is being sought is a transfer of image such that the initial mismatch is resolved by shifting desired aspects of the event's image to the destination.

In order to address both brand image enhancement and brand image change, any prescription must be able to specify what engenders a match-up and what renders some potential for image change. In other words, what constitutes an appropriate basis for selecting and using events to obtain a desired effect on the destination's image? To address that question, it is useful to consider the psychological basis of brand equity. Cognitive psychologists have for some time held that knowledge is represented as associative networks (e.g. Anderson, 1983; Collins and Loftus, 1975; Halford et al., 1998). Accordingly, knowledge consists of a set of nodes that are connected through a network of associations. The nodes and their relations form an 'association set'. Association sets have been found to be useful descriptors of brand image (Henderson, Iacobucci and Calder, 1998; Keller, 1993). When two brands are paired, the image of one brand can be strengthened when its association set shares common elements with the association set of the brand with which it is paired (Gwinner and Eaton, 1999). Further, a transfer of brand image from one brand to another occurs when consumers assimilate a node from one brand's association set into the association set for the brand with which it is paired (Till and Shimp, 1998).

By way of illustration, consider the hypothetical set of relationships depicted in Figure 10.1. The figure represents a fictitious market segment's association set for holiday destinations in south-eastern Queensland, Australia. For this segment, two destinations are represented as nodes – the Gold Coast (located to the south of Brisbane) and the Sunshine Coast (located to the north). In this example, the Gold Coast enjoys a more complex set of associations than does the Sunshine Coast. The key point of differentiation is that the Gold Coast is seen to be more urbanized and, consequently, more exciting. The destination is also seen to offer rainforest settings, but that aspect is unelaborated in this particular association set. The Sunshine Coast, on the other hand, is seen to be more family oriented than the Gold Coast. Nevertheless, in this example, the two destinations are linked in memory – directly and through the shared features of beach and sun, as well as the shared disadvantage that this market segment perceives the cultural amenities to be poor.

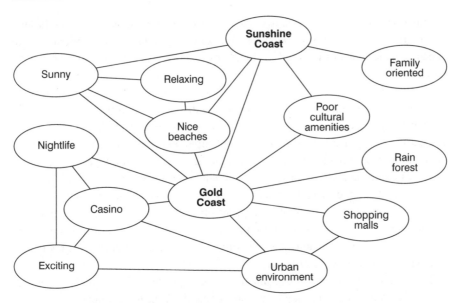

Figure 10.1   Hypothetical association set for vacations in south-eastern Queensland

The strategic use of events

Now, let us consider how each destination represented in Figure 10.1 might consider its choice of events in order to enhance or change its image among the market segment. Let us further consider how either destination might use events to enhance its strategic position relative to that market segment. If either destination wishes to use events to strengthen its existing brand image, it will choose events for which the association set is consistent with one or more aspects of the current destination image. Thus, either destination could benefit by choosing events that highlight its beaches and/or its sunny climate – for example, a beach volleyball tournament, a surfing competition, or a triathlon. Assuming that the event obtained some exposure to the target segment through media (via stories or advertising), it would strengthen the aspects of brand image associated with sun and beach. It would not, however, differentiate one destination from the other. If the Gold Coast sought to strengthen its point of differentiation from the Sunshine Coast, it would include events on its calendar that accentuate urban excitement or nightlife. For example, motorcycle or auto racing along a city course could showcase the destination as an exciting urban locale. A music festival with night-time concerts could highlight the destination as a place with exciting nightlife. On the other hand, the Sunshine Coast could accentuate its competitive advantage over the Gold Coast by adding events with a strong family theme. For example, events requiring siblings or a parent and child to participate jointly would further that aspect of the destination's image.

Either destination might seek to enhance or to further elaborate its image through events that it includes on its calendar. For example, the Gold Coast might seek to enhance the saliency of the rainforest node by elaborating that node through events. Orienteering competitions through the rainforest might be used to feature the distinctive plant life and landscapes of the rainforest. A birdwatching competition or festival might contribute nodes associated with distinctive wildlife of the rainforest. Similarly, either destination might seek to change its image by using events to alter a negative aspect of its brand image. For example, in order to counter the image of poor cultural amenities, events designed to showcase cultural performances or activities could be added. These might include a performing arts festival or an art contest. Finally, either destination could seek to introduce an entirely new node into its association set. For example, the Sunshine Coast might seek to counter the nightlife elements of the Gold Coast's image by building a node for fine dining. In that instance, an event featuring competitions among leading chefs or a festival of fine wines might prove useful.

The example elaborated above illustrates the requisite logic for linking events to destination branding. Four key conclusions emerge from the example:

- In order to build events into destination branding, destination managers should seek to develop a portfolio of events. Different events may be used to strengthen, enhance, or change particular aspects of the destination's brand image in particular market segments.
- Before destination managers can determine which events will meet their destination's branding needs, they must determine how the destination is perceived in the marketplace. They need to map (through market research) the relevant association set of target market segments (cf. Henderson, Iacobucci and Calder, 1998).
- In order to determine what kinds of events to consider, destination managers must decide which aspects of their destination's brand image they wish to strengthen, enhance or change.
- In order to select and use an event appropriately, the destination manager needs to identify the association set by which target markets are likely to encode and interpret the event.

It is not being suggested here that events are sufficient in and of themselves to build a destination's brand. Rather, events represent a tactically leverageable component of the destination's product mix. The key insight is that destination managers can be strategic in their choice of events and in the ways they build events into the destination's marketing communications campaign. This latter point is worth exploring a bit further. It is unlikely that all nodes of a destination's association set will be valued by a market segment. Each market segment will value particular aspects more than others. Returning to the example in Figure 10.1, the market segment being illustrated might place a high value on outdoor settings, but might not value shopping, nightlife or gambling. If so, then marketing communications to that market segment should feature visuals or mentions of events that play up the beach or rainforest nodes, and should not feature visuals or mentions of events that play up urban excitement or nightlife. In other words, the marketing communications campaign should focus on those aspects of a destination's brand that are attractive to the target market.

This facet of marketing communications illustrates an important aspect of events. Each event can be used beyond the time in which it takes place. The event's role in destination branding need not be limited to whatever media or visitor experiences are obtained while the event is happening. Visuals about the event and/or mentions of the event can be incorporated into marketing communications (advertisements, brochures, video postcards, media releases) throughout the year in order to support the destination's desired brand image. By placing event images or mentions alongside images or mentions of other elements of the destination's product mix that highlight comparable aspects of brand image, the overall impact should be enhanced (cf. Baloglu and McCleary, 1999; MacKay and Fesenmaier, 1997; Washburn, Till and Priluck, 2000).

Events and destination branding: exploring the relationship in Australia

The Australian Co-operative Research Centre for Sustainable Tourism (CRC Tourism) is a partnership between the federal government, the tourism industry and university tourism researchers. It was formed in 1997 to facilitate strategic tourism research. The mission of CRC Tourism is 'developing and managing intellectual property to deliver innovation to business, community and government to enhance the environmental, economic and social sustainability of tourism' (www.crctourism.com.au). Research in the CRC Tourism programme is project based, and in 2000 funding was made available to examine the role of events in destination branding. The project sought to answer questions about:

- how, and to what degree destination marketers incorporate events into their marketing strategies
- how events have an impact on the image or 'brand' of the destination
- whether events could be used more effectively to build a destination's brand image.

It was decided to conduct an initial scoping study in order to better understand the current situation by consulting widely with tourism and event management professionals throughout Australia. It represented an attempt to gain an industry perspective and to determine the type of research that was considered necessary to assist future decision making. The ultimate objective was to provide information for destination marketing managers and event organizers which will allow them to use events more strategically in creating an image for their destination, and thereby to support their marketing of the destination. It should be noted that the current project complements other CRC Tourism projects which are investigating the impact of the 2000 Sydney Olympic Games on awareness of, and interest in Australia.

Destination marketing, and the promotion and marketing of events is predominantly a function of the second and third tiers of government in Australia. In fact, most state governments have established special entities to bid for and manage events. These include the Queensland Events Corporation and the Australian Major Events Company (which is an agency of the South Australian state government, despite the national-sounding name). Local governments also provide financial support for events which they feel may help induce tourism into their region. Because of the predominant role of state government in the bidding, funding and managing of events, it was decided to use state-based organizations as primary sources of information on current knowledge and practices in the industry. Consultation with senior staff in these organizations, and in organizations involved in general marketing of the tourism destination was achieved by holding workshops in capital cities throughout Australia.

Efficiency of the process was achieved by gathering information in one sitting. The cost of having a number of stakeholders in one room at one time was that they might not venture opinions or thoughts in an open forum that they would offer in private. A consistent approach to consultation was achieved by running each workshop using a standard protocol for group decision making and problem solving (see Chalip, 2001). This protocol consisted of five phases:

1 *Introduction*. A brief explanation of the project was followed by the participants being asked to write down on provided notepad three events/destinations where the event has enhanced the imaging of the destination, three events/destinations where this enhancement has not occurred, and reasons in each case.
2 *Mixed breakout session*. Participants were divided into two groups, with a mixture of destination marketers and event organizers in each group. The purpose of breaking into smaller groups was to allow discussion to occur based upon the events/destinations on each person's list, and the reasons that they have written down. Each group nominated one of their number to be a group leader and spokesperson. Each group session was attended by someone from the research team who recorded the discussion points.

3 *Feedback and discussion*. Each spokesperson presented to the reassembled group a summary of the discussion of their respective breakout group. This phase was intended to explore commonalities of events and reasons why some events work and some do not in branding the destination.

4 *Specialist breakout session*. Destination marketers were formed into one group, event organizers into another. Each appointed a spokesperson. Discussion focused on the nature of professional relationships between the two groups, how each views the activities of the other from 'over the fence' and how the use of events in destination branding could be better organized and managed.

5. *Conclusion*. The group reassembled, with each group's spokesperson summarizing the issues.

Throughout the process, members of the research team took notes and/or recorded the discussion on audiotape for future transcription. After a number of such sessions, many common themes were observed regarding how events help brand the destination. There was also discussion within more than one group of whether tourism destinations had single or multiple brand images, and whether destinations should strive for a strong single brand or whether they should be flexible and support all markets.

The general findings from the process have been that events can be successful in branding a destination and enhancing its image, particularly those that possess the following characteristics:

1 *Longevity*. The passage of time was needed to allow the event to become associated with the destination in the minds of potential visitors. The Melbourne Cup was mentioned favourably in this regard by most workshops, both in Melbourne and elsewhere. Although an almost organic process seemed to be described in the case of some events which seemed to grow into the local environment over time, it needs to be recognized that single events can have a major impact on the image of a destination especially if leveraged appropriately.

2 *Community support*. Events which had strong support in their host communities were more successful as image makers. Host communities tended to celebrate such events, to join in the festivities, to decorate streets and buildings, thereby raising the awareness of others about the destination, especially the awareness of media. Psychologically, an event may have an impact on self-identity. This will be a positive outcome if people enjoy being associated with an event that has an image that matches the way they wish to be seen. It was also said that long-running home-grown events were more likely to get strong community support than events which were foisted on the community by outsiders. However, this was recognized as being the case only for recurring events. Once again, one-off events

such as the Sydney Olympics could also generate strong community support if correctly organized.

3 *Professionalism of organization.* Where an event had a reputation for professional management, this professionalism was seen to 'rub off' on to the image of the destination. However, if the event was not compatible with the destination, this advantage was lost. Some motorsport events were seen as having this characteristic in that the management and organization was seen as world class, thereby enhancing the image. The same events were often thrust upon their host destinations without regard for the nature of the tourism product of the host. Successful events that grow in size and complexity may require specialist expertise to be brought into the area. This may be accompanied by concerns about a loss of 'local' control in terms of the way the event is organized and promoted and the way images about the host environment are projected.

4 *Compatibility with the destination.* An event needed to 'fit' with the destination in order to be successful in imaging. Thus outdoor, water sport events seemed to fit well with Queensland which already had an image as a 'sun, sea and sand' destination, whereas theatre, opera and cultural events seemed to fit well with Adelaide, which hosts Australia's longest running arts festival. Ongoing tourism benefits accrue if an event serves to stimulate visitation throughout the year. For example, this will occur if skiers are attracted to a particular resort because it hosted a ski event. Retail outlets and other industrial sectors in the resort can take advantage of the consistency between the market appeal of the event and the activities supported by the location where it occurs. However, the scope to attract a number of target markets may be compromised by an approach that focuses exclusively on a single type of event.

5 *Media coverage.* It was universally agreed that media coverage was essential for an event to play a role in destination branding. To achieve international coverage, the event needed to be large and have unique characteristics. Brisbane's Goodwill Games was given as one example. The need for media management will be discussed in more detail in the context of the Sydney Olympics.

6 *Research.* The industry representatives expressed a desire to learn more about information flows and information processing. There was concern about whether information was communicated adequately between the different tourism and event stakeholders and a recognition that little understanding exists about the way potential tourists are influenced by the images they receive about an event.

In the discussion of the interaction between destination marketers and event managers, it was noted that in each city there were good channels of communication between the two. However, there was an expressed need for wider communication with the tourism industry and the community. The latter was seen as important where events were receiving public funding. There was also a suggestion that there needed to be a network of event managers/organizers so that there could be more sharing of skills and knowledge.

In addition to the workshops conducted in the capital cities, one workshop has been conducted in a regional centre. Many of the same issues emerged. However, it was suggested that association with a location that has a clearly defined image is a particularly critical factor if events are to be successful in smaller communities. This was illustrated by explaining that the East Coast Blues and Roots Festival has become known as the Byron Blues Festival, and the Northern Rivers Writers Festival is referred to as the Byron Writers Festival. In both cases, these events have come to be seen as intrinsically linked with Byron Bay which has an iconic status as a tourist destination and as a community with a unique lifestyle.

In conclusion it should be noted that many workshop participants struggled to separate the success of the event per se from its success as an image builder. This may have been because the concept of using events as destination image builders is new to them. The tendency in Australia to emphasize the economic impact of events (Mules and Faulkner, 1996) may have blinded the tourism industry to more subtle ways of benefiting from events.

A case that examines some of the subtle opportunities presented by an event and the considerable work required to exploit these opportunities will now be described. It is, in some ways, exceptional due the scale of the event and the period of time spent in its planning and preparation. However, the Sydney Olympic Games shows how destination branding can be achieved as an outcome of communications associated with an event. It provides insight of relevance to other locations and lessons that are applicable to other events.

The Sydney Olympics and Brand Australia

At the closing ceremony of the 2000 Olympics, the Sydney Games were declared 'the best ever' by the IOC's President, Juan Antonio Samaranch, and Australia's Olympic tourism strategy had been described as a role model for future host cities. The IOC's Director of Marketing had suggested that 'Australia is the first Olympic host nation to take full advantage of the Games to vigorously pursue tourism for the benefit of the whole country. It's something we've never seen take place to this level before, and it's a model that we would like to see carried forward to future Olympic Games in Athens and beyond' (Payne, 1998). The Managing Director of the ATC has claimed that the Games changed forever the way the world sees Australia and that Australia's international tourism brand had been advanced by ten years (Morse, 2001). It is undeniable that television coverage raised the profile of Australia, with an estimated 3.7 billion people watching events, set against backdrops such as the Opera House, Sydney Harbour and Bondi Beach. Although this coverage was a destination marketer's dream, these images conformed to the existing stereotypes held about

175

Australia and may have done little to broaden understanding about the country. This is significant as broadening understanding about Australia in international markets was one of the main objectives of the ATC's Brand Australia campaign.

Brand Australia was launched by the ATC in 1995, two years after Sydney had been awarded the right to host the 2000 Olympic Games. It was the culmination of two years of research that had identified the need to broaden Australia's image and promote the holiday experience rather than specific cities and regions. It was also to be used to oversee strategies attempting to capitalise on the 2000 Olympics (ATC, 1996). A logo, featuring a kangaroo, the country's most recognizable symbol, set against a red sun and blue waves, was used as a unifying link to help cement the brand image. The relationship between the brand and the Olympics was acknowledged explicitly at the launch of a three-year brand advertising campaign in 1998. 'With this campaign we have the opportunity to use the extraordinary interest in Australia surrounding the 2000 Olympic Games to build awareness and add depth and dimension to the country's image' (Morse, 1998).

The ATC's US$6.7 million, four-year Olympic strategy focused on promoting Australia through a media relations programme and the development of alliances with Olympic organizations and partners such as broadcast rights holders and sponsors (Figures 10.2 and 10.3). Underpinning the strategy was a desire to add new dimensions by promoting more than the typical images and themes. This was achieved by bringing together Brand Australia, the Olympic Brand and the brands of Olympic partners. This process was predicated on the establishment of an effective relationship between the ATC and the Sydney Organizing Committee for the Olympic Games (SOCOG). It was SOCOG and the IOC that referred sponsors, broadcast rights holders, National Olympic Committees (NOCs) and the media to the ATC, providing opportunities for the ATC to give advice about marketing and brand imagery. The ATC sought to convince members of The Olympic Program (TOP) – sponsors – of the benefits of linking their Olympic promotions with Brand Australia. The resulting projects included collaborations on competitions, hospitality packages and advertising campaigns. These activities generated US$170 million in additional exposure for Australia (ATC, 2001b).

The most significant relationship for the ATC with a single sponsor was with Visa. This resulted in television commercials that were screened around the world, supplements in magazines, travel offers distributed to cardholders worldwide and billboard advertising featuring Australian images that dominated the waterfront area of Shanghai for a year. All carried the slogan 'Australia prefers Visa'. This designation was the product of an alliance signed in 1997 between Visa and tourism organizations in Australia, including the ATC. American Express voiced concern that it implied government endorsement (Washington, 1997b) but from Visa's perspective it was a perfect fit. Sydney's 'aspirational value' as a destination had been the central and integrative theme of the long-term marketing strategy conducted by Visa in conjunction with its member banks (Smythe, 1999).

The Managing Director of the ATC countered arguments against the exclusive nature of the arrangement with Visa by claiming that funds from Olympic sponsors enhanced the ATC's ability to promote Australia overseas (McMahon, 1998). It was supported in the press as 'an example of the innovative "partnering" sponsors are using to enhance the value of their Olympic sponsorship. The tourism industry appears to be a major winner from the "partnering" trend' (Washington, 1997a: 5). From Visa's perspective the partnership was also regarded as a success. It helped produce an increase of 23 per cent in card usage by overseas visitors to Australia in 1999 and, during the Games, transaction levels at official Olympic sites surpassed those recorded by Visa at the Atlanta Games. At Olympic Park, AUS$20 million was spent on Visa cards at point of sale transactions and more than AUS$5 million was withdrawn from Visa automated teller machines.

By working with the world's broadcasters, the ATC had aimed to make the Olympics a two-week documentary on all aspects of Australian life. Heightened interest in Australia in the lead-up to the Games was also exploited wherever

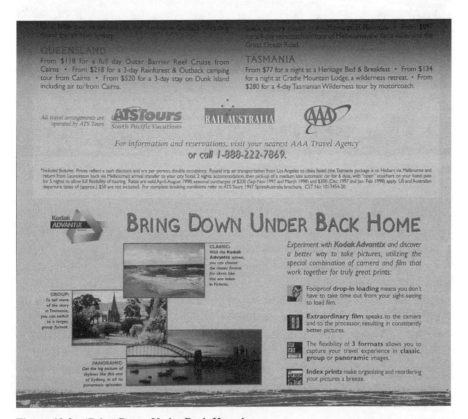

Figure 10.2 'Bring Down Under Back Home'

Figure 10.3 'Taste of Australia' – Visa advertising

possible. For instance, the UK's leading travel show, *The Holiday Programme*, focused its tenth anniversary programme on Australia, in January 1999. It was watched by 8.2 million viewers and featured Sydney, as the Olympic city, but also showed other destinations around the country. In 1996, when the television rights were under negotiation, NBC agreed to provide US$6 million in free commercial airtime to promote Australia as host country of the Olympics. The ATC assisted the American broadcaster in the production of a highly effective advertisement that linked the Olympic Brand with Brand Australia. This was an attempt by NBC to build interest in the forthcoming Games in the USA market and it was achieved by linking colours of the Australian landscape with the colours of the Olympic rings. It was considered, by the ATC, to be critical that the images projected by NBC and the other broadcasters were consistent with the values of the brand, and this required presenting Australia as a vibrant, friendly, colourful, free-spirited place that offers a sophisticated lifestyle. The tactics employed to ensure this was achieved took many forms but included the preparation of a detailed *Film Locations Guide* and the provision of story ideas and profiles of colourful characters and places to direct interest to a variety of regions throughout Australia.

In the five years leading up to the Games, the ATC hosted around 5000 media personnel, with many invited as part of the Visiting Journalist Program. This programme generated US$2.1 billion in coverage in the period 1997–2000 in magazines, newspapers, radio and television around the world (ATC, 2001b). It is claimed that trends in media coverage have increasingly shown Australia's contemporary urban culture, food and wine, arts and cultural themes as well as a strong interest in the lifestyle of Australian people (ATC, 2001a). Media initiatives by the ATC, during the Games, included assisting in the design of the Main Press Centre at Olympic Park by incorporating images reflective of Brand Australia. The ATC was also one of five public sector agencies (with the Department of Foreign Affairs and Trade, Tourism New South Wales, the Sydney Harbour Foreshore Authority, and the New South Wales Department of State and Regional Development) that developed a media centre in the city for non-accredited media. It was considered to be particularly important to provide facilities and information to support the activities of journalists who would not have access to Olympic venues and events. It was thought that their focus would inevitably be more on the city, its people and broader issues about the impact of the Games in Australia.

It would seem that the relationship between a national brand and a major event, such as the Olympic Games, is influenced by a heightened level of interest in the host country. This can be translated into additional opportunities for the tourism industry to communicate with a receptive audience using a variety of media. However, a more sophisticated approach is that which takes advantage of opportunities to consciously integrate mutually compatible elements of a number of brands including the destination brand. This requires the selection of suitable partners, the identification of markets that will respond favourably to the mix of brand values and a desire among the different parties to think creatively in an environment that is subject both to many rules and a very focused temporal horizon. Brown (2000) has advocated the need for research to better understand the outcomes of complementary brand development with sponsors of major events.

The final, critical issue concerns the impact of the visitor experience. Despite all the media coverage, many people who attend the event will return to their homes to give firsthand accounts of their experience. The destination brand is inevitably implicated by the success of the event and the level of satisfaction experienced by people who, in the case of the Olympics, attended the event as spectators, corporate guests, athletes, officials and, of course, the media. All will hold values associated with the destination brand that will affect their desire to return as tourists in the future and the type of word-of-mouth promotion that accompanies every story they recount about their Games experience.

Conclusion

Despite the significant role that events have come to play in tourism, there has been little research that addresses the use of events in destination branding. Nevertheless, as the Olympic example shows, even a one-time event can have a significant impact on a destination's brand. Further, workshops with destination marketers and event organizers have demonstrated that both groups seek a deeper understanding of the ways that events can assist the development of a destination's brand. The conceptual frameworks from which to start construction of relevant models and methods have been formulated in the work on co-operative branding.

The experience, research, and theory described in this chapter suggest the value of further work on the role of events in strengthening, elaborating or changing a destination's brand. More work is needed that examines the ways in which to use event visuals and mentions most effectively in a destination's marketing communications – before, during and after the event. Further work is needed to develop appropriate measures of event impacts on brand image. The use of added partners in co-operative branding activities – particularly event sponsors – needs to be explored. The best means to leverage one-time versus recurring events need to be identified. The relevant considerations when building an event portfolio for a destination need to be determined. Events have a distinctive capacity to excite residents and to appeal to target markets. They become the basis for images, stories and emotions. The challenge to destination marketers is to find the best ways to use event images, stories, and emotions to capture the consumer's attention and build the destination's brand.

References

Anderson, J. R. (1983). *The Architecture of Cognition*. Harvard University Press.

Arcodia, C. and Robb, A. (2000). A taxonomy of event management terms. In *Events Beyond 2000: Setting the Agenda* (J. Allen, R. Harris, L. Jago and A. Veal, eds) pp. 154–160, Proceedings of Conference on Event Evaluation, Research and Education, UTS, Sydney.

Australian Tourist Commission (ATC) (1996). *Annual Report 1995/96*. ATC.

Australian Tourist Commission (ATC) (2001a). *Australia's Olympics. Special Post Games Tourism Report*. ATC.

Australian Tourist Commission (ATC) (2001b). *Olympic Games Strategy: Overview*. March. ATC.

Backman, K., Backman, S., Uysal, M. and Mohr Sunshine, K. (1995). Event tourism: an examination of motivations and activities. *Festival Management and Event Tourism*, **3**(1), 15–24.

Baloglu, S. and McCleary, K.W. (1999). A model of destination image formation. *Annals of Tourism Research*, **26**, 868–897.

Berg, L. van den, Braun, E. and Otgaar, A. H. J. (2000). *Sports and City Marketing in European Cities*. Euricur.

Boyle, M. (1997). Civic boosterism in the politics of local economic development: 'institutional positions' and 'strategic orientations' in the consumption of hallmark events. *Environment and Planning A*, **29**, 1975–1997.

Bramwell, B. (1997). Strategic planning before and after a mega-event. *Tourism Management*, **18**, 167–176.

Brown, G. (2000). Emerging issues in Olympic sponsorship. *Sport Management Review*, **3**(1), 71–92.

Burgan, B. and Mules, T. (2000). Event analysis: understanding the divide between cost benefit and economic impact assessment. In *Events Beyond 2000: Setting the Agenda* (J. Allen, R. Harris, L. Jago and A. Veal, eds) pp. 46–51, Proceedings of Conference on Event Evaluation, Research and Education, UTS, Sydney.

Burns, J., Hatch, J. and Mules, T. (eds) (1986). *The Adelaide Grand Prix: The Impact of a Special Event*. Centre for South Australian Economic Studies.

Chacko, H. and Schaffer, J. (1993). The evolution of a festival: Creole Christmas in New Orleans. *Tourism Management*, **14**(6), 475–482.

Chalip, L. (2001). Group decision making and problem solving. In *The Management of Sport: Its Foundation and Application* (B. L. Parkhouse, ed.), 3rd edn, pp. 93–110, McGraw-Hill.

Collins, A. M. and Loftus, E. F. (1975). Theory of semantic processing. *Psychological Review*, **82**, 407–428.

Commonwealth Department of Tourism (1992). *Tourism, Australia's Passport to Growth: A National Tourism Strategy*. Australian Government Publishing Service.

CRC Tourism web site: www.crctourism.com.au

Crompton, J. and McKay, S. (1997). Motives of visitors attending festival events. *Annals of Tourism Research*, **24**(2), 425–439.

Evans, G. (1995). The role of the festival in urban regeneration: planning for the British Millennium Festival. Paper presented at International Festivals Association Second European Research Symposium, 17 August, Edinburgh.

Faulkner, B. (1993). *Evaluating the Tourism Impact of Hallmark Events*. Occasional Paper No. 16, Bureau of Tourism Research.

Fredline, E., Mules T., Raybould M. and Tomljenovic R. (1999). Sweet little rock and roller: the economic impact of the 1998 Wintersun Festival. *Proceedings of the Ninth Australian Tourism and Hospitality Research Conference*. Bureau of Tourism Research.

Getz, D. (1989). Special events: defining the product. *Tourism Management*, **10**(2), 125–137.

Getz, D. (1991). *Festivals, Special Events, and Tourism*. Van Nostrand Reinhold.

Getz, D. (1994a). Event tourism: evaluating the impacts. In *Travel, Tourism, and Hospitality Research* (J. Ritchie and C. Goeldner, eds), pp. 437–450, Wiley.

Getz, D. (1994b). Event tourism and the authenticity dilemma. In *Global Tourism: The Next Decade* (W. Theobald, ed.), pp. 313–329, Butterworth-Heinemann.

Getz, D. (1994c). In pursuit of the quality tourist. Paper presented at Tourism Down-under Conference, Massey University, Palmerston North, December.

Getz, D. (1997). *Event Management and Event Tourism*. Cognizant Communications Corporation.

Getz, D. (2000). Developing a research agenda for the event management field. In *Events Beyond 2000: Setting the Agenda* (J. Allen, R. Harris, L. Jago and A. Veal, eds) pp. 10–21, Proceedings of Conference on Event Evaluation, Research and Education, UTS, Sydney.

Getz, D. and Wicks, B. (1993). Editorial. *Festival Management and Event Tourism*, **1**(1), 1–3.

Getz, D. and Wicks, B. (1994). Professionalism and certification for festival and event practitioners: trends and issues. *Festival Management and Event Tourism*, **2**(2), 103–109.

Goeldner, C. and Long, P. (1987). The role and impact of mega-events and attractions on tourism development in North America. *Proceedings of the 37th Congress of AIEST*, Calgary, 28, 119–131.

Gunn, C. (1994). *Tourism Planning*. 3rd edn. Taylor and Francis.

Gwinner, K. P. and Eaton, J. (1999). Building brand image through event sponsorship: the role of image transfer. *Journal of Advertising*, **28**(4), 47–57.

Halford, G. S., Bain, J. D., Maybery, M. T. and Andrews, G. (1998). Induction of relational schemas: common processes in reasoning and complex learning. *Cognitive Psychology*, **35**, 201–245.

Hall, C. (1987). The effects of hallmark events on cities. *Journal of Travel Research*, **26**(2), 44–45.

Hall, C. (1990). The impacts of hallmark tourist events. Workshop Paper at Metropolis 90, third International Congress of the World Association of the Major Metropolises, Recreation and Tourism Development Branch of the City of Melbourne, Melbourne.

Hall, C. (1992). *Hallmark Tourist Events: Impacts, Management and Planning*. Belhaven Press.

Hall, C. (1996). Hallmark events and urban reimaging strategies. In *Practising Responsible Tourism; International Case Studies in Tourism Planning, Policy and Development* (L. Harrison and W. Husbands, eds), pp. 366–379, Wiley.

Henderson, G. R., Iacobucci, D. and Calder, B. J. (1998). Brand diagnostics: mapping branding effects using consumer associative networks. *European Journal of Operational Research*, **111**, 306–327.

Hodges, J. and Hall, C. (1996). The housing and social impacts of mega-events: lessons for the Sydney 2000 Olympics. In *Tourism Down Under II: Towards a*

More Sustainable Tourism (G. Kearsley, ed.), pp. 152–166, Centre for Tourism, University of Otago.

Hughes, H. (1993a). Olympic tourism and urban regeneration. *Festival Management and Event Tourism*, **1**(4), 157–162.

Hughes, H. (1993b). The role of hallmark event tourism in urban regeneration. Paper presented at The First International Conference on Investments and Financing in the Tourism Industry, Jerusalem.

Jago, L. and Shaw, R. (1994). Categorisation of special events: a market perspective. In *Tourism Down Under: Perceptions, Problems and Proposals*, conference proceedings, pp. 682–708, Massey University.

Jago, L. and Shaw, R. (1998). Special events: a conceptual and differential framework. *Festival Management and Event Tourism*, **5**(1/2), 21–32.

Janiskee, R. (1994). Some macroscale growth trends in America's community festival industry. *Festival Management and Event Tourism*, **2**(1), 10–14.

Janiskee, R. (1996). Historic houses and special events. *Annals of Tourism Research*, **23**(2), 398–414.

Kang, Y. and Perdue, R. (1994). Long-term impact of a mega-event on international tourism to the host country: a conceptual model and the case of the 1988 Seoul Olympics. In *Global Tourist Behaviour* (M. Uysal, ed.), pp. 205–225, International Business Press.

Kaspar, C. (1987). The role and impact of mega-events and attractions on national and regional tourism development: introduction into the general topic of the 37th AIEST Congress. *Proceedings of the 37th Congress of AIEST*, Calgary, 28, 11–12.

Keller, K. L. (1993). Conceptualizing, measuring, and managing customer-based brand equity. *Journal of Marketing*, **57**, 1–22.

Law, C. (1993). *Urban Tourism; Attracting Visitors to Large Cities*. Mansell.

Light, D. (1996). Characteristics of the audience for 'events' at a heritage site. *Tourism Management*, **17**(3), 183–190.

Lynch, R. and Veal, A. (1996). *Australian Leisure*. Addison Wesley Longman.

MacKay, K. J. and Fesenmaier, D. R. (1997). Pictorial element of destination image formation. *Annals of Tourism Research*, **24**, 537–565.

McCann, C. and Thompson, G. (1992). An economic analysis of the first Western Australian State Masters Games. *Journal of Tourism Studies*, **3**(1), 28–34.

McDaniel, S. R. (1999). An investigation of match-up effects in event sponsorship advertising: the implications of consumer advertising schemas. *Psychology and Marketing*, **16**, 163–184.

McMahon, I. (1998). AmEx, QH clash with ATC over marketing. *Travel Week*, 28 October, 3.

Mihalik, B. (1994). Mega-event legacies of the 1996 Atlanta Olympics. In *Quality Management in Urban Tourism: Balancing Business and Environment* (P. Murphy, ed.), pp. 151–161, proceedings, University of Victoria.

Morse, J. (1998). $150 million campaign set to boost tourism arrivals and export earnings. *Brand Australia: A New Image for a New Millennium.* ATC.

Morse, J. (2001). The Olympic Games and Australian tourism. Presentation made at the Sport Tourism Conference, Barcelona, 23 February.

Mules, T. and Faulkner, B. (1996) An economic perspective on special events. *Tourism Economics,* **2**(2), 107–117.

Murphy, P. and Carmichael, B. (1991). Assessing the tourism benefits of an open access sports tournament: the 1989 B.C. Winter Games. *Journal of Travel Research,* **29**(3), 32–36.

National Institute of Economic and Industry Research (2000). *The 2000 Qantas Australian Grand Prix.* Victorian Department of State and Regional Development.

Payne, M. (1998). Presentation at the Regent Hotel, Sydney, 14 October.

Pyo, S., Cook, R and Howell, R. (1988). Summer Olympic tourism market; learning from the past. *Tourism Management,* **9**(2), 137–144.

Rao, A. R. and Ruekert, R. W. (1994). Brand alliances as signals of product quality. *Sloan Management Review,* **36**(1), 87–97.

Ritchie, B. (1996). How special are special events? An impact study of the National Mutual New Zealand Masters Games on Dunedin's economy. In *Tourism Down Under II: Towards a More Sustainable Tourism* (G. Kearsley, ed.) pp. 73–79, Centre for Tourism, University of Otago.

Ritchie, J. (1984). Assessing the impact of hallmark events: conceptual and research issues. *Journal of Travel Research,* **23**(1), 2–11.

Ritchie, J. and Beliveau, D. (1974). Hallmark events: an evaluation of a strategic response to seasonality in the travel market. *Journal of Travel Research,* **13** (2), 14–20.

Ritchie, J. and Smith, B. (1991). The impact of a mega-event on host region awareness: a longitudinal study. *Journal of Travel Research,* **30**(1), 3–10.

Ritchie, J. and Yangzhou, J. (1987). The role and impact of mega-events and attractions on national and regional tourism: a conceptual and methodological overview. *Proceedings of the 37th Congress of AIEST,* Calgary, 28, 17–58.

Robinson, A. and Noel, J. (1991). Research needs for festivals: a management perspective. *Journal of Applied Recreation Research,* **16**(1), 78–88.

Roche, M. (1994). Mega-events and urban policy. *Annals of Tourism Research,* **21**(1), 1–19.

Simonin, B. L. and Ruth, J. A. (1998). Is a company known by the company it keeps? Assessing the spillover effects of brand alliances on brand attitudes. *Journal of Marketing Research,* **35**, 30–42.

Smythe, S. (1999). Personal communication with the Vice-President, Sponsorship and Event Marketing, Visa.

Speed, R. and Thompson, P. (2000). Determinants of sports sponsorship response. *Journal of the Academy of Marketing Science,* **28**, 226–238.

Spethmann, B. and Benezra, K. (1994). Co-brand or be damned. *Brandweek*, **35**(45), 20–25.

Spilling, O. (1996). Mega-event as a strategy for regional development: the case of the 1994 Lillehammer Olympic Games. *Proceedings of Institute of Tourism and Service Economics,* International Centre for Research and Education in Tourism, International Conference, Innsbruck, 128–154.

Till, B. D. and Shimp, T. A. (1998). Endorsers in advertising: the case of negative celebrity information. *Journal of Advertising*, **27**(1), 67–82.

Tourism South Australia (1990). *Planning of Festivals and Special Events*. Tourism South Australia.

Tourism Victoria (1993). *Strategic Business Plan 1997–2001: Building Partnerships*. Tourism Victoria.

Tourism Victoria (1997). *Strategic Business Plan 1997–2001: Building Partnerships*. Tourism Victoria.

Travis, A. and Croize, J. (1987). The role and impact of mega-events and attractions on tourism development in Europe: a micro perspective. *Proceedings of the 37th Congress of AIEST*, Calgary, 28, 59–78.

Uysal, M. and Gitelson, R. (1994). Assessment of economic impacts: festivals and special events. *Festival Management and Event Tourism*, **2**(1), 3–9.

Washburn, J. H., Till, B. D. and Priluck, R. (2000). Co-branding: brand equity and trial effects. *Journal of Consumer Marketing*, **17** 591–604.

Washington, S. (1997a). Visa opens fire in card games. *Australian Financial Review*, 17 November, p. 5.

Washington, S. (1997b). Visa deal sparks major card row. *Australian Financial Review*, 18 November, p. 4.

Wells, J. (1994). Floriade: a study in re-imaging Australia's capital through event tourism. Working paper at Tourism Down-Under Conference, Massey University, Palmerston North.

Whitson, D. and Macintosh, D. (1996). The global circus: international sport, tourism, and the marketing of cities. *Journal of Sport and Social Issues*, **20**, 278–297.

Wicks, B. and Fesenmaier, D. (1995). Market potential for special events: a midwestern case study. *Festival Management and Event Tourism*, **3**(1), 25–31.

Williams, P., Hainsworth, D. and Dossa, K. (1995). Community development and special event tourism: the men's World Cup of skiing at Whistler, British Columbia. *Journal of Tourism Studies*, **6**(2), 11–20.

Witt, S. (1988). Mega-events and mega-attractions. *Tourism Management*, **9**(1), 76–77.

11

Destination branding and the Web

Adrian Palmer

Introduction

Tourism destinations are probably one of the most difficult 'products' to market, involving large numbers of stakeholders and a brand image over which a destination marketing manager typically has very little control. The diversity and complexity of tourism destinations is well documented (Heath and Wall, 1991; Leiper, 1996; Palmer and Bejou, 1995), and this makes brand development very difficult for national, regional and local tourism organizations. Destination branding necessarily involves the focused attention of all tourism-related organizations in a destination, and this can create major challenges in getting all stakeholders to develop a coherent theme for the destination brand. There have been many notable successes in developing strong tourist destination brands (for example, the brand development programmes for New York and Spain), but equally many efforts at co-operative marketing have failed to gain momentum. This chapter reviews the challenges and opportunities arising from the emerging technologies of high-speed data transmission (comprising, among others, the WWW, the Internet, e-commerce and m-commerce) for the marketing of tourism destinations.

Co-operative promotion of tourism destinations has conventionally focused on the production of joint publicity brochures, often distributed through shared stands at exhibitions (although of course many organizations have done much more, such as operating booking services). The development of electronic commerce now offers new opportunities for collaboratively marketing tourism destinations. There is the potential to create 'virtual co-operation', whereby potential tourists can browse through web sites of individual facilities at a destination and develop a coherent picture of the destination experience on offer. The creative linking of web sites facilitates the profiling of enquiries in a way that allows potential tourists to develop their own package of experiences from a visit to a destination.

There is a strong consensus that 'image' is a pivotal aspect of a marketing strategy for a destination and numerous authors have investigated the use of image in brand formation for destinations (Chon, 1991; Heath and Wall, 1991). It is argued that despite a multiplicity of products and services under the one brand umbrella, the formation of a brand identity can be achieved to give the destination a common marketing purpose and direction. Examples include the Brand Australia initiative to gain partnerships between all state tourism bodies within Australia; Queensland's 'Destination Queensland : Beautiful One day, Perfect the Next!' campaign and the Brand Ireland campaign to promote Eire and Northern Ireland as a single tourism destination. The development of a central brand for a destination faces new challenges and opportunities from evolving electronic distribution channels. While the Internet can allow suppliers in a destination to come together to create a strong centralized site, the Internet can also facilitate a stronger presence for individual tourism suppliers in the marketplace, who are now able to reach their potential markets more directly.

Electronic marketing of tourism destinations

Tourism-related services have emerged as a leading product category to be promoted and distributed to consumer markets through the Internet (see Connolly, Olsen and Moore, 1998; Millman, 1998; Sussman and Baker, 1996; Williams and Palmer 1999). The nature of consumers' search activity, involving multiple choice of suppliers and comparison of facilities, prices and availability is facilitated by the search capabilities of the Internet. Increasingly, tourism suppliers are able to profile consumers and provide a selection that is based on their needs. Electronic commerce offers great flexibility for tourism suppliers operating in volatile markets. The promotional message can be changed much more quickly than is the case where the requirement to print brochures leads to long lead times between a policy decision being made and the implementation of that decision. Electronic commerce is very good at handling clearance of perishable capacity close to the time of use and for managing yields effectively. Customers benefit from such channels by gaining immediate gratification of their requests, greater choice, multisensory, accurate and up-to-date information, and an easy to use interface. Similarly, the costs of obtaining information are reduced for customers and the wide diversity of information can be represented on one terminal. Many tourism destination marketing organizations have developed web sites with varying levels of interactivity. An interactive web site provides a good opportunity for the multiple suppliers involved in a tourism destination to uniquely fashion together the specific components of a destination offer, which are sought by individual visitors.

Faced with a rapid increase in information availability through the Internet, a crucial role is played by the methods used to guide individuals through the enormous range of destination options available. In this sense Internet-based marketing is no different to traditional marketing in that consumers seek to simplify their choice by using a combination of intermediaries, trusted brand names and established business relationships. Within the tourism sector, the role of tour operators has simplified the purchase process of tourism buyers by prepackaging the elements of a vacation that might otherwise be difficult to assemble individually. The use of trusted brand name tour operators and the emergence of branded virtual intermediaries have helped to reduce the perceived riskiness of tourism purchases. The complexity of a tourist destination's 'routes to market' in an electronic environment are illustrated in Figure 11.1.

The fundamental distribution channel in the travel industry is made up of three important players – principals, intermediaries and customers. Principals provide travel services to end users. Intermediaries pass on information about these services to potential customers and try to influence targeted customers to use their channel. They also facilitate in customizing the principal's services to the end-user's needs and handling paperwork and after-sales enquiries. An early move to create an electronic distribution channel was provided by global distribution systems (GDS), which represented a closed, dedicated connection of terminals displaying travel information about airlines, hotels, car rentals, cruises and other travel products. Used almost exclusively by travel agents, the GDS created a linear distribution chain. In present-day terms, however, the GDS has been reduced to just one component of a much larger system of networked travel information with advances in communication and software. The four leading global distribution systems are Sabre, Galileo, Amadeus and Worldspan. Increasingly, Internet-based travel companies, on-line access providers and other virtual communities appeal directly to consumers and travel agents, thereby circumventing the traditional GDS. The WWW has made this possible. Global distribution systems are being transformed into global distribution networks (GDNs). This is the larger 'ecosystem' in which the constituents of a distribution system unite and it is dramatically affecting how travel products are

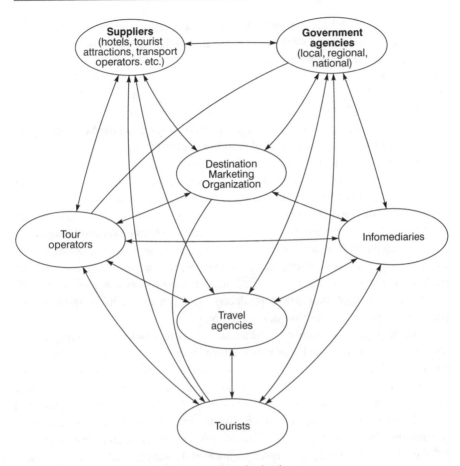

Figure 11.1 'Routes to market' for a tourism destination

distributed in the travel industry. This emerging distribution channel facilitates the multidimensional flow of information and transactions – with any organization in the channel able to distribute travel information and complete a transaction directly with customers. However, direct booking of travel services is not always a feasible option for service principals due to the complexity and sensitivity of channel partners, in addition to the extra costs incurred by maintaining specialized call centres.

With the evolution of the Internet, 'shelf space' has grown exponentially and has become much more complex, and indeed crowded. Many service principals, tour and travel companies, virtual agents and travel agents maintain web sites and conduct business over the Internet. In addition, some web sites offer various levels of travel information and advice, many of which are linked to one or more of the above booking agents.

Forrester Research has estimated that in 1998 4 per cent of holidays were reserved and purchased over the Internet (Forrester Research, 1999). Consumers have a tendency to use the Internet as a means of gathering information, but not actually using it to reserve services. The adoption of the Internet as a transaction facilitator has been impeded by consumers' concerns over security and privacy. Nevertheless, with Internet proliferation, splintering of audiences and the rise of a heterogeneous, information-technology literate society, channels of distribution have been changing rapidly, with direct marketing and relationship marketing strategies being incorporated into many distribution systems.

Tourist destinations can benefit from the Internet by developing a coherent position in the marketplace, increasing their market share by getting closer to customers (actual and potential) and, subsequently, by ensuring delivery of high levels of customer satisfaction. The role of information integration and brokerage is especially applicable to destination marketing organizations (state tourism departments, national tourism offices, and city convention and visitor bureaux) as they rarely have a product of their own to sell. Instead, their role is to match buyers with sellers, demand with supply and producers with consumers by positioning and promoting a place as a tourism destination brand.

A WWW page is essentially an electronic document which allows multiple users (consumers) to access and download information from the page to their own computers. Each web page can be stored on numerous computer servers all connected to the Internet, which in effect broadens the distribution of the web page to a larger number of potential users around the world. The flexibility to update and then distribute a web page electronically has created some exciting marketing possibilities for tourism suppliers. The WWW can be compared with a product brochure that is constantly up to date, graphical and colourful, capable of text, audio and video images, cheap and easy to copy, and accessible by millions of readers around the world. Tourism suppliers can thus create their own electronic brochures to market their products and services quickly and cheaply on a global scale.

Other opportunities arise through the development of destination databases that can be used for customer targeting and request fulfilment. These databases can offer full product information, interactive booking capability and real-time price and availability information. Several destination databases have been developed worldwide, often involving large investment costs, and with varying degrees of success, including the BOSS system in Canada, GULLIVER in Ireland, SWISS-LINE in Switzerland and ATLAS in Queensland, Australia. With further developments in technology, there are great opportunities for linking picture and video images of destinations and accommodation which could alter the purchasing procedures of consumers in the tourism sector. An advantage of an electronic brochure for tourism destinations is the ability for consumers to select only the information that appeals to them. Similarly suppliers have the opportunity to reduce costs of distribution at the same time as reaching more directly into the consumer's home where decisions are made, thus creating new and more direct channels of distribution for destination brands.

Against these opportunities, the Internet can pose challenges for destination marketing organizations. One of the most notable effects of electronic commerce is to facilitate direct access between a supplier and its customers, without the need to resort to an intermediary. There has been considerable development in many service sectors of direct-sell organizations that are able to deal with many thousands of customers on an individual basis. At the same time, there is evidence of the effects these direct channels have had on the number and profitability of remaining intermediaries. In the context of tourism destination brands, it is quite possible that individual companies who make up a tourist destination may seek to open up direct channels with their existing and prospective customers, rather than channelling more effort into the development of a central brand or the destination. This may be a real possibility where an operator offers a unique facility such as a theme park whose appeal is not directly related to the area in which it is located. Search engines are increasingly allowing Internet users to search out types of activity. Once the web site for a favoured activity is found, that web site may suggest other attractions in the area that appeal to the needs of the type of person who typically takes part in the preferred activity. Hotlinks may take an individual to related activities without the intervention of a centralized tourism brand.

Many Internet-based destination marketing initiatives have created conflict among members where commissions charged to individual businesses for handling booking requests are perceived as being too high. Of course, such arguments are not new, as commissions charged by more conventional co-operative booking initiatives have frequently been challenged. The Internet may, however offer more routes to the final consumer, and so an individual organization's dependency on the destination marketing organization may be lessened by the presence of Internet portals. Challenges may arise when individual tourism suppliers attempt to develop their own individual brand identities on a global scale via the Internet. Consumers may be faced with multiple tourism suppliers each doing their own thing and promoting to multiple market segments (i.e. lots of channels of distribution/communication), thereby further confusing the consumer. Other challenges for this medium arise from the complexity of information to new users, copyright and legal issues, and security and privacy of information.

The rapid development and dissemination of WWW sites created by suppliers and intermediaries potentially increases the amount of confusion faced by consumers when seeking travel information about a destination. The implications of such confusion are that destination marketing organizations have a great opportunity to bring together the relevant suppliers of tourism services in their region under one brand identity. The destination marketing organization would act as a 'filter' for customers seeking professional travel advice in their region and thus add value to existing services for both customers and suppliers in terms of a strong centralized brand. The destination marketing organization could significantly reduce the amount of potential confusion for suppliers and consumers. The challenge for destination marketing organizations is to act as a better 'filter' than other portals or web site operators who similarly set out to be a trusted source of information.

Pollock (1996: 25) noted that 'the distance between suppliers and consumers is closing. It appears safe to suggest that the winning destinations will be the ones that close the gap fastest'. Tourism destination marketing organizations are likely to play a significant role in helping to close that gap through active promotion of a destination to create awareness and also through electronic distribution channels to facilitate customers' demands for speed, accuracy and up-to-date information when making enquiries. Distribution channels are the 'final link' in the tourism marketing system by getting messages and services to the market. However, closing this gap is not an easy task and strategies must adapt to embrace the new technology. For a tourism destination merely to have an electronic presence is not adequate. It must also have a strategy to bring that presence close to potential customers, and this typically involves alliances with portals and other information intermediaries, and advertising of its presence through new and traditional media.

The Internet and the development of 'virtual' destination marketing organizations

The 1990s saw growing interest in a new form of organization, often referred to as the virtual organization. The virtual organization in this context refers to a network of independent companies, suppliers, customers, even one-time rivals linked by information technology to share skills and cost, and to access to one another's markets and resources. A characteristic is that they may have no central office or internal hierarchy (Byrne, 1993; Davidow and Malone, 1992). Electronic commerce has facilitated the development of virtual organizations. Hale and Whitlam (1997) define as 'virtual' any organization that is continually evolving, redefining and reinventing itself for practical business purposes. The aim of such organizations is to deliver services through structures and processes that are fast, flexible and flat. Virtual organizations can use computer-mediated communication to become more flexible and responsive than traditional organizational structures (Barnatt, 1997; Hoffman and Novak, 1995). They can allow small businesses to collaborate with minimal bureaucracy and can create value cost-effectively. The virtual organization has great relevance to the marketing of tourism destinations, particularly where they are dominated by small businesses whose limited resources require the outsourcing of many specialist functions. By drawing together essentially freelance individuals, virtual organizations can benefit from an inherent responsiveness to change in the business environment.

There are many variants of virtual organization, which capitalize upon the prominence of knowledge and information as key inputs and outputs. Due to the intangibility of the resources they process, there is no necessity for many virtual organizations to exhibit or support a definite physical architecture nor a clear bureaucracy; a tight employment structure, nor a dedicated resource base which characterize conventional organizational structures. Here, the term 'virtual organiza-tion' can be used to describe the network of independent companies that constitute and market a tourist destination. The outcome of this co-operation is the composite tourism destination product which consumers experience. It should be possible for all businesses within a tourist destination to link their web sites so that a visitor to one site would easily be able to find out about related facilities at other companies' web sites. Recent growth in accessibility to information technology has fuelled the development of virtual web sites, with particularly rapid growth in travel-related sites (Anon., 1999). However, despite the potential for creating virtual destinations out of the component organizations, the marketing of many tourist destinations appears to remain dominated by the central role of a hierarchical tourist board.

Evidence of virtual electronic tourism destinations

There is disappointing evidence so far of tourism destination marketing organiza-tions' ability to create 'virtual' organizations using the Internet. In a study undertaken in Northern Ireland during 1998, a very low level of reciprocation of links between tourist suppliers' own web sites was observed (Palmer and McCole, 2000). The study examined each possible link between tourism businesses within the Greater Belfast area which had a web site; this entailed a total of 2200 possible links. Out of this theoretical maximum number of links, only eleven (0.5 per cent of the total) had reciprocated hypertext links between them. What was most disappointing was the observation that if a potential tourist 'landed' on an individual web site that is not reciprocated or linked to surrounding amenities, the opportunity for that particular surfer to gain a holistic view of the totality of experiences available in that destination is lost.

The structure of the system of web sites studied indicated a dominant role played by the two regional web sites, especially the long-established site operated by Northern Ireland Tourist Board (NITB), and a newer one operated by Belfast City Council. The NITB site provided a comprehensive top-down facility for tourism businesses within the study area, but the level of linkages back to the site from individual businesses was very low. This regional web site adopted a profiling technique and listed attractions, accommodation, restaurants and public houses. An additional link then provided information on 'what you can do around here', and

193

listed fishing, car rental, birdwatching, horse riding, golf, sailing, adventures on foot and recreational courses available. The visitor to the site is given the opportunity to avail of a holiday planner by administering a login name and password at the beginning of the search. If a particular service or amenity is of interest it may be added to the itinerary which is automatically produced on request. An important implication is that once the visitor has entered this site he or she should have no need to undertake an additional search for other web sites relating to the area.

The result of the analysis of linkages is surprising considering that the impact of individual web sites may be of little value for potential tourists wishing to gain a holistic impression of all that is on offer at the destination. Therefore, if an Internet user landed on the site of a particular tourism constituent from outside the system studied, they would most likely *not* be linked back to either the NITB or Belfast City Council, the two main regional web sites. From initial searches using the Yahoo! search engine, these two web sites were not immediately apparent in the top ten results of a search for 'Belfast' and 'tourism'. However, the sites could be accessed from other indirect channels, some of which were not primarily related to hospitality and tourism (for example, newspapers hosting their own web-based travel sections).

The NITB and Belfast City Council play a key role in promoting tourism to Belfast. In both regional web sites the study found a top-down approach for promoting individual tourism businesses. Tourism marketing was therefore driven by a central organization in which enquiries may be made, accommodation reserved and information gathered on particular amenities. Bookings could be made through these web sites. However, no link was provided from the regional site to individual businesses' own web sites, despite the latter usually containing a lot more information than was contained in the very basic information given in the regional web sites. The rationale may have been to prevent the regional web site losing revenue by customers booking directly with the service provider, but it served to highlight the hierarchical nature of the web site. Developing a value chain which incorporates the efforts of destination marketing organizations as well as individual businesses remains a challenge. Some regional sites (and commercial booking agencies) have developed systems where the regional site (or central booking agency) charges a commission for each 'click through' from the site to individual businesses' web sites. Nevertheless many businesses remain suspicious of the auditing of these transactions and resentful of paying a 'click through' fee, especially when a regional site is financed by government agencies or members' own subscriptions.

For the future, the development of application service providers (ASPs) presents further opportunities and challenges for small and medium-sized tourism businesses. Numerous commercial companies now allow a small or medium-sized hotel to operate a sophisticated on-line booking system, hosted by an ASP. A destination marketing organization's booking service is only one 'route to market' for a small and medium-sized tourism business. While the quality of destination marketing organizations' sites will undoubtedly improve, the alternatives open to individual businesses are also likely to increase.

New technology or old principles?

While new technology offers exciting challenges and opportunities for destination marketing, we should not lose sight of basic principles that underlie the co-operative efforts which are a prerequisite for success. In particular, it is likely that if the stakeholders in a destination do not trust each other with a conventional marketing programme, then merely adding new technology is in itself unlikely to bring about success. Trust and leadership will remain key issues in electronic destination marketing (Palmer, 1998).

Trust is a major factor in determining the level of activity within groups. The existence of 'hidden agendas' that individual members bring into a group can undermine mutual trust. Unless the motives which underlie these agendas are controlled by mutual agreement, implicit or explicit, there may be little chance of getting a collaborative spirit within a group and the group's development may become impeded. Successful collaboration depends upon the commitment of the group to goals and the degree of trust that is generated within the group. Destination marketing organizations typically involve a member being both a competitor and collaborator with fellow group members. A delicate balance exists between the needs of individuals to advance the interests of the business that they represent and the collective needs of the group. Where the balance is seen to favour the individual's own business, a perception of mistrust based on a lack of reciprocity may harm relationships. The development of Internet based co-operation will not change the issue of managing relationships between collaborators, for example in determining the marketing strategy of a destination web site or the emphasis that it should assign to different interest groups.

Numerous studies have shown that strong leadership is important for achieving a group's objectives (Adair, 1986; Blake and Mouton, 1978; Mintzberg, 1973) but such leadership may not be sought by individuals who seek essentially social benefits from a co-operative marketing association. Like conventional destination marketing activities, an electronic strategy is unlikely to happen without an effective champion who can lead teams of people in developing and executing an Internet strategy. In studies of leadership, it has been noted that being able to follow is an important contributor to good leadership (Handy, 1976). A common problem with co-operative ventures is the apparent difference in individuals' goals. Co-ordination of co-operative activities can thus prove challenging and necessitate a style of leadership that will accommodate individuals' characteristics. Small-business owners who typically comprise the membership of co-operative marketing groups may find the transition to followship of one of their peers a difficult challenge. It may be essential for the leader to become part of a social group and to occasionally alienate members by actions which may be sound commercially, but unacceptable socially within a small network of members.

A key task of leadership is to raise finance for an electronic marketing initiative, and to maintain interest in the initiative during the early teething periods. Destination marketing web sites have not been immune from cynicism by stakeholders in the destination who may be quick to seize on high development costs and poor reliability. The issue of paying for access to a destination site has caused tension in many destinations, as noted above, and effective leadership is crucial to reconcile the interests of multiple stakeholders.

Conclusion

The Internet offers tremendous opportunities for developing strong destination marketing organizations. The advantages over traditional methods of promoting the destination brand and fulfilling information requests which are specifically aimed at the needs of individual tourists, are numerous. However, this chapter has pointed out that having a web site in itself is not enough to enjoy continuing success of a tourist destination. In an age when all destinations can develop a web site, there must be a coherent strategy to develop, position and promote an electronic presence. Individual tourism operators have never before had so many routes to get to their target markets, and destination marketing organizations are just one means of reaching potential customers.

Of course, even the best electronic strategy will ultimately fail if it is not matched by a consistent delivery of promises. In the early development of the Internet, tourism sector businesses have been accused of overpromising on their web sites in a way which they might have been more reluctant to do through printed media. Repeat business is only likely to develop if tourists' expectations are met. And if they are not met, there are increasing numbers of web sites where potential visitors can go to see 'warts and all' accounts of a destination.

References

Adair, J. (1986). *Effective Team Building*. Gower.

Anon. (1998). 'Our friends electric', *Marketing*, 29 January, 28–31.

Barnatt, C. (1997). Virtual organisation in the small business sector: the case of Cavendish Management Resources. *International Small Business Journal*, **15**(4), 36–47.

Blake, R. and Mouton, J. (1978). *The New Managerial Grid*. Gulf.

Byrne, J. (1993). The virtual corporation. *Business Week*, February, 98–102.

Chon, K. S. (1991). Tourism destination image modification process: marketing implications. *Tourism Management*, **12**, 68–72.

Connolly, D. J., Olsen, M. D. and Moore, R. G. (1998). The Internet as a distribution channel. *Cornell Hotel and Restaurant Administration Quarterly*, **8**(4), 42–54.

Davidow, W. H. and Malone, M. S. (1992). *The Virtual Corporation*. HarperCollins.

Forrester Research (1999).
http://www.forrester.com/ER/Marketing/0,1503,138,FF.html
(accessed 29 November 1999).

Hale, R. and Whitlam, P. (1997). *Towards the Virtual Organization*. McGraw-Hill.

Handy, C. (1976). *Understanding Organisations*. Penguin.

Heath, E. and Wall, G. (1991). *Marketing Tourism Destinations: A Strategic Planning Approach*. Wiley.

Hoffman, D. L. and Novak, T. P. (1995). *Marketing in Hypermedia Computer-Mediated Environments: Conceptual Foundations*.
(http://www2000.ogsm.vanderbilt.edu)

Leiper, N. (1996) *Tourism Management*. RMIT Publications.

Millman, H. (1998). Online travel arrangements begin to catch on. *Infoworld*, **20**(9), 78.

Mintzberg, H. (1973). *The Nature of Managerial Work*. Harper and Row.

Palmer, A. (1998) Evaluating the governance style of marketing groups. *Annals of Tourism Research*, **25**(1), 185–201.

Palmer, A. and Bejou, D. (1995). Tourism destination marketing alliances. *Annals of Tourism Research*, **22**(3), 616–629.

Palmer, A. and McCole, P. (2000). The virtual re-intermediation of services: a conceptual framework and empirical investigation. *Journal of Vacation Marketing*, **6**(1), 33–47.

Pollock, A. (1996). The role of electronic brochures in selling travel: implications for businesses and destinations. *Australian Journal of Hospitality Management*, **3**(1), 25–30.

Sussmann, S., and Baker, M. (1996). Responding to the electronic marketplace: lessons from destination management systems. *International Journal of Hospitality Management*, **15**(2), 99–112.

Williams, A. P. and Palmer, A. (1999). Tourism destination brands and electronic commerce: towards synergy? *Journal of Vacation Marketing*, **5**(3), 263–275.

Index